Highland Park

Frederick Law Olmsted's Living Landscape
in Rochester, New York

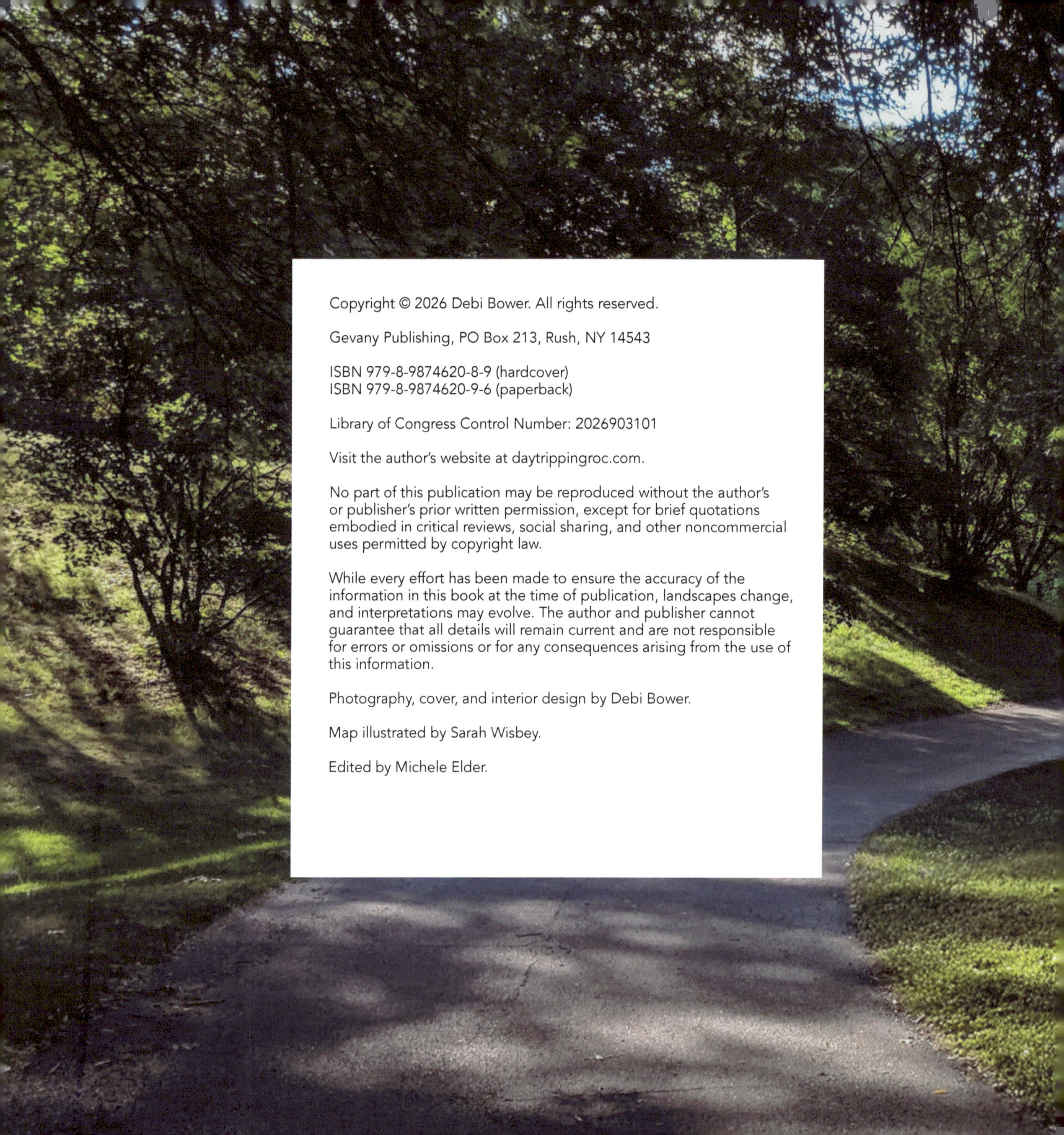

Gevany Publishing, PO Box 213, Rush, NY 14543

ISBN 979-8-9874620-8-9 (hardcover)
ISBN 979-8-9874620-9-6 (paperback)

Library of Congress Control Number: 2026903101

Visit the author's website at daytrippingroc.com.

While every effort has been made to ensure the accuracy of the information in this book at the time of publication, landscapes change, and interpretations may evolve. The author and publisher cannot guarantee that all details will remain current and are not responsible for errors or omissions or for any consequences arising from the use of this information.

Photography, cover, and interior design by Debi Bower.

Map illustrated by Sarah Wisbey.

Edited by Michele Elder.

Highland Park

Frederick Law Olmsted's Living Landscape
in Rochester, New York

Debi Bower

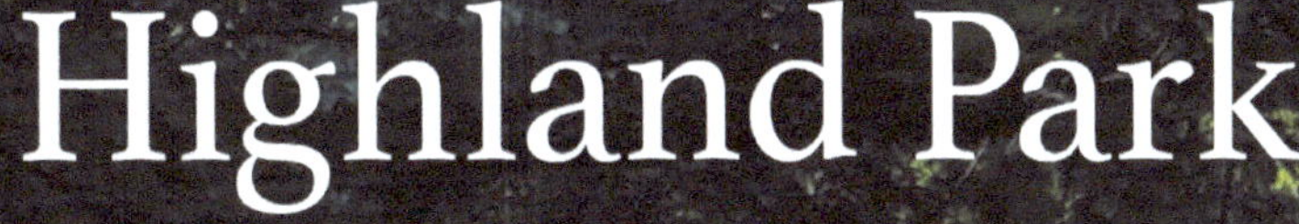

gevany
PUBLISHING

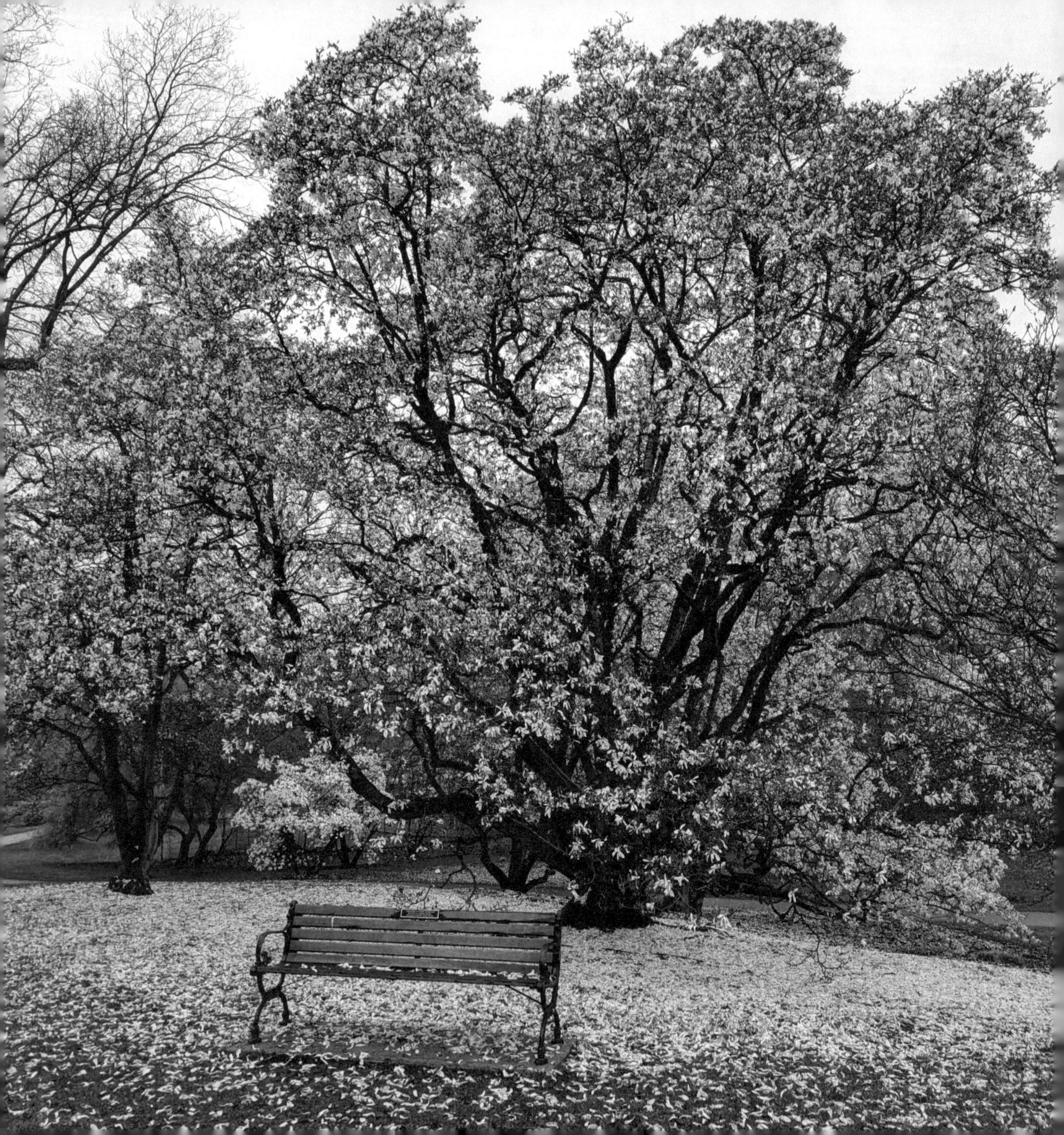

Author's Note

Photography, for me, is a way of paying attention; writing is how I make sense of what I've noticed. Together, they form a quiet record of a place shaped by design, stewardship, and time—shared not as a guide, but as a conversation with past, present, and future visitors.

This book is not meant to catalog every feature or explain every detail. It is an act of caring—a way of showing up for a place that matters to us.

More than a simple photo book, this is a love letter to a place that rewards patience, invites attention, and reminds us that preservation begins with presence.

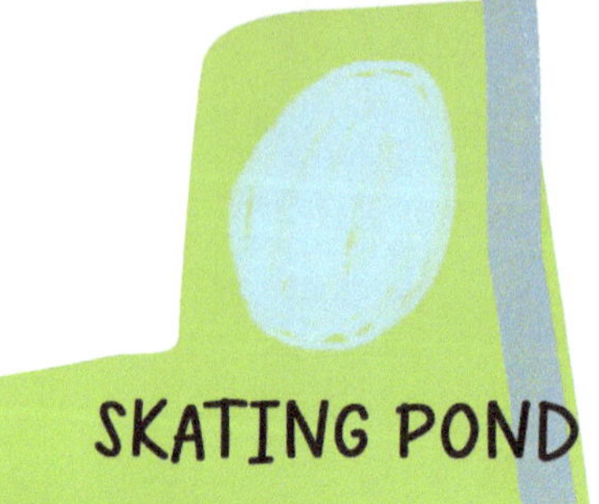
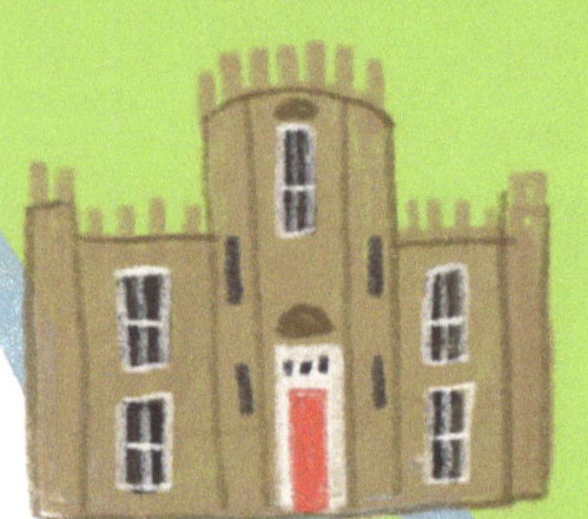

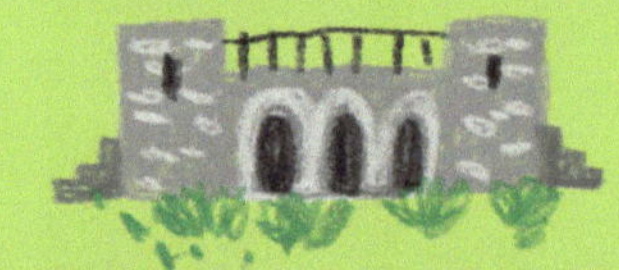
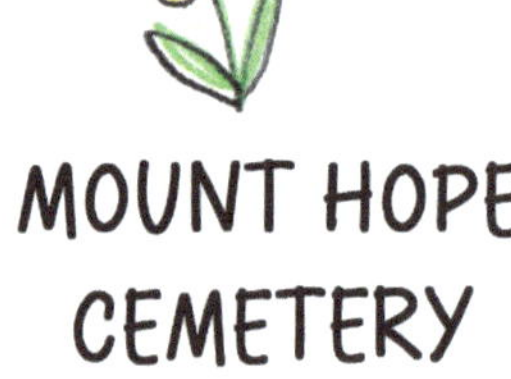
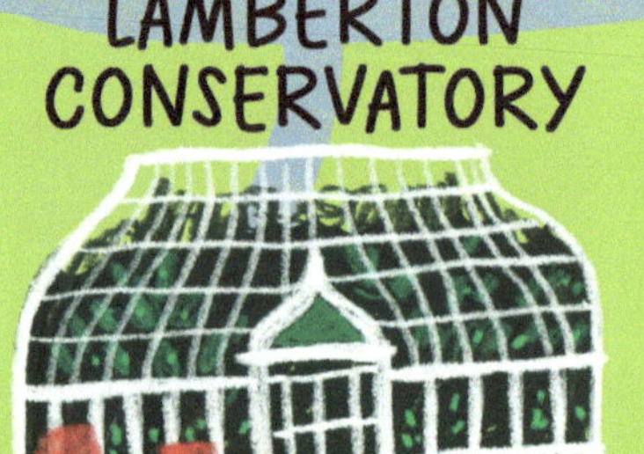
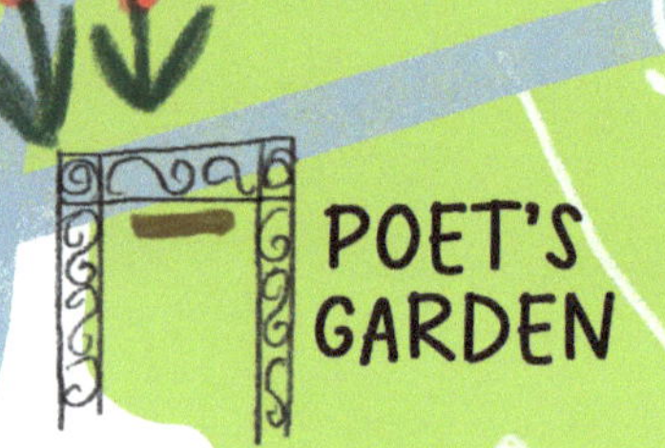
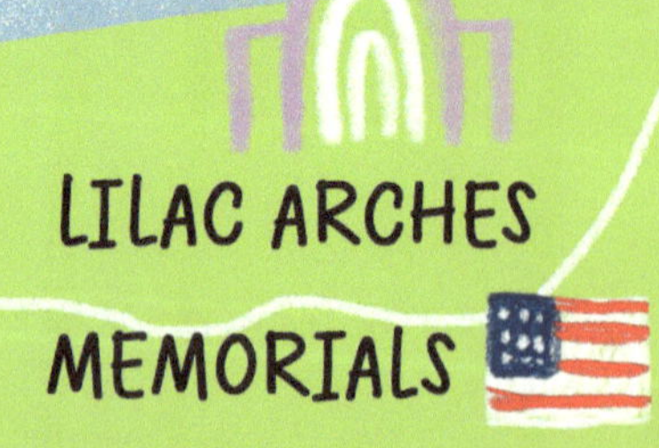

SKATING POND
ROBINSON DRIVE
LAMBERTON CONSERVATORY
HIGHLAND BOWL
WARNER CASTLE
SUNKEN GARDEN
POET'S GARDEN
MOUNT HOPE CEMETERY
MT HOPE AVENUE
SOUTH AVENUE
MAGNOLIAS
LILAC ARCHES
MEMORIALS

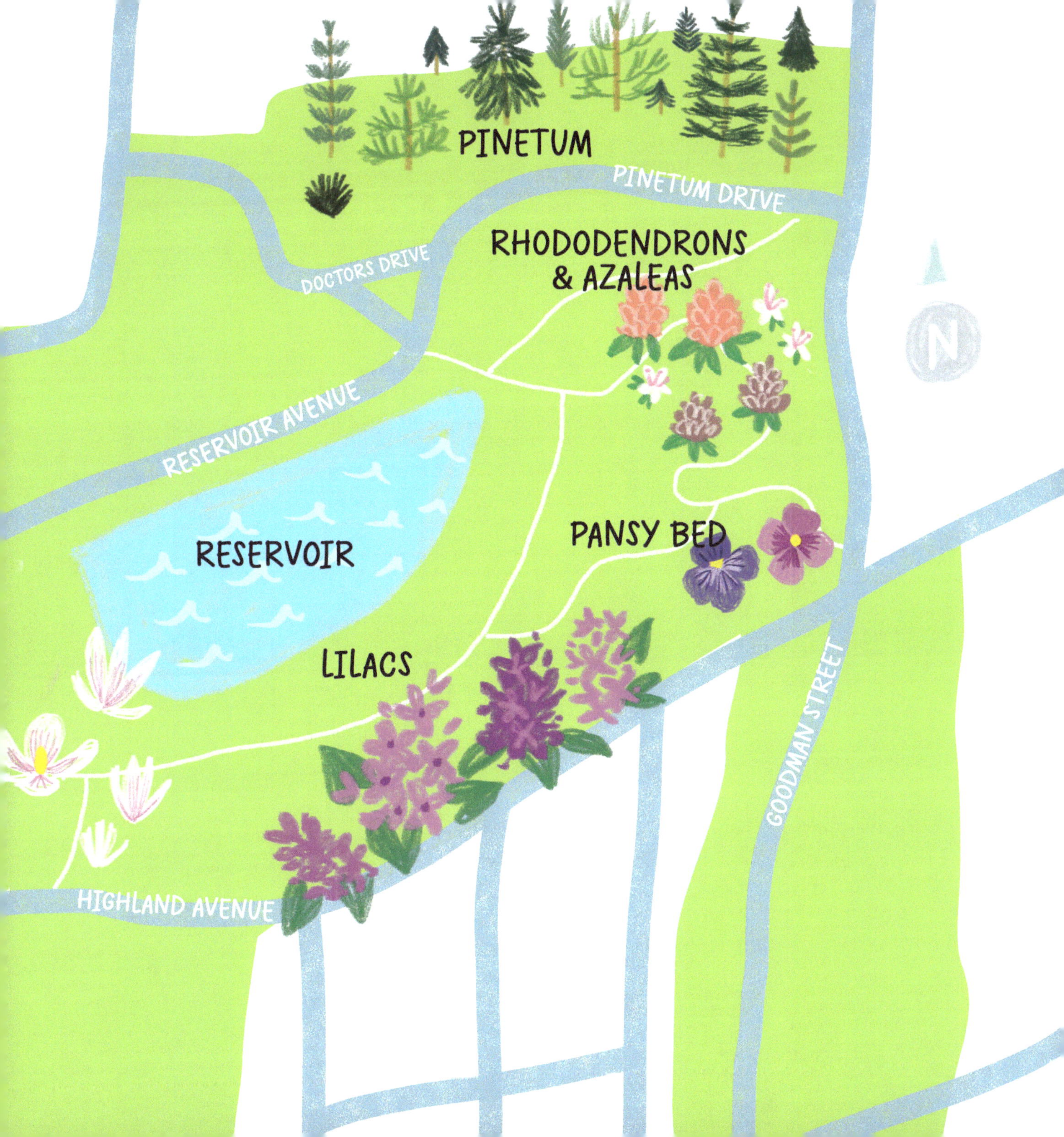
PINETUM
PINETUM DRIVE
DOCTORS DRIVE
RHODODENDRONS & AZALEAS
RESERVOIR AVENUE
RESERVOIR
PANSY BED
LILACS
GOODMAN STREET
HIGHLAND AVENUE
N

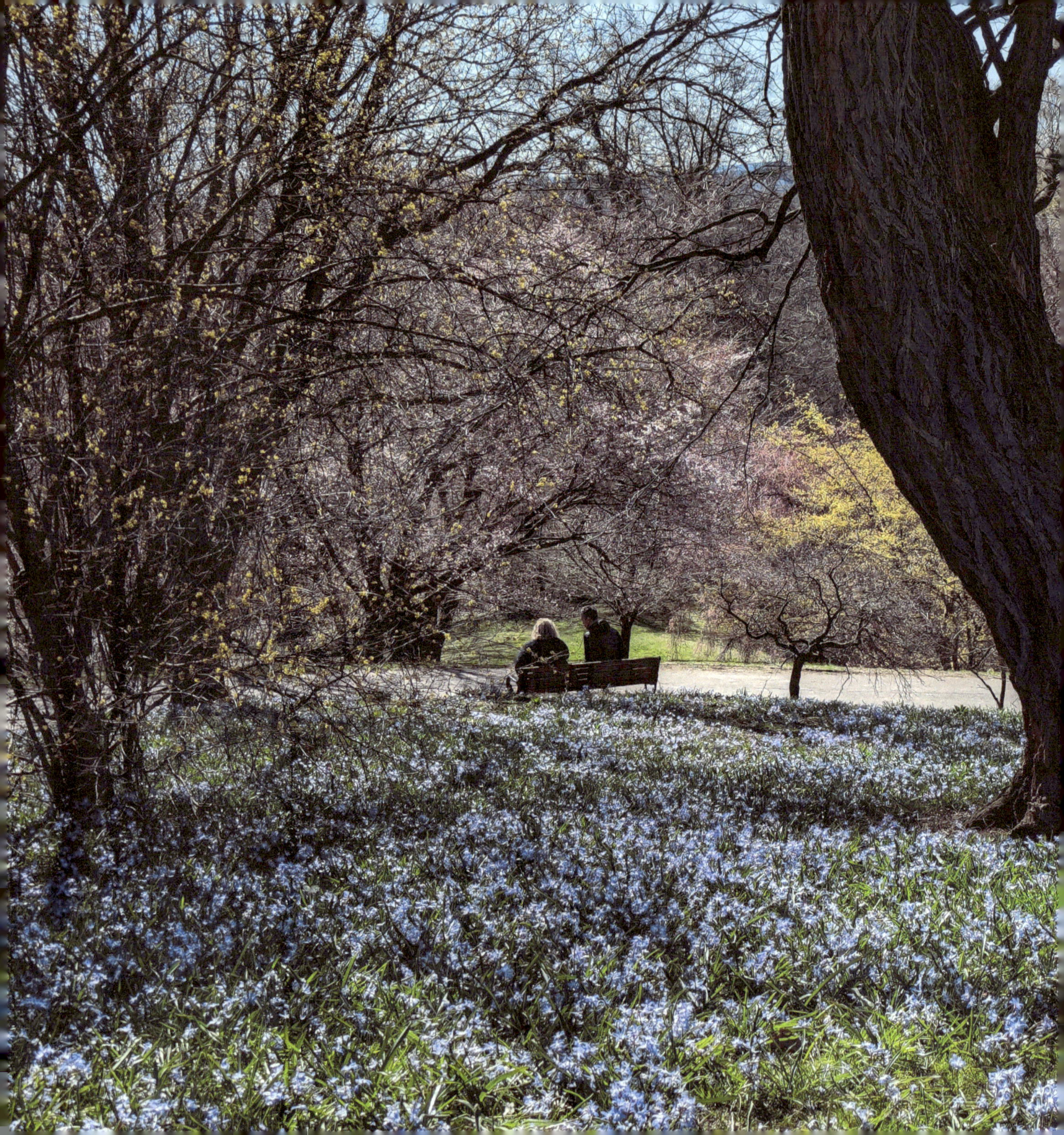

Welcome to Highland Park

Highland Park in Rochester, New York, is more than a destination. It's a rhythm of movement along curving paths, a gentle pause beneath mature trees, and a deep breath of lilac-scented air as the landscape opens and closes around each turn.

Frederick Law Olmsted and his firm planned Highland in the late nineteenth century, but they never intended it to be an arboretum frozen in time. They imagined a place that would grow—season by season, generation by generation—offering beauty freely and without expectation. It was designed as a living landscape, where careful planning and everyday use continually shape one another.

Through photography and reflection, this book lingers in those moments of movement and pause, returning to Highland Park again and again as the seasons shift and the landscape reveals itself in new ways.

Highland Park may not match the scale of Olmsted's work at Central Park, the drama of his preservation vision at Niagara Falls State Park, or the grandeur of the gardens at the Biltmore Estate, yet it offers something equally enduring: an intimate demonstration of how Olmsted's democratic vision thrives at a human scale. Here, paths are close enough to walk in an afternoon, views are low enough to meet the eye, and the details are near enough to touch.

Whether you've walked these paths a hundred times or are planning your first visit, may these pages offer what Highland has always given: moments of peace, sparks of wonder, and the quiet understanding that nature, when thoughtfully designed and freely shared, is an act of love.

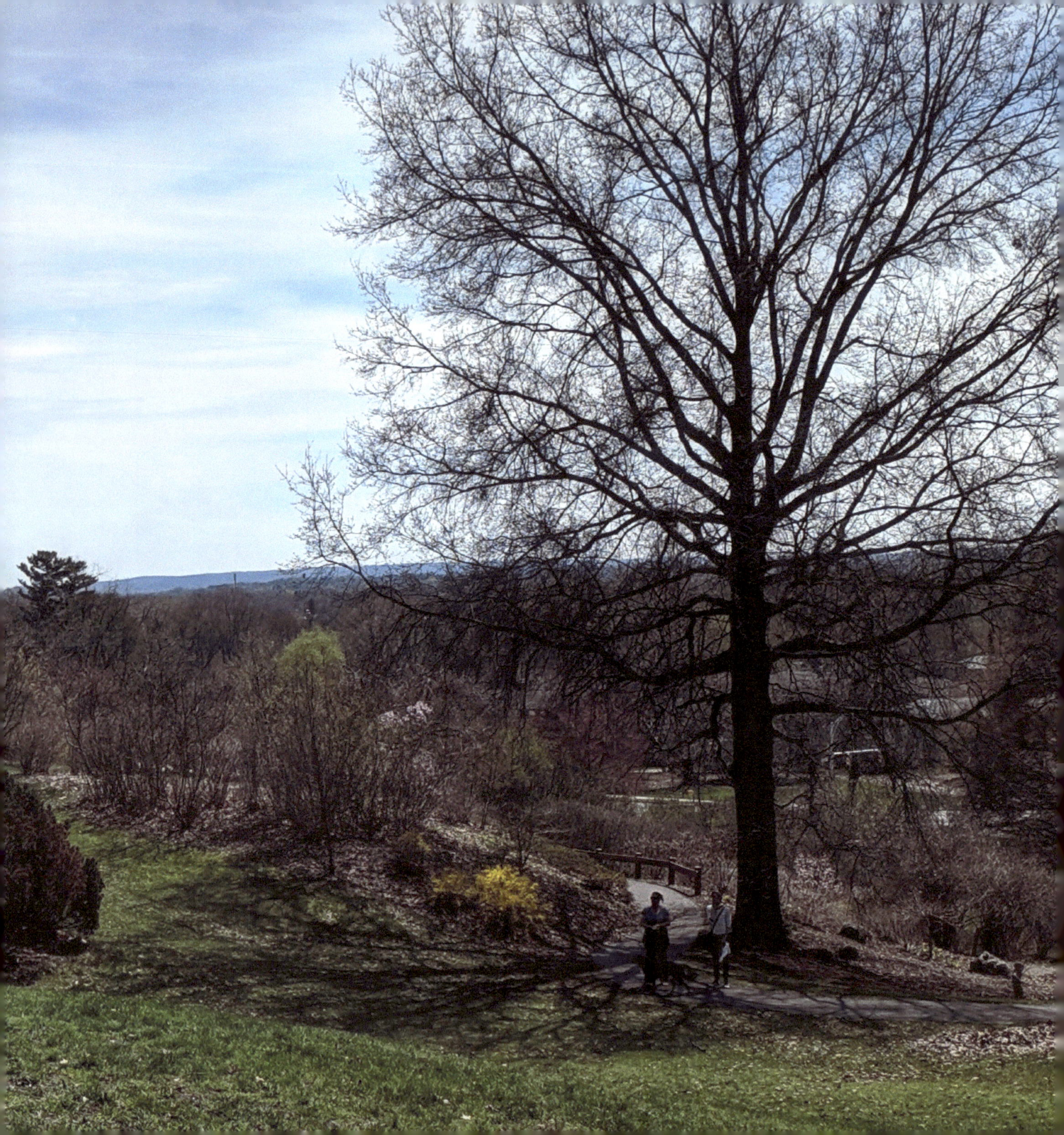

Rochester's Olmsted Legacy

Highland Park (formally known as Highland Botanical Park) did not emerge by accident. It was the product of a particular moment in Rochester's history—one shaped by rising industry, expanding wealth, and a growing belief that prosperity entailed civic responsibility.

In the final decades of the nineteenth century, Rochester was undergoing rapid transformation. Mills, nurseries, and manufacturers fueled the city's economic momentum. New fortunes were being made, the population grew, and civic ambitions expanded alongside the city's skyline. With that growth came an essential question: what should a prosperous city give back to itself?

For Rochester's civic leaders and horticultural visionaries, the answer included parks, not as ornamental luxuries, but as essential civic infrastructure. At a time when many American cities concentrated wealth behind gates and private estates, Rochester invested in landscapes designed for shared use, where health, beauty, and dignity were available to all.

Highland Park stands as one of the most explicit expressions of that ethic. When renowned nurserymen George Ellwanger and Patrick Barry donated the land surrounding the city reservoir in 1888, their intent was clear. The site was to become a public arboretum, financed, owned, and managed by the city, placing horticultural knowledge and scientific study within reach of everyday life. Unlike private estates or university collections, Highland Park was something new: a living archive created for the public good.

Ellwanger and Barry stipulated not only that the land be maintained as an arboretum, but that the city retain a professional landscape architect to shape it. In response, Rochester turned to Frederick Law Olmsted. Though Olmsted generally resisted formal botanical collections in public parks, he made a rare exception here. Constrained by both topography and intent, he transformed a scientific collection into a landscape, arranging specimen trees in sweeping masses and naturalistic groupings rather than rigid rows. The result was neither museum nor meadow, but something distinct: a designed landscape that balanced study with experience and order with freedom.

This approach reflected Olmsted's broader philosophy. He believed parks were civic acts, places designed not to impress but to restore. Long, curving paths invited reflection. Open spaces offered relief and sky. Wooded slopes provided shade and stillness. In an era of rapid industrial growth, Olmsted argued that access to nature was essential to a healthy democracy. In his view, parks were not indulgences but necessities.

The establishment of the Rochester Park Commission in 1888 and the hiring of the Olmsted firm formalized that belief. Rochester's park system would become one of the last comprehensive systems shaped under Olmsted's direct guidance. Each park was assigned a distinct purpose: Genesee Valley Park emphasized pastoral openness and river views; Seneca Park highlighted the dramatic wildness of the Genesee River gorge; and Highland Park served as a horticultural showcase and quiet retreat. Tree-lined parkways connected these spaces, weaving them into a cohesive whole that shaped how residents moved through and experienced the city.

Highland Park's location reinforced its civic role. Set within reach of growing neighborhoods and connected by emerging streetcar routes, it was designed to be part of daily life, not a distant destination reserved for special occasions. Drives and paths followed the land's natural contours, rising to elevated views of Rochester to the north and the Bristol Hills to the south, with the reservoir anchoring the landscape at its center.

As Olmsted's health declined in the early 1890s, his sons and their firm carried the work forward, adapting the framework he established. Under park superintendent Calvin Laney and horticulturist John Dunbar, planting strategies evolved, shifting toward ornamental displays and seasonal color. The lilac collection that would come to define Highland Park emerged not as a departure from Olmsted's vision but as an expression of its flexibility.

That adaptability is part of the park's enduring strength. Olmsted's designs were never rigid prescriptions; they were frameworks meant to grow, change, and respond to stewardship. Highland Park endures not because wealth once existed, but because the idea of shared beauty took root and was carried forward by generations who believed public space matters.

Seen through this lens, Highland Park is more than a scenic destination. It is living proof of Rochester's identity as the Flower City—a place where horticulture, science, and civic pride are inseparable and where cultivation is understood not as a luxury but as a public good.

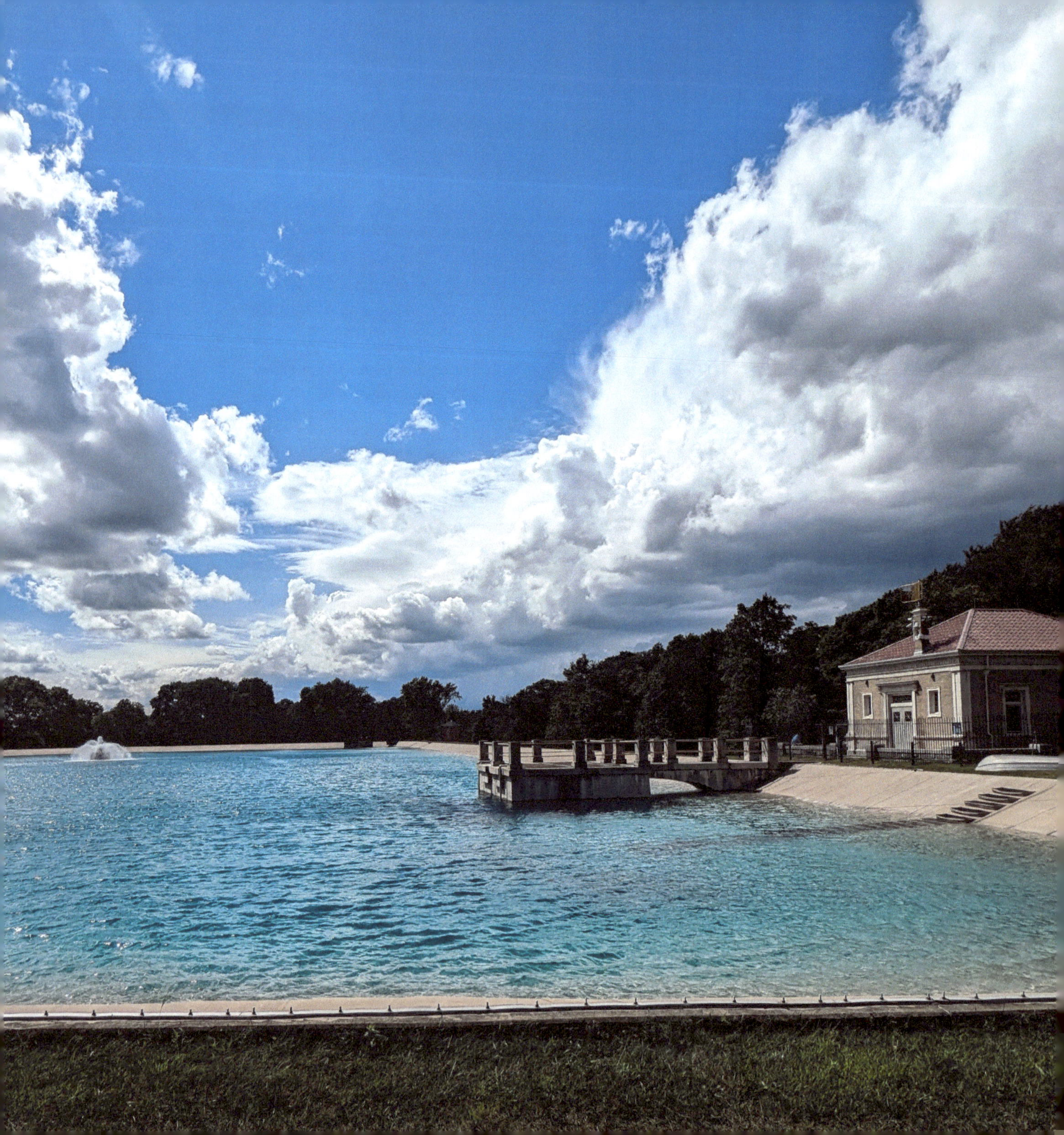

Highland Reservoir

Completed in 1876, the Highland Reservoir was one of Rochester's earliest public water systems. Supplied by gravity from Hemlock and Canadice Lakes, it remains an essential part of the city's infrastructure and a quiet reminder of long-term civic planning.

When Ellwanger & Barry donated the surrounding land a decade later, the reservoir became the heart of Highland Park. Elevated above the city and bordered by mature trees, the water creates an expansive mirror reflecting the sky.

Walking paths trace the reservoir's edge. From this high ground, views extend north toward the city and south toward the rolling Bristol Hills. The reservoir is one of Highland Park's most contemplative spaces—a place to pause, breathe, and take in a landscape shaped to feel both purposeful and unforced.

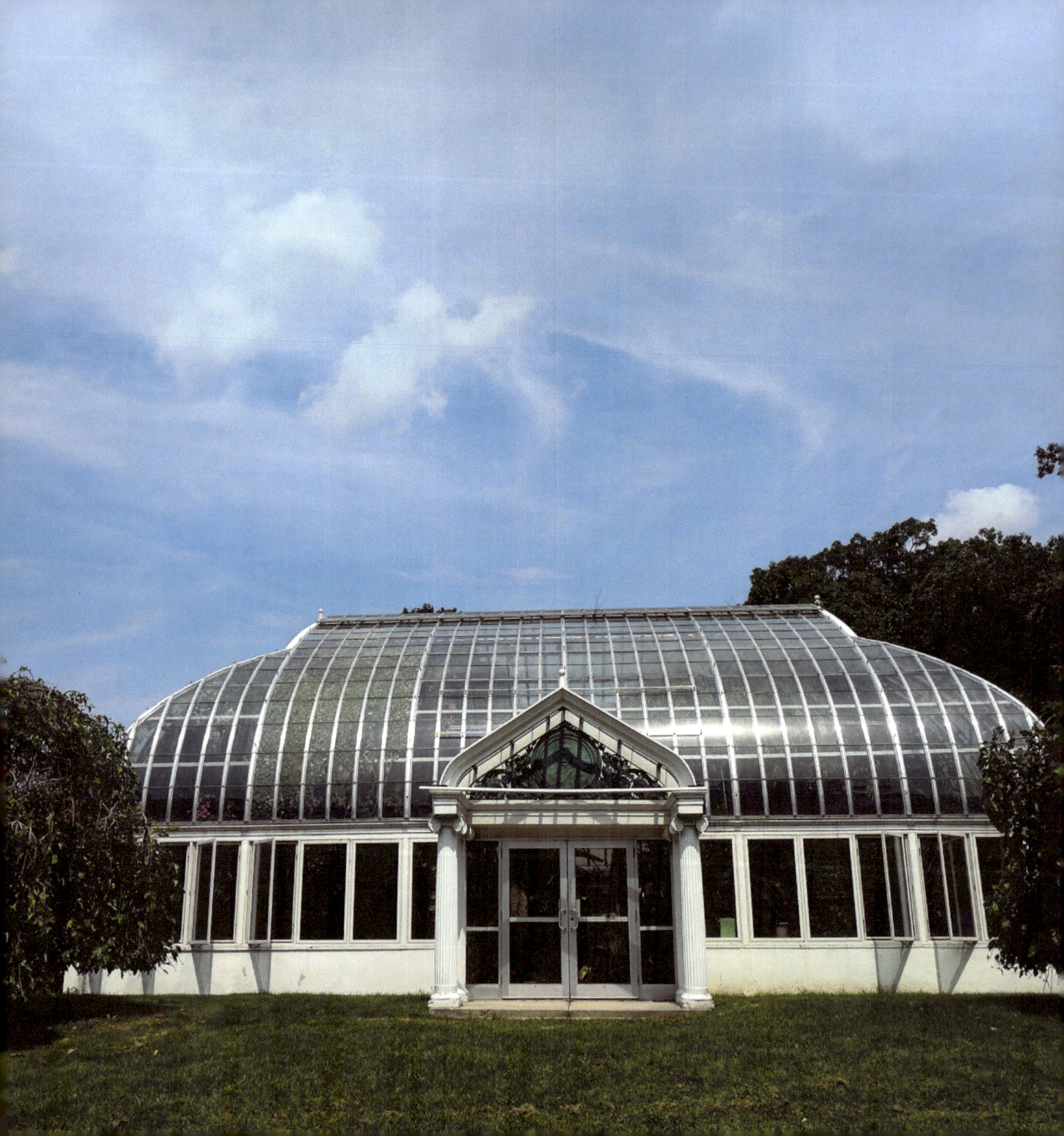

Lamberton Conservatory

At the edge of South Avenue stands the Lamberton Conservatory, a year-round refuge first built in 1911 and named for Alexander Lamberton, then president of the Parks Board. Glass-walled and light-filled, it offers warmth in winter, shade in summer, and blooms year-round.

Though it appears unchanged from its original structure, what visitors see today is a replica of the historic Lord & Burnham conservatory. In 2007, the building was fully dismantled to its foundation. The original steel framework—damaged by decades of constant humidity—was used as a pattern to fabricate a new galvanized steel frame engineered to match the historic form.

Inside, a small pond shelters turtles, while button quail move quietly through the undergrowth. Running water softens the air and slows the pace. Each room maintains its own climate. The seasonal display house shifts with the calendar—poinsettias in winter, tulips and lilies in spring, and rotating plantings through summer and fall. Beyond it, palms and banana trees rise in the humid air, while the cactus house glows dry and bright with slow-growing forms shaped by time.

The conservatory invites lingering. Whether on a cold January morning or a humid summer afternoon, a visit here offers a quiet reminder that preservation, like growth itself, depends on renewal, and that even familiar places endure through careful, often unseen work.

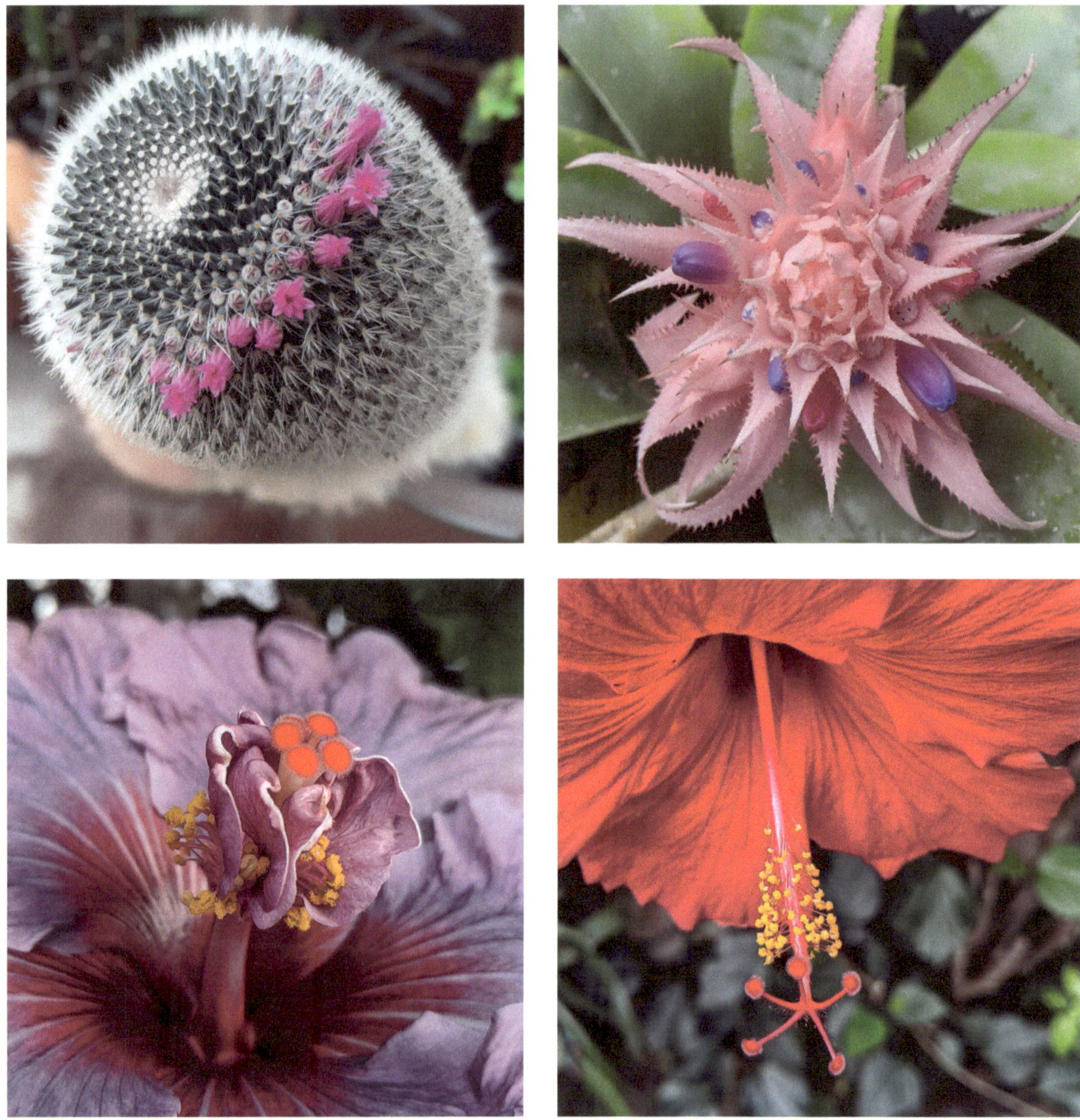

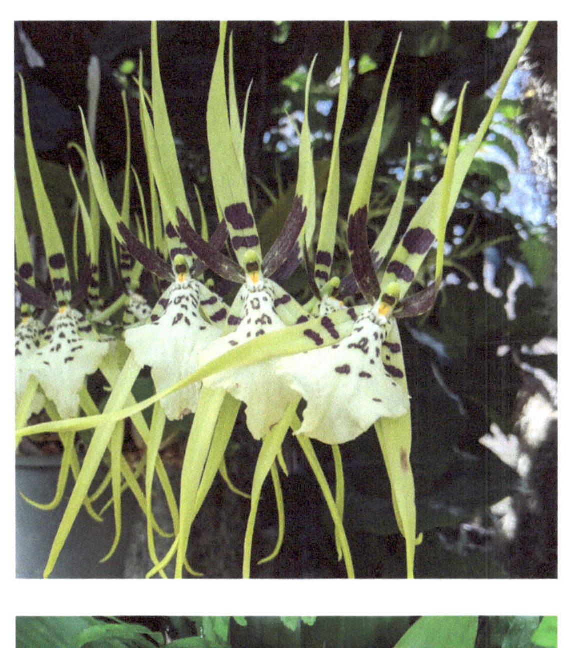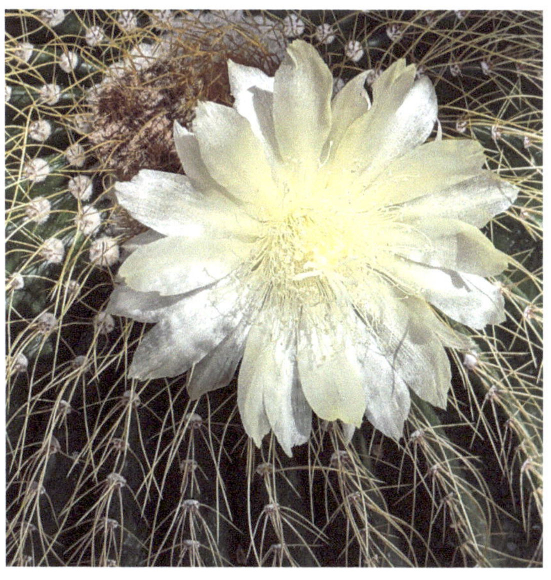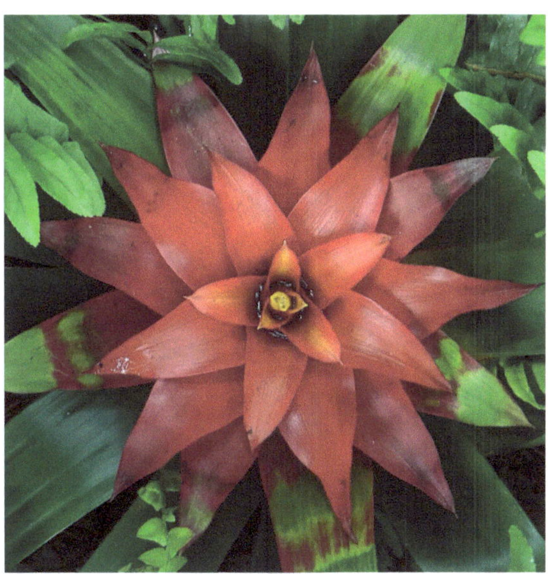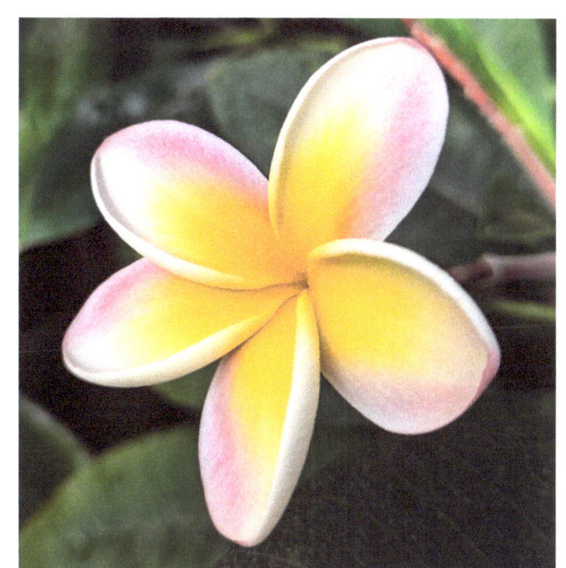

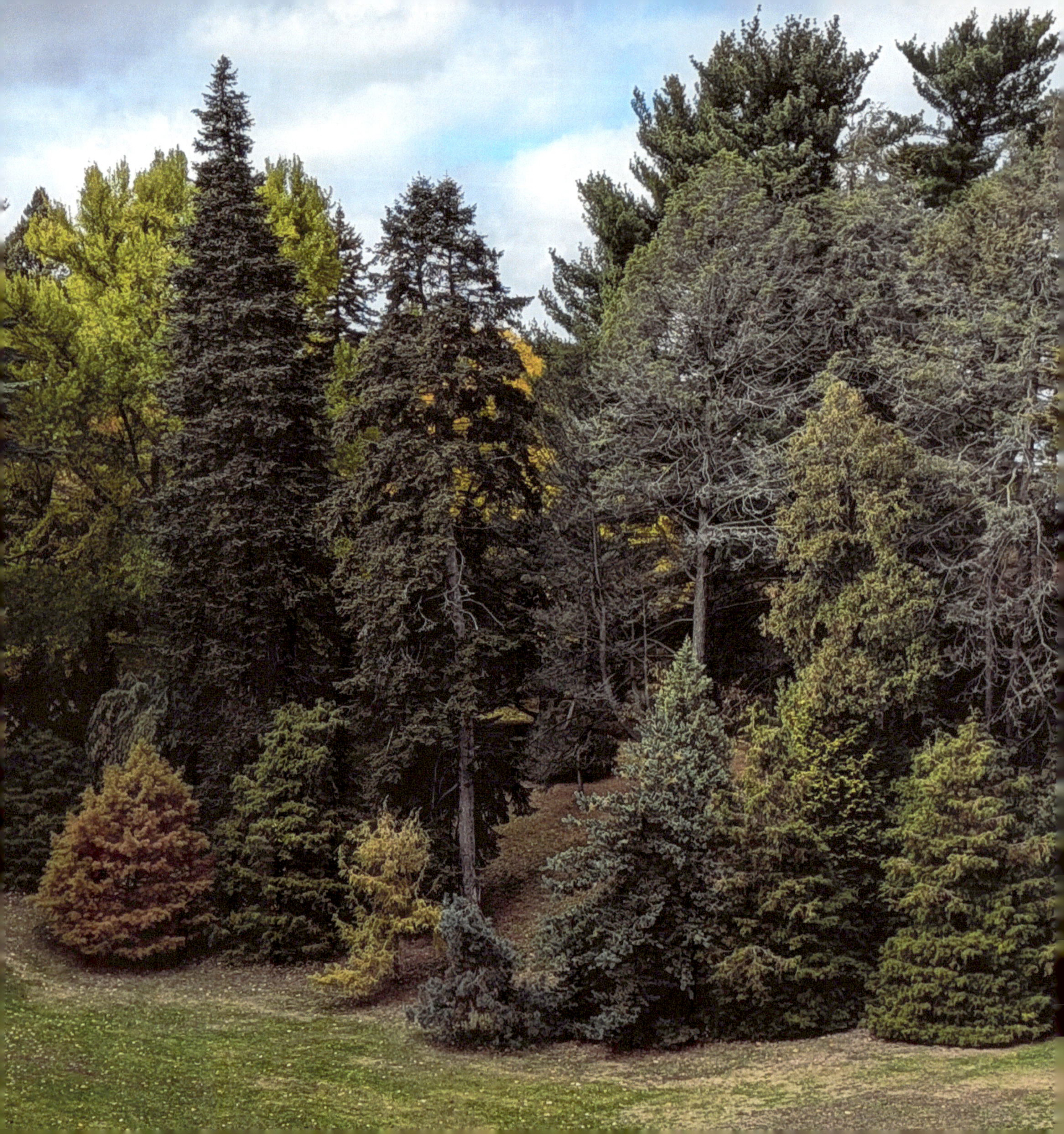

The Pinetum

Encircling the park's upper reaches, the pinetum offers a deeper immersion into nature. Established more than a century ago, its collection of cone-bearing trees and shrubs includes more than 300 species and varieties collected from around the world. Most plantings belong to the evergreen family—pines, spruces, firs, and hemlocks—but the collection also includes deciduous conifers such as larch, dawn redwood, and bald cypress, which shed their needles each autumn. Nearby, ancient ginkgo trees add another layer of texture and history to the landscape.

Walking the loop along Pinetum Drive, visitors move through shifting shades of green: blue-gray spruce beside deep hemlock, airy larch beside towering white pine. In summer, the grove offers cool shade and a faint resin scent. In winter, when much of the park rests, the pinetum holds its quiet, enduring presence with color and structure.

The pinetum's steadiness is not accidental. It reflects decades of careful tending—work that is rarely noticed, yet essential to the tranquility the space provides.

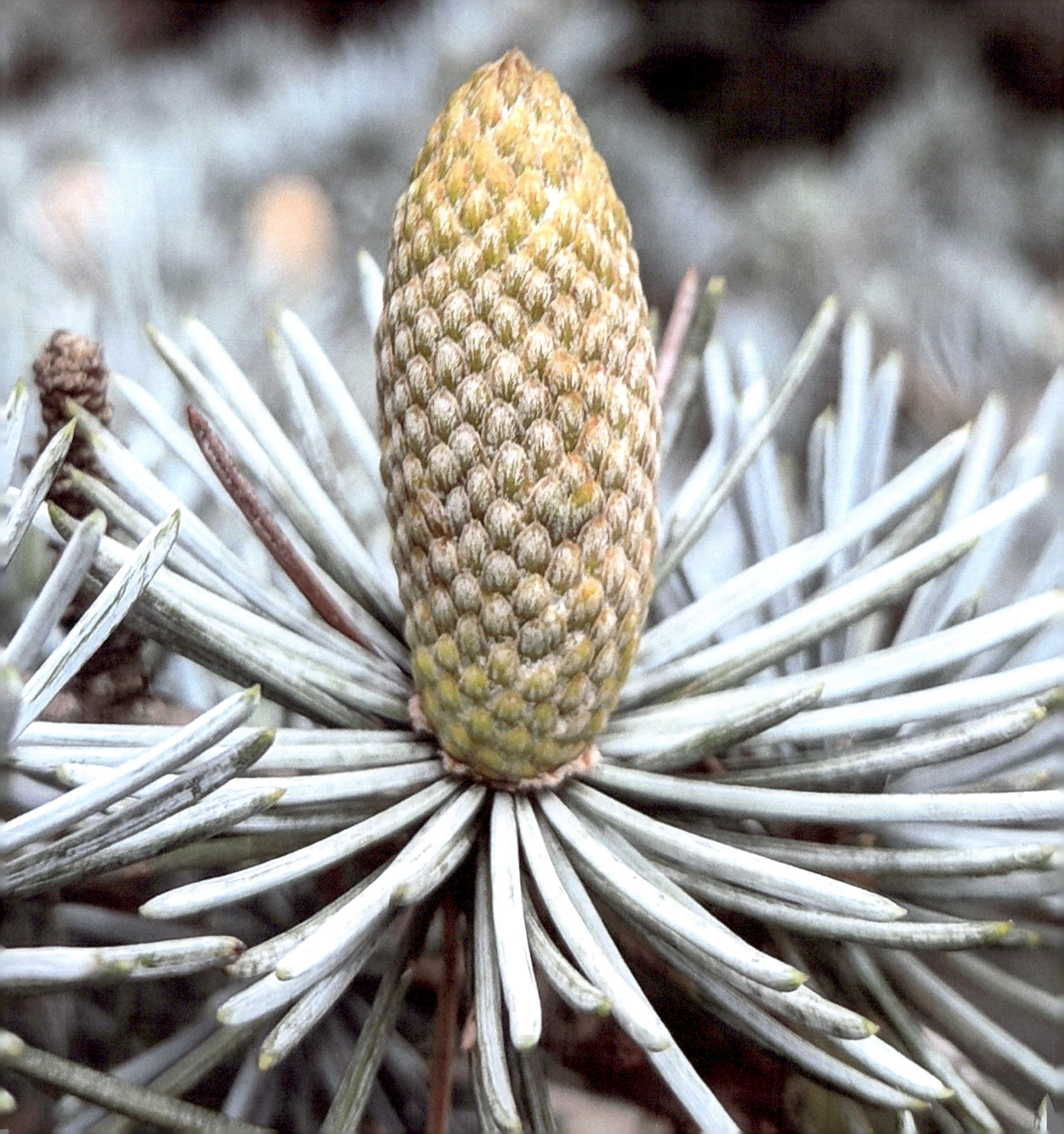

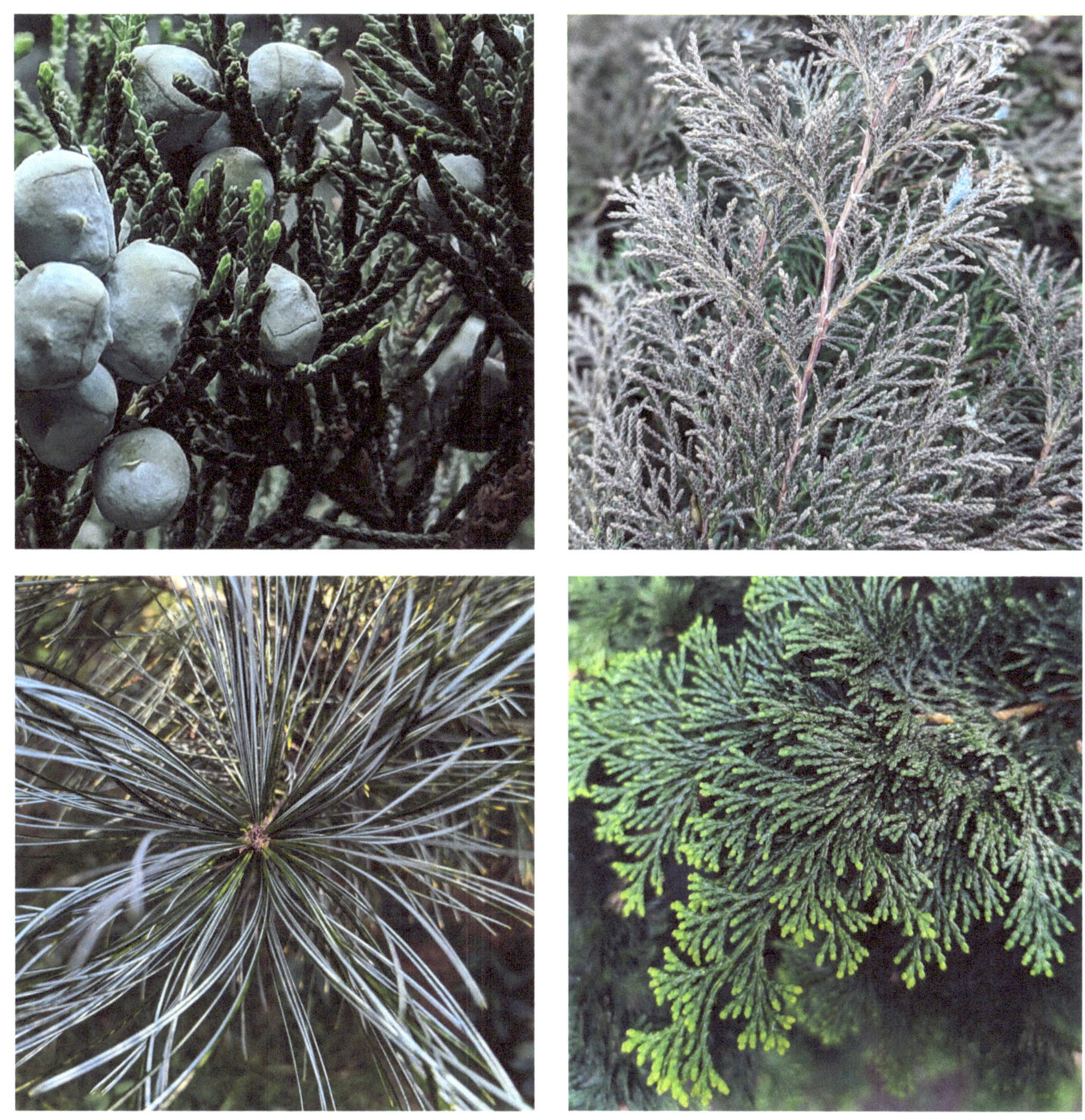

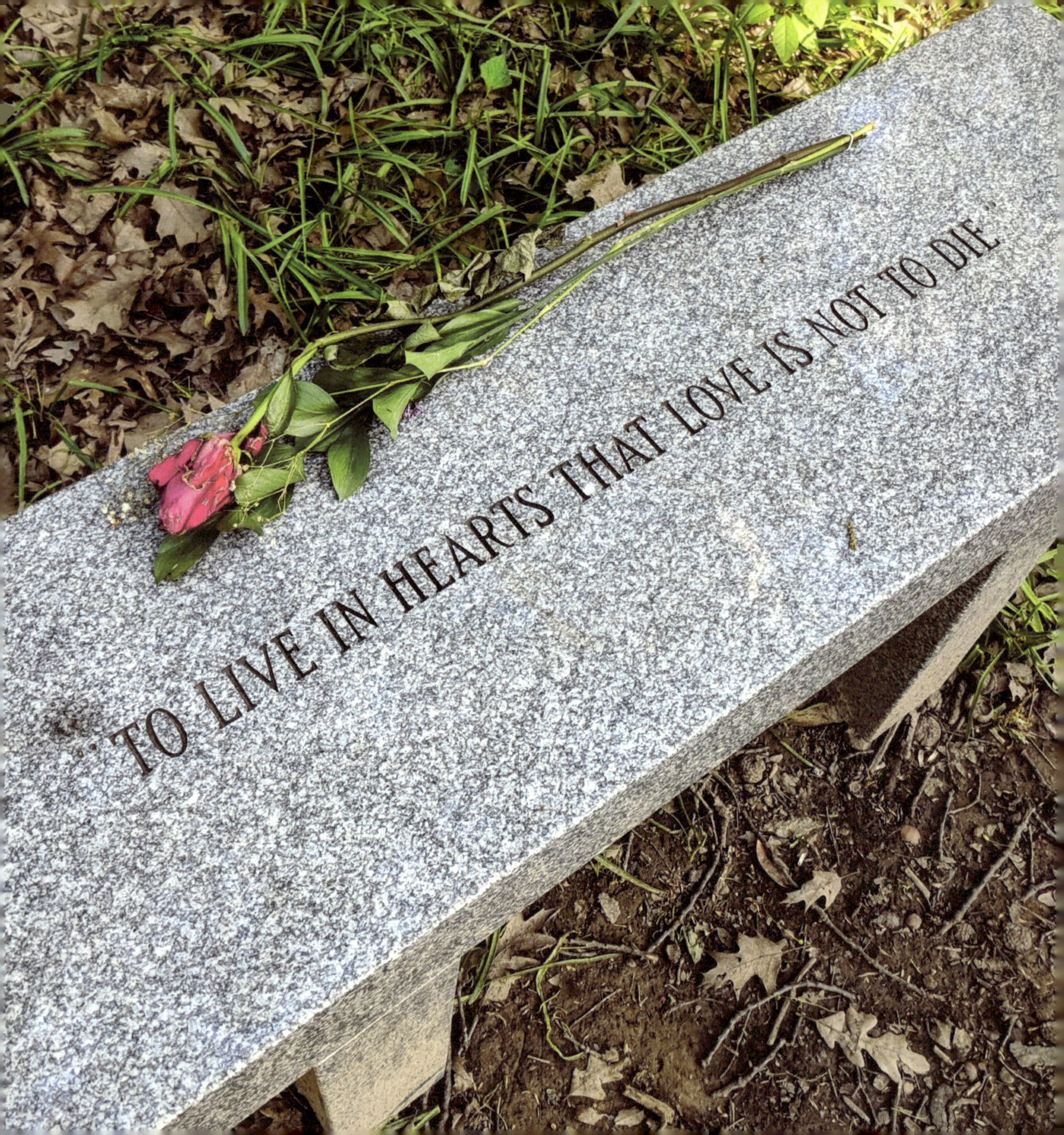

TO LIVE IN HEARTS THAT LOVE IS NOT TO DIE

The Poet's Garden

Across Reservoir Avenue from the Lamberton Conservatory, a narrow path with wrought-iron portals at either end leads into the Poet's Garden, a quiet space shaped by more than a century of community devotion. Established in 1916 to mark the 300th anniversary of William Shakespeare's death, the garden began as a project of the Rochester Garden Club, inspired by plants mentioned in Shakespeare's plays and sonnets. Volunteers planted the border and added stone benches etched with quotations, a bird bath, and a sundial.

Over time, the garden evolved. Many of Shakespeare's plants struggled in Rochester's climate, and the focus shifted toward native trees, shrubs, ferns, and wildflowers better suited to the land. What began as Shakespeare's Garden became the Poet's Garden, shaped as much by place as by poetry.

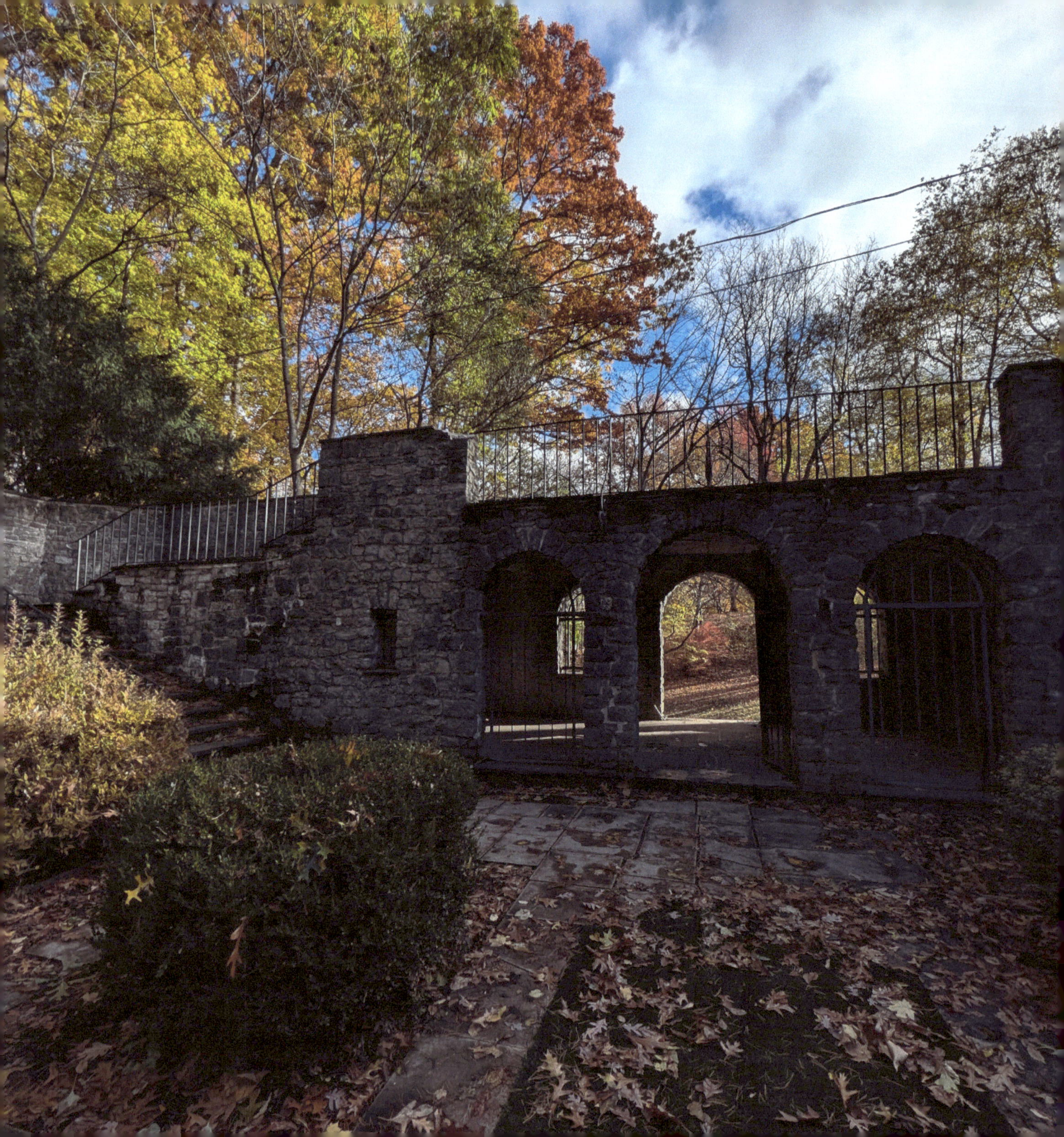

Warner Castle & the Sunken Garden

On the park's western edge stands Warner Castle, built in 1854 as the private residence of Horatio Gates Warner. Designed to resemble a Scottish manor, the stone structure adds a distinct architectural presence to Highland Park's largely naturalistic landscape. The city acquired the property in 1951, extending the park's reach and character.

Behind the castle lies the Sunken Garden, designed in 1930 by landscape architect Alling S. DeForest. As reflected in his earlier work on the grounds of the George Eastman House, DeForest drew inspiration from the English Renaissance style, creating a space that feels like a sheltered outdoor room—enclosed by limestone walls, terraced steps, and formal plantings that stand in sharp contrast to the surrounding hills and trees.

Managed by the Highland Park Conservancy garden stewards, the estate's gardens extend beyond the Sunken Garden, with perennial displays that wrap around the castle's stone walls and continue along connecting pathways. Together, they create a tapestry of color and texture that evolves from spring through autumn.

Today, Warner Castle is home to the Landmark Society of Western New York. Although access to the building varies, the grounds and the Sunken Garden remain open to the public. It is one of Highland Park's most unexpected spaces—intimate, structured, and quietly elegant.

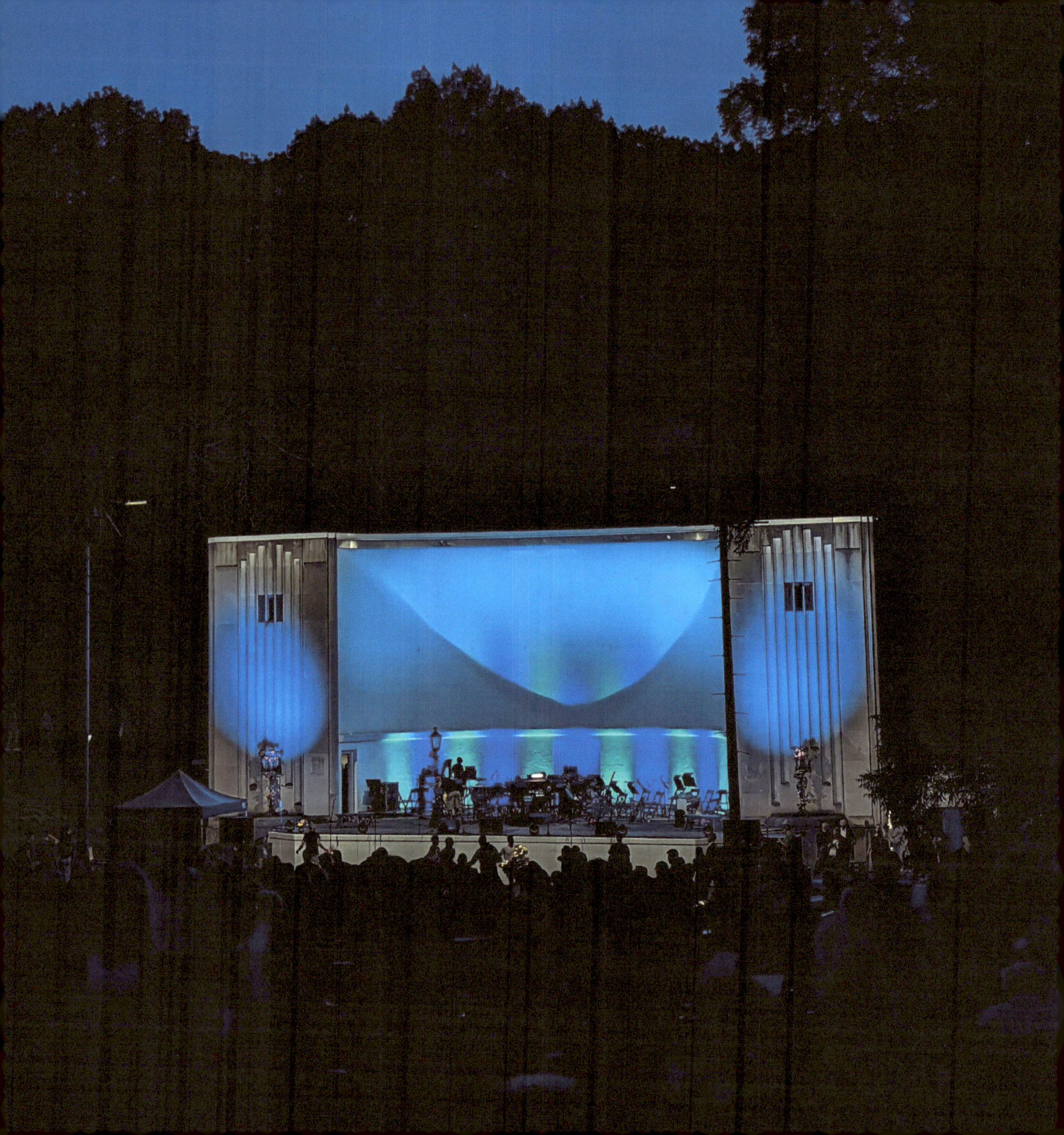

Highland Bowl

Downhill from South Avenue, the land opens onto a broad slope known as Highland Bowl—a grassy hillside that forms a natural amphitheater.

The Works Progress Administration built the concrete stage shell in the late 1930s and dedicated it as the John Dunbar Music Pavilion. Its curved form and modest scale reflect the era's investment in public spaces, adding a functional element to a landscape intended initially to let the land speak for itself.

Backed by mature trees, the pavilion remains understated. Each summer, audiences spread blankets on the hillside for concerts, poetry readings, film screenings, and other gatherings. Since 1997, the Rochester Community Players have presented their annual Shakespeare in the Park production here in a continuing tradition of shared cultural experience beneath the open sky.

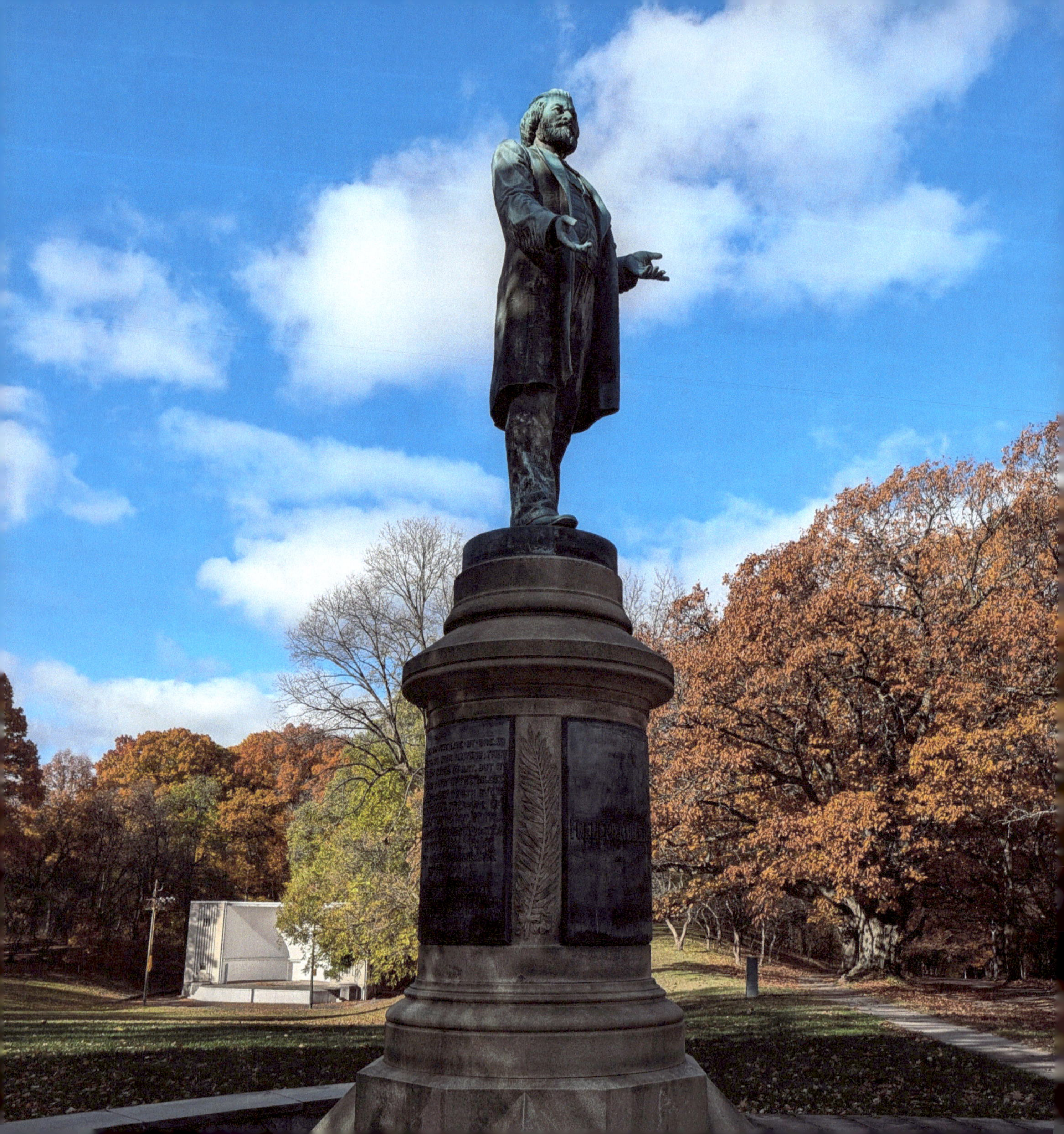

Frederick Douglass Memorial Plaza

Overlooking Highland Bowl, the Frederick Douglass Memorial Plaza honors one of Rochester's most influential residents and one of America's most powerful voices for freedom and justice. Douglass chose Rochester deliberately. From 1847 to 1872, he published *The North Star* here and helped shape national conversations about abolition and civil rights from the city he called home—one that, as a significant stop on the Underground Railroad, earned his trust. His residence stood just down the street from this hillside, where he raised his family on a small farm, anchoring his national work in this very neighborhood.

The bronze statue at the plaza's focal point is widely regarded as the first public monument in the United States to honor an African American man. Sculpted by Sidney W. Edwards and unveiled in 1899—just four years after Douglass's death—it was created while those who had known him were still alive, making it closer to a memorial made in grief than a distant historical tribute.

The statue has been moved several times, a quiet record of the city's evolving relationship with Douglass's legacy. In 1941, the City of Rochester relocated it to Highland Park, placing his likeness within the landscape of his adopted city, not far from the farm he once called home. Now Douglass stands elevated against the open sky, his outstretched arms suggesting welcome and resolve. Facing an illuminated North Star sculpture, he appears in dialogue across the centuries, reminding visitors that remembrance is not static and that the work he began continues to this day.

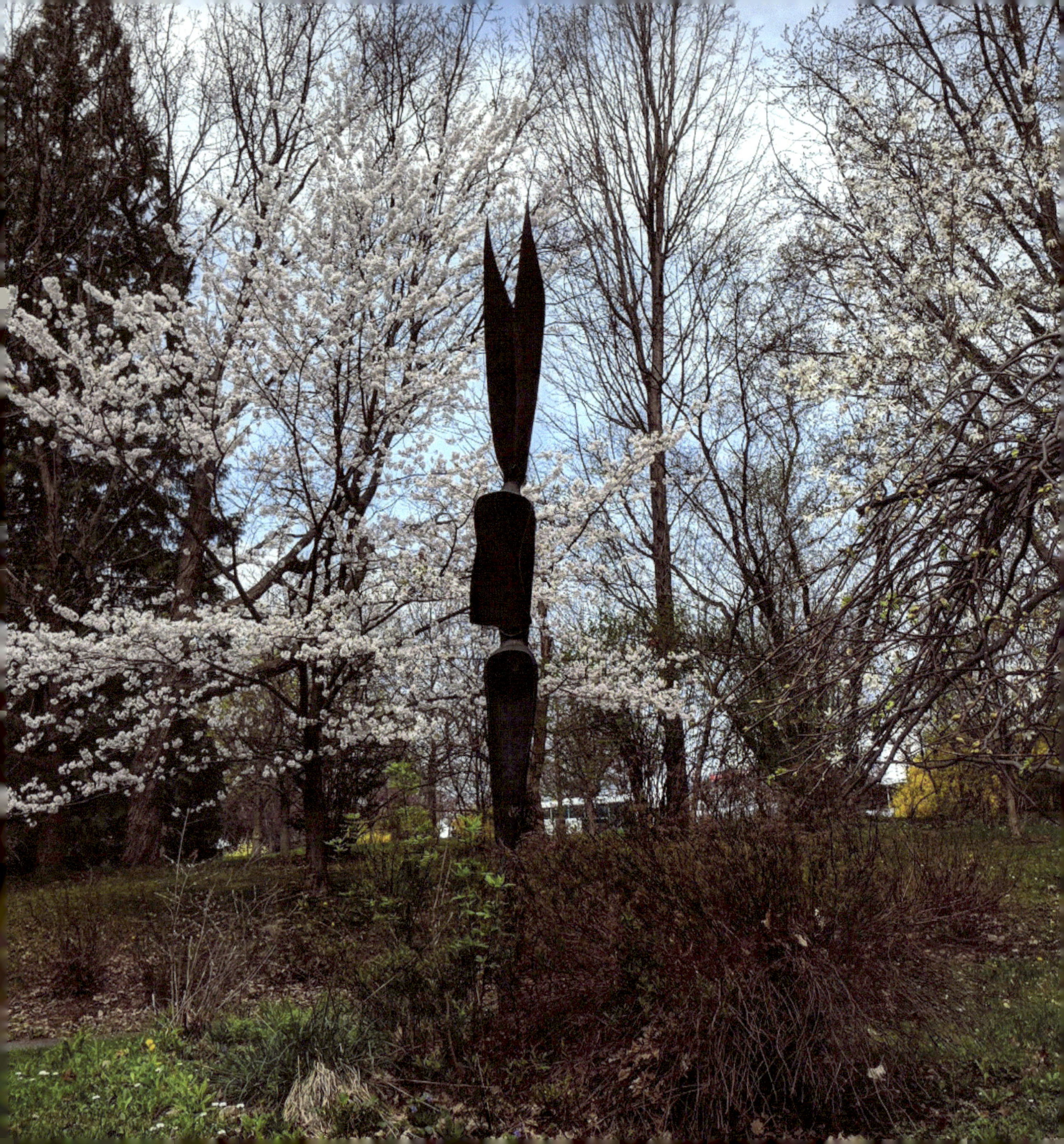

Beikirch Park

South of Highland Avenue lies Beikirch Park, a memorial landscape honoring Sergeant Gary Beikirch, a Vietnam veteran, combat medic, and Medal of Honor recipient.

Within Beikirch Park, a series of memorials honors service and remembrance, including monuments dedicated to Vietnam veterans, those lost in the War on Terror, victims of AIDS, crime victims, and workers' rights. At its heart lies the Remember Garden, a quiet tribute to residents of the nineteenth-century institutions that once stood on this site and whose unmarked graves rest beneath it. Together, these spaces form a landscape of gratitude and grace—a place where memory and renewal coexist.

Nearby, the Lilac Arches create a welcoming threshold. A sequence of pale arches holds festival energy in May, and frames quieter, more intimate moments the rest of the year.

Left: AIDS Remembrance Garden

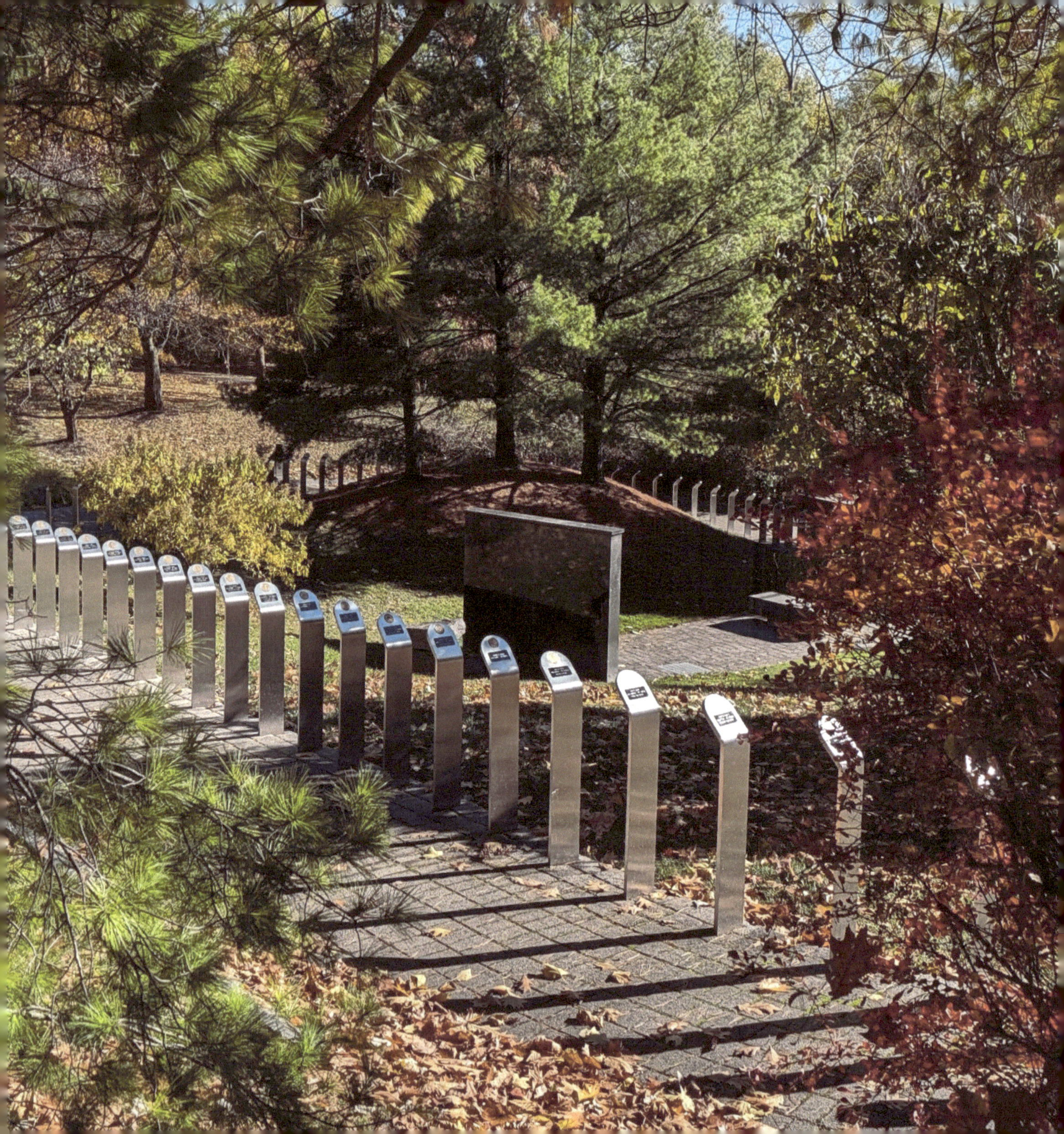

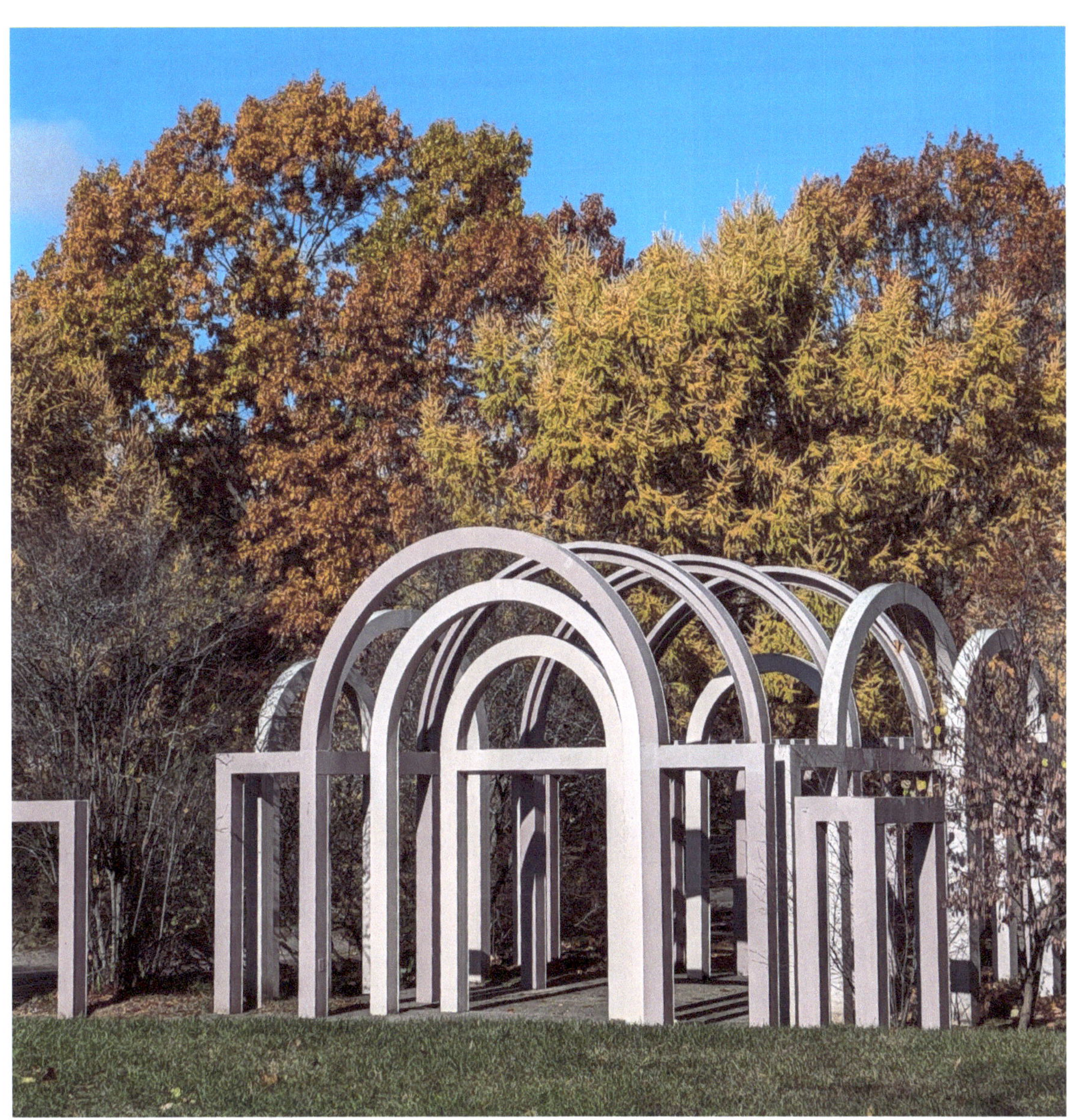

Left: Vietnam Veterans Memorial; above: Lilac Arches

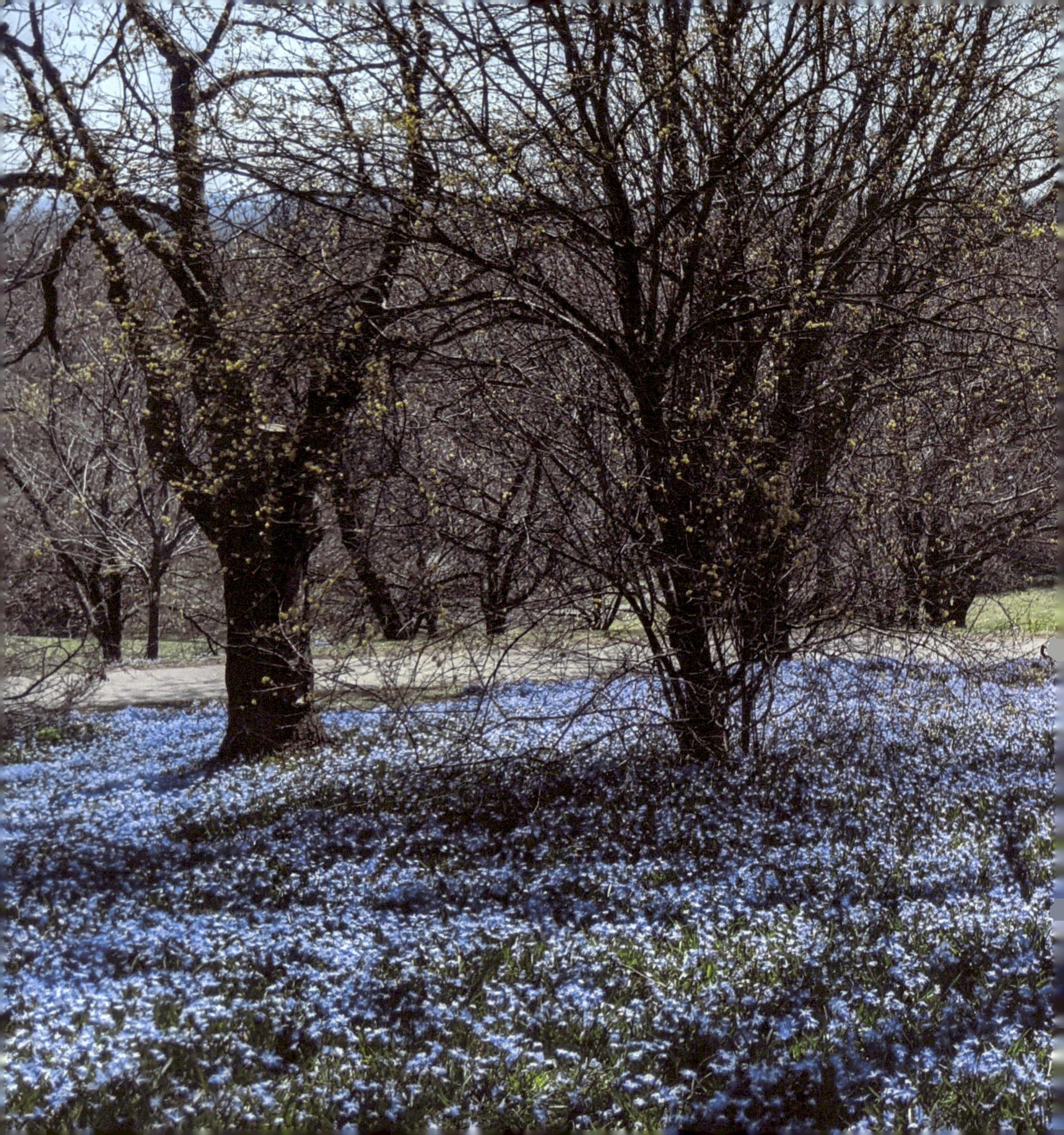

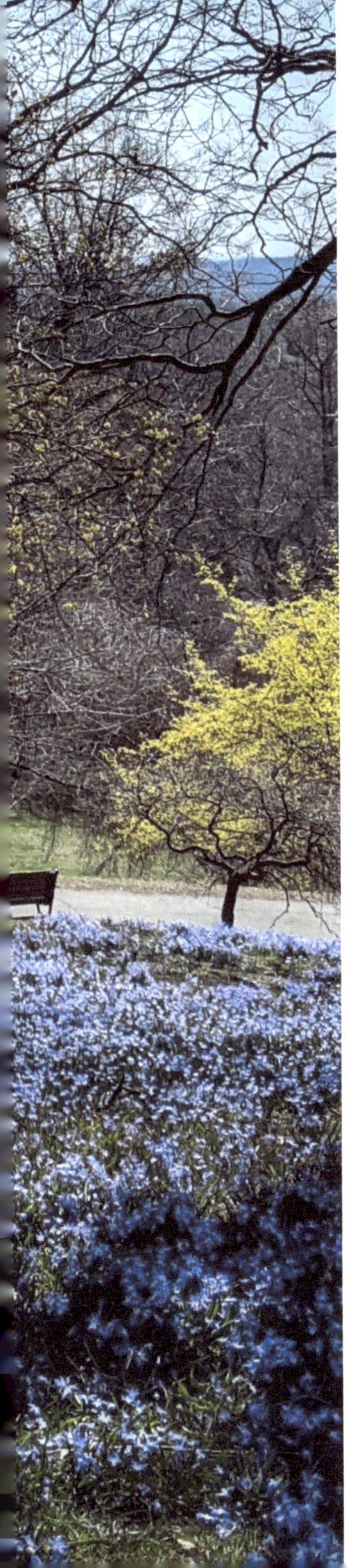

Spring

The park awakens subtly, then unmistakably, rewarding return visits with small changes that unfold with each passing day. The soil softens. Buds swell. Paths are slowly unveiled from winter's quiet hold.

Visitors wander uphill, guided as much by anticipation as by sight. Old stone steps reemerge beneath leaf litter. Light slips through bare branches, tracing the park's curves and terraces. Carpets of early glory-of-the-snow and Siberian squill—tiny blue signs of spring—give way to cherries, crabapples, and the promise of lilacs still weeks away. Nothing here blooms by chance.

There is movement everywhere: gardeners tending beds, photographers shifting position to frame a scene, walkers slowing their pace without quite knowing why.

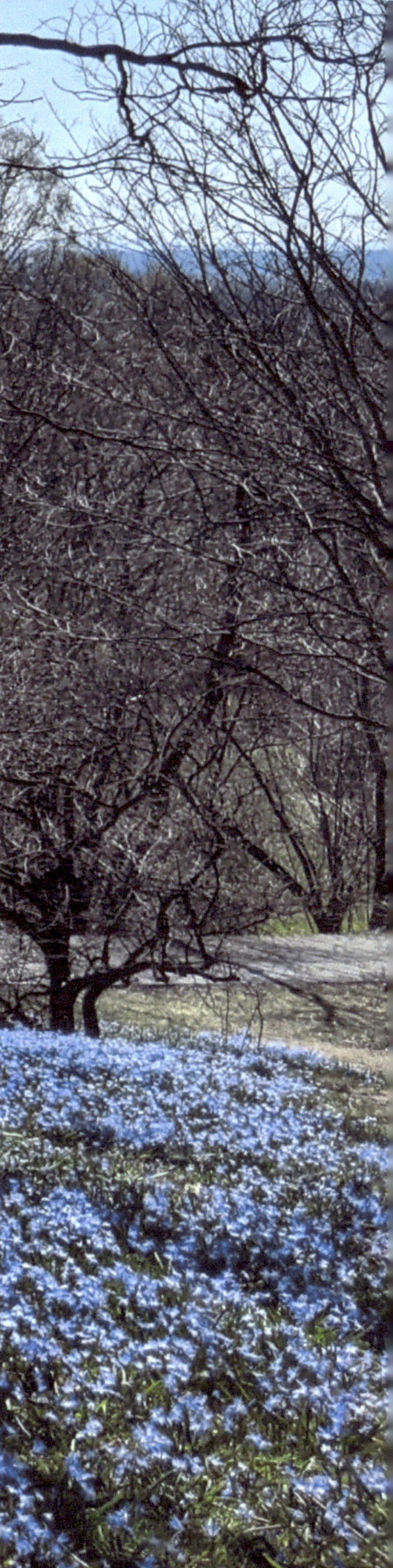

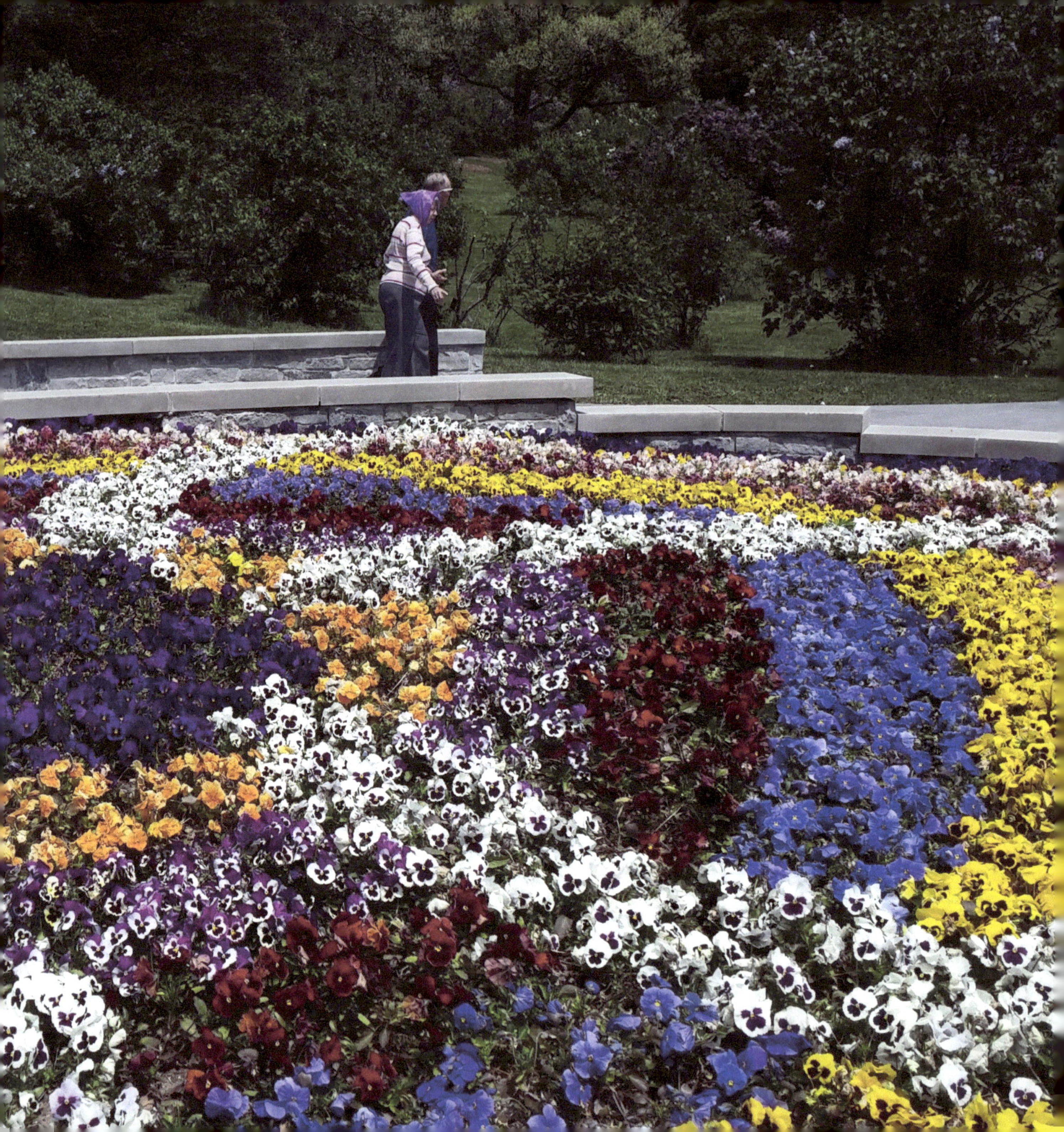

The Pansy Bed

Since 1904, the Pansy Bed has been one of Highland Park's most deliberate expressions of design. This oval bed of blooms is planned and planted each spring by the Monroe County Parks horticultural staff. No two designs are ever repeated, with each season bringing a newly imagined pattern shaped by careful color choices and geometric order that ultimately gives way to a bold display of summer annuals in June.

More than 20,000 pansies are grown in Monroe County greenhouses for the display, then planted by hand to form a dense, early-season mosaic. The layout is designed by Kent Millham, whose decades of work with Monroe County Parks have shaped the Pansy Bed into a living tradition. His approach to the design—rooted in precision, continuity, and care—continues to define the display each spring.

The result is playful yet disciplined: a formal counterpoint to the park's rolling lawns and naturalistic slopes, and one of the first unmistakable signs that spring has arrived.

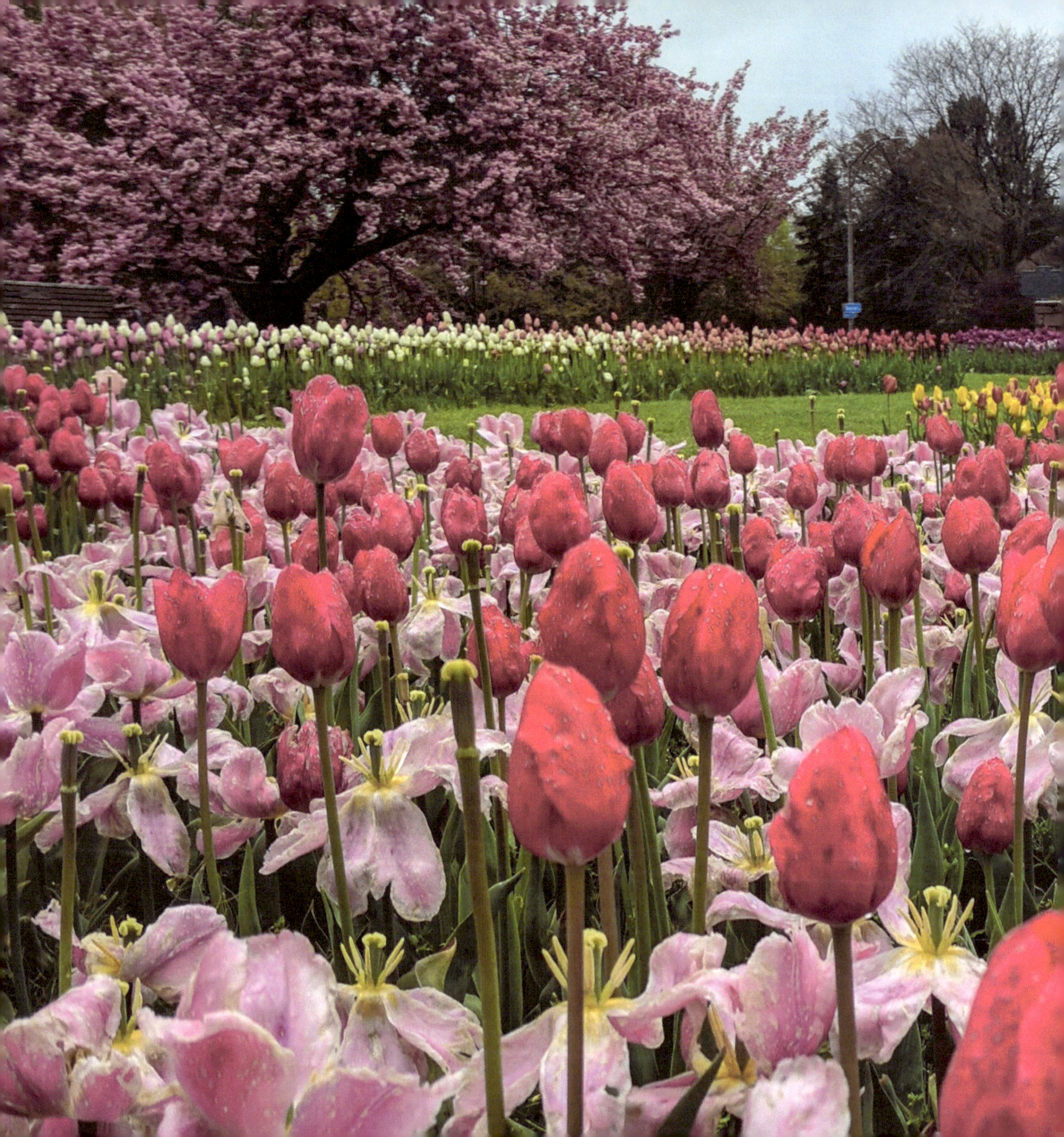

The Tulip Beds

Alongside the Lamberton Conservatory, sweeping bands of tulips announce spring in bold form. Each year, approximately 10,000 tulip bulbs are planted in beds of varied shapes, creating a kaleidoscope of color that peaks in late April and early May.

Set along busy South Avenue, the beds are designed to be read in motion—drivers and pedestrians alike take in the display at a glance. Up close, individual varieties reveal subtler differences in height, petal shape, and tone.

To preserve the display's intensity and uniformity, the tulips are treated as annuals. Once their brief but vibrant season ends, the bulbs are removed, and the beds—like the pansy beds—are replanted with summer annuals, ensuring this prominent corner remains colorfully engaging through early autumn.

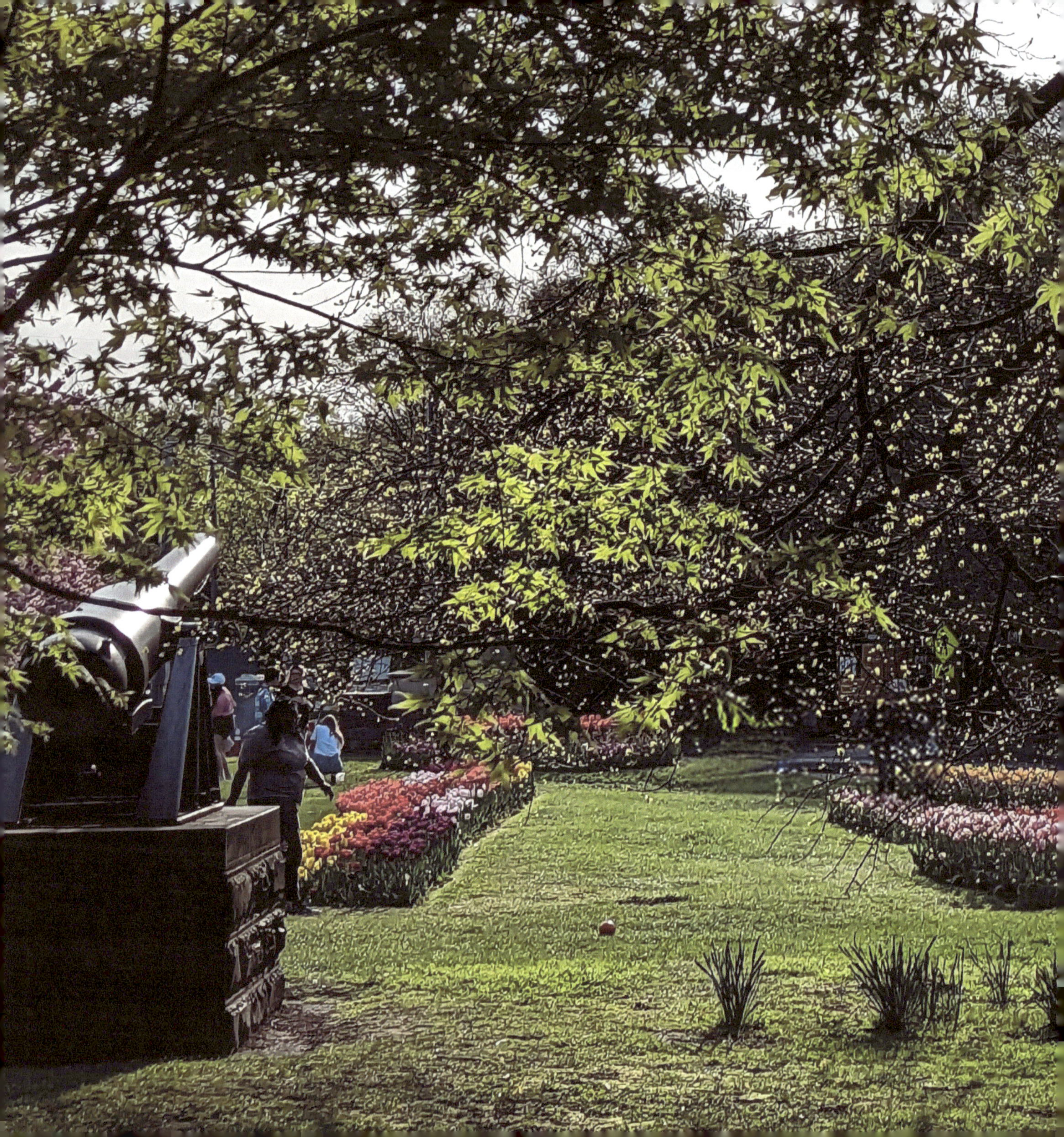

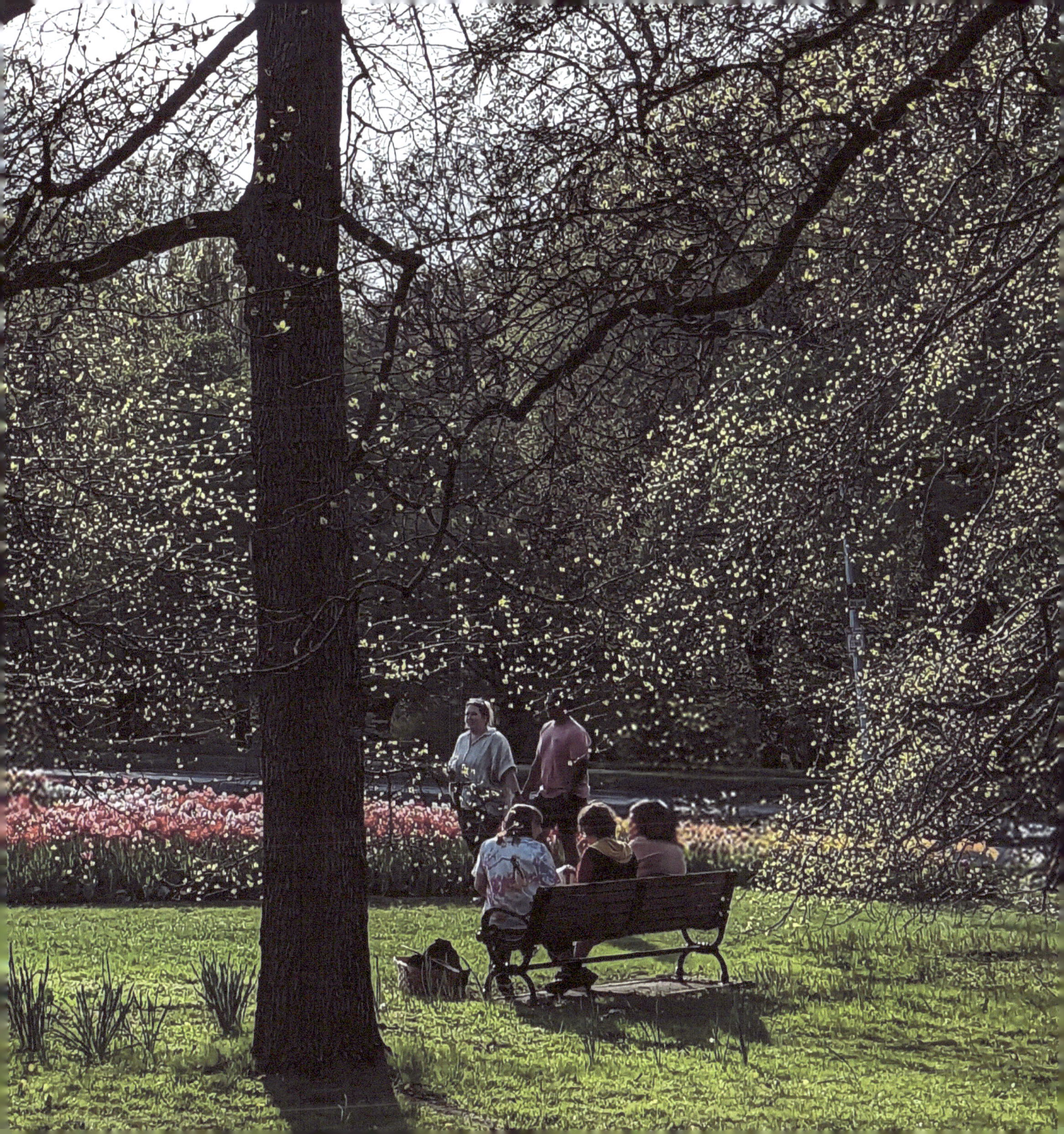

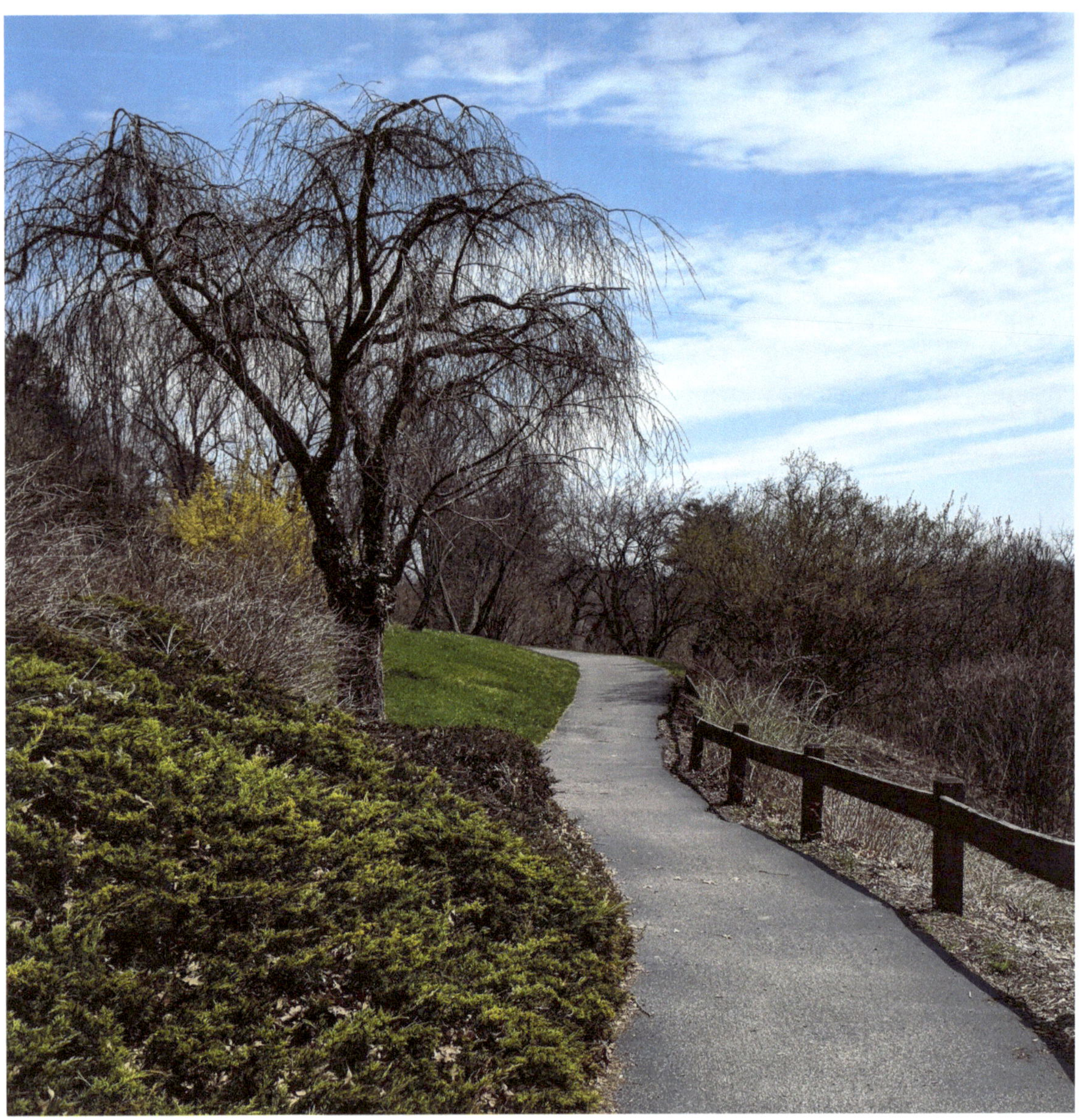

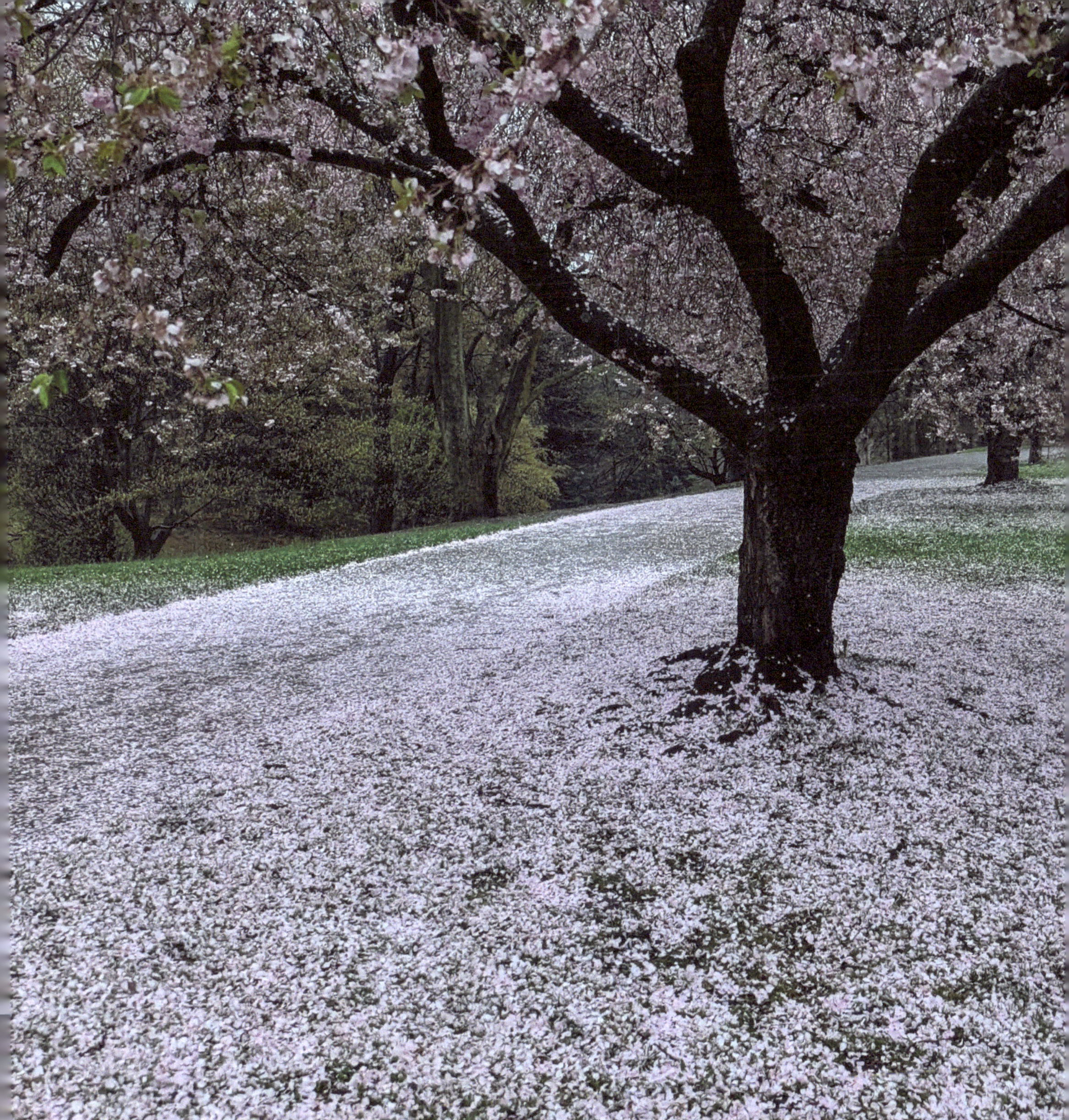

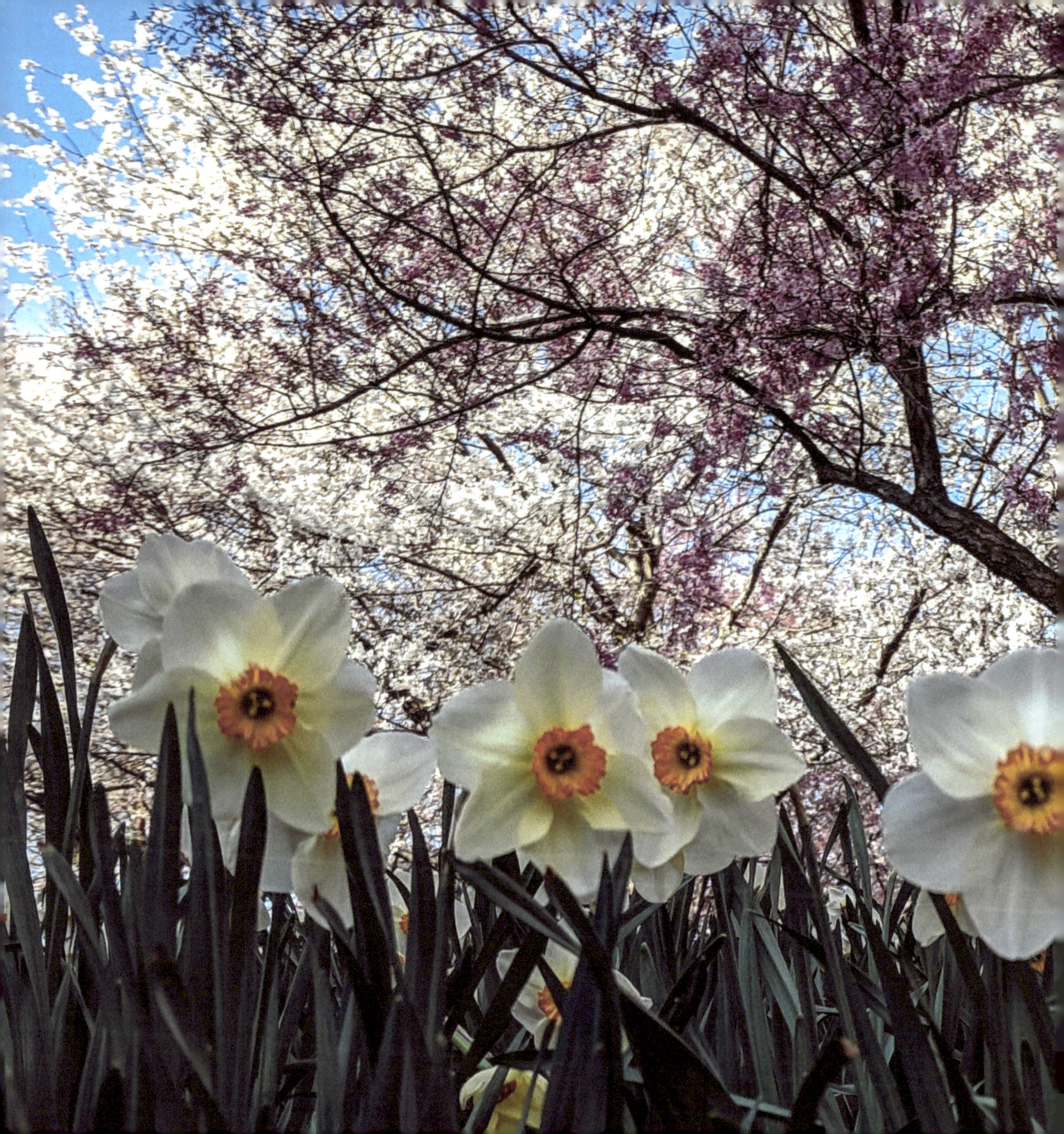

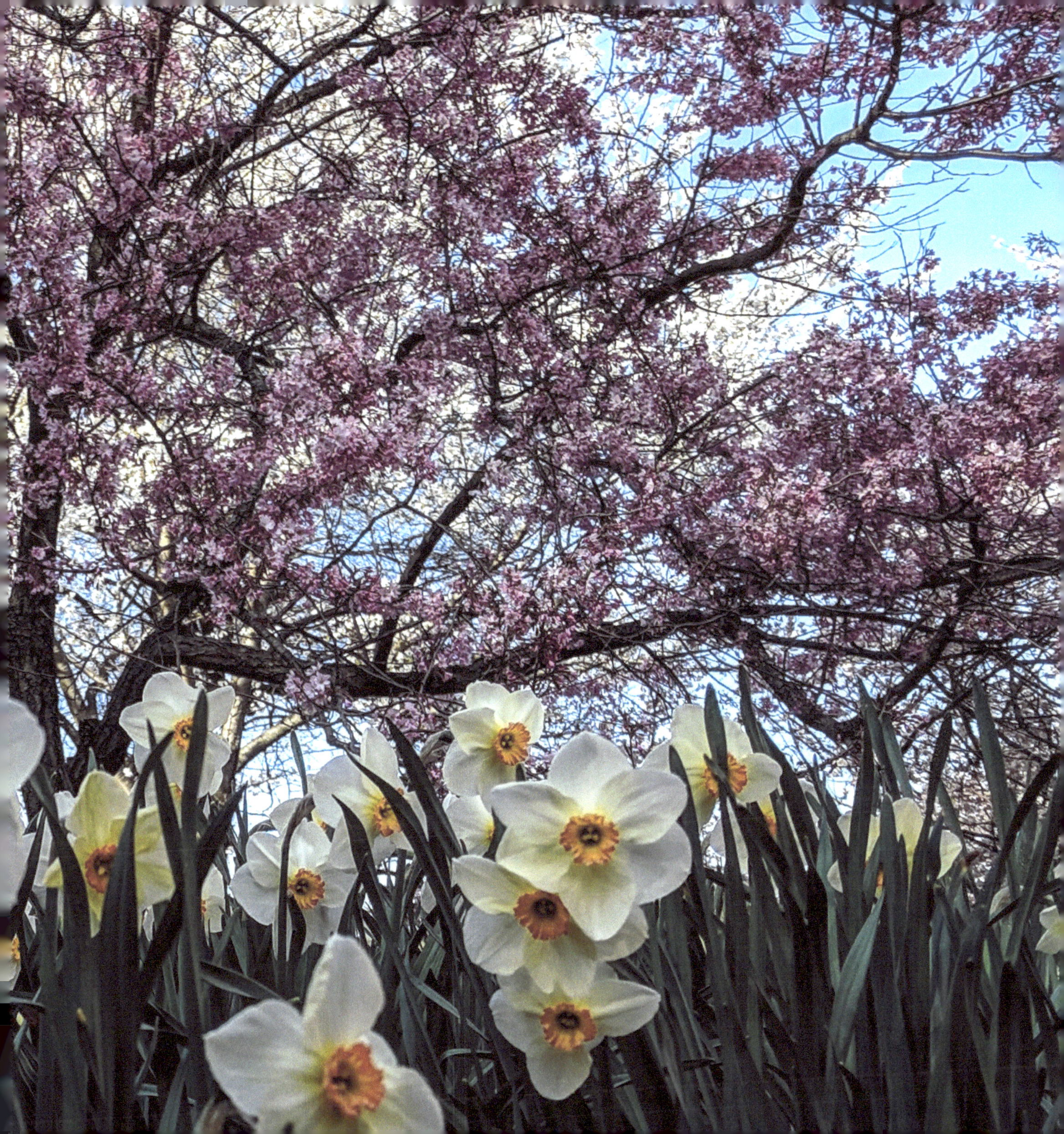

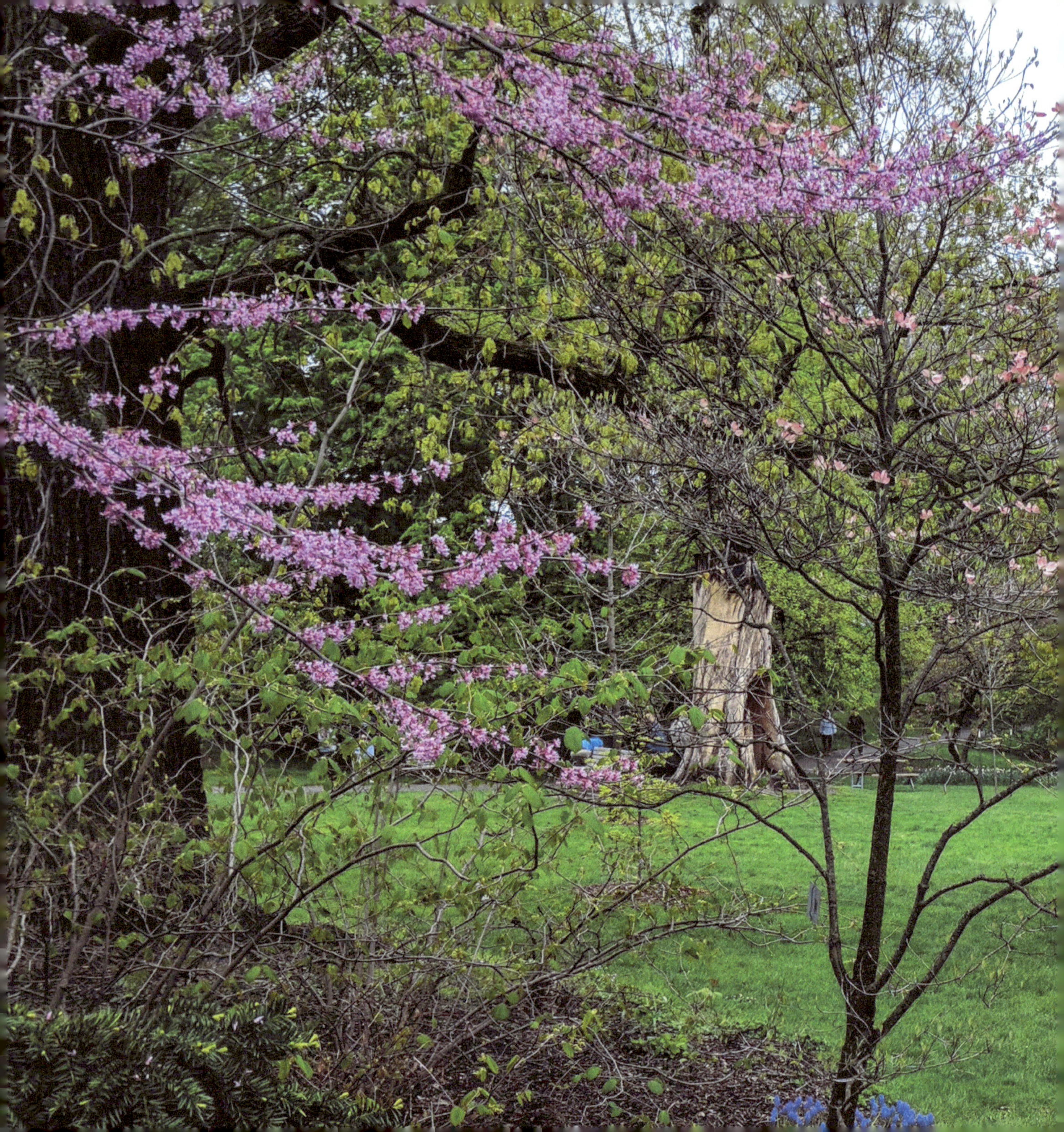

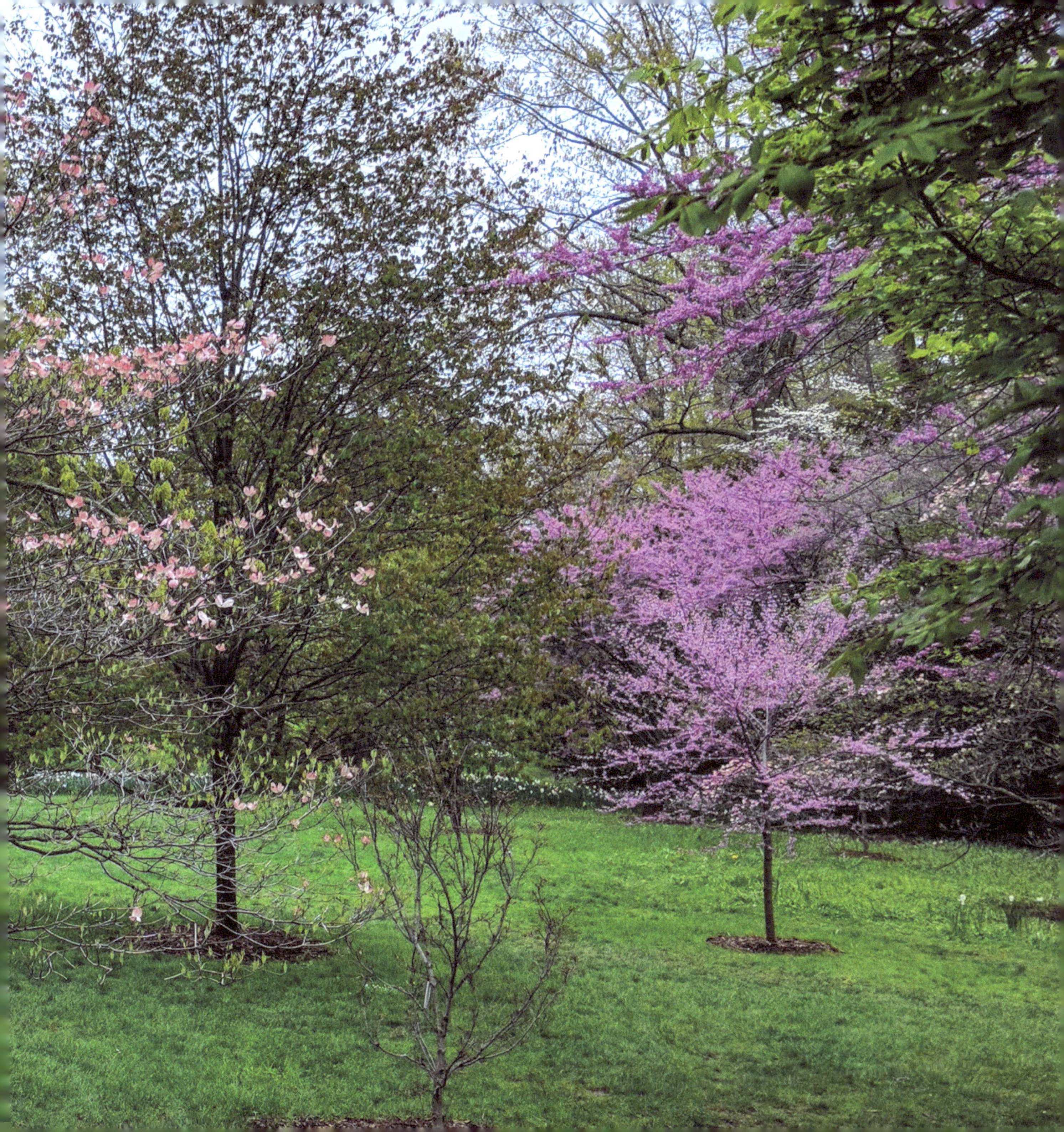

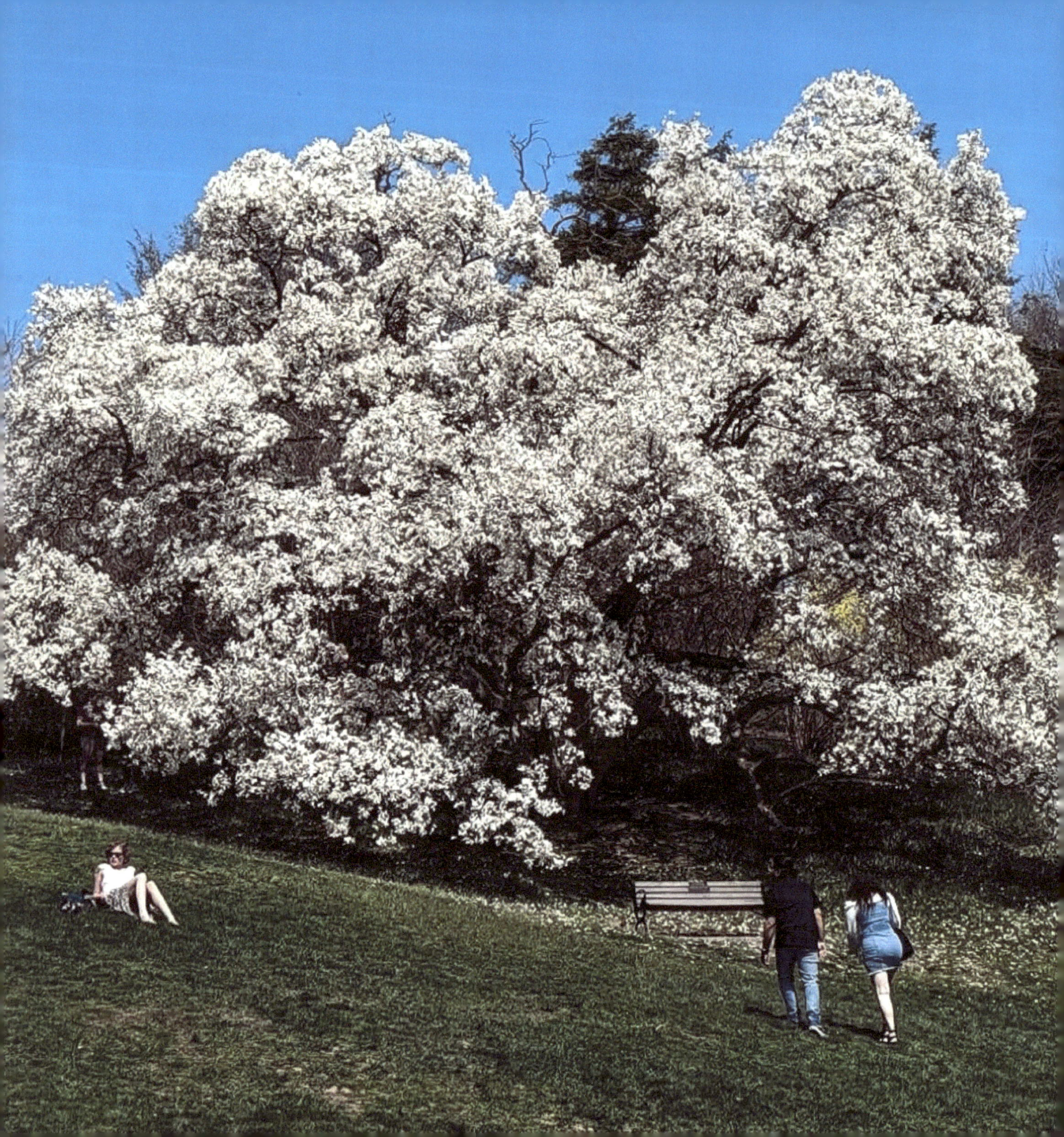

Rose Valley

East of the reservoir, Rose Valley blooms in late April. Flowering pear and cherry trees cover the hillside with soft whites and pinks, transforming the open lawn into one of Highland Park's most beloved spring scenes.

Petals drift across the grass and paths, marking the true arrival of spring. Designed for ornamental effect, the valley's gentle slopes and open center form a natural amphitheater of bloom. Families gather beneath the trees, picnics return to familiar spots, and the park settles into the rhythm of the new season.

Rose Valley is not hidden. It is well loved, visited year after year by those who come to mark the season and savor a shared moment of beauty.

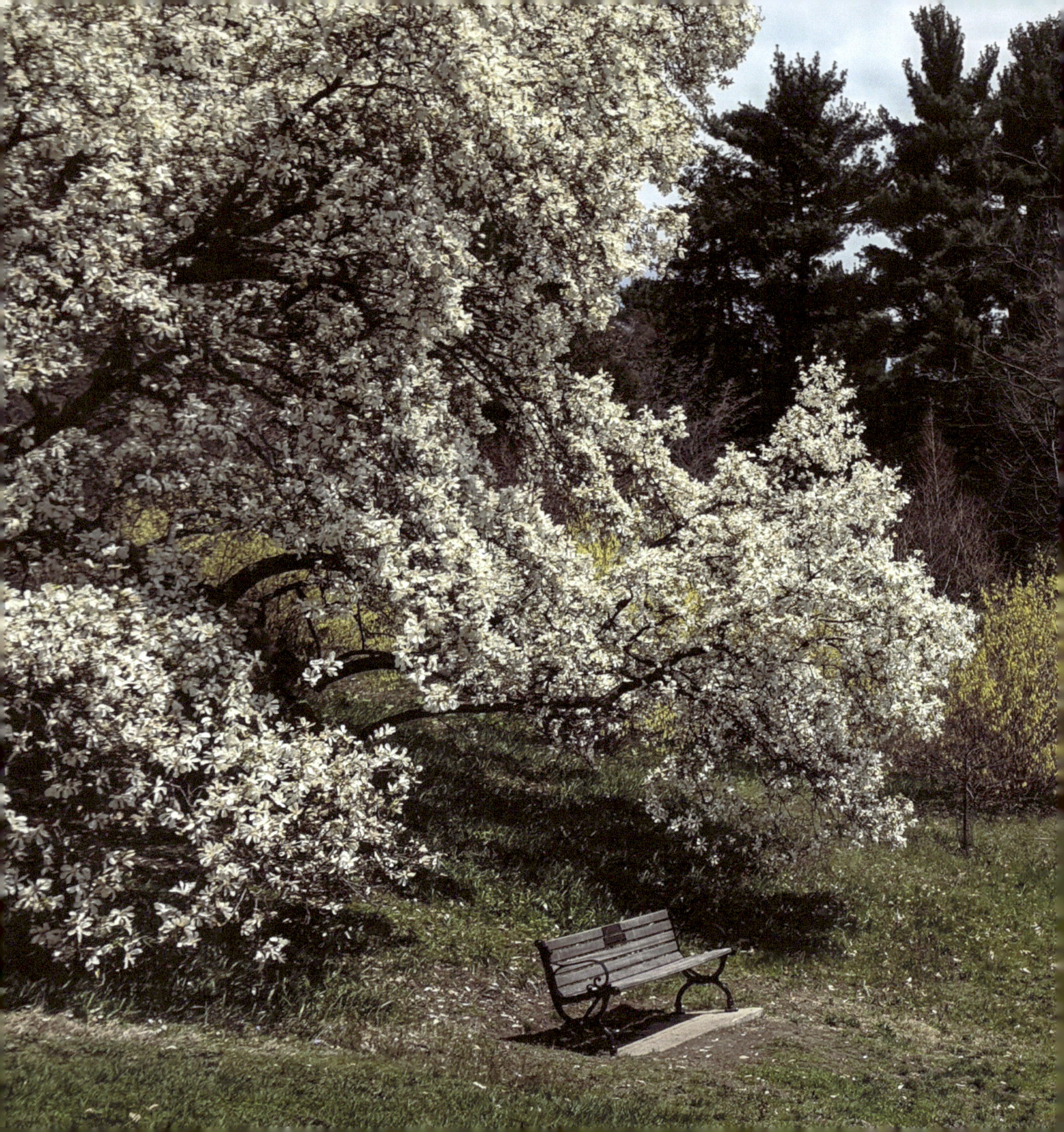

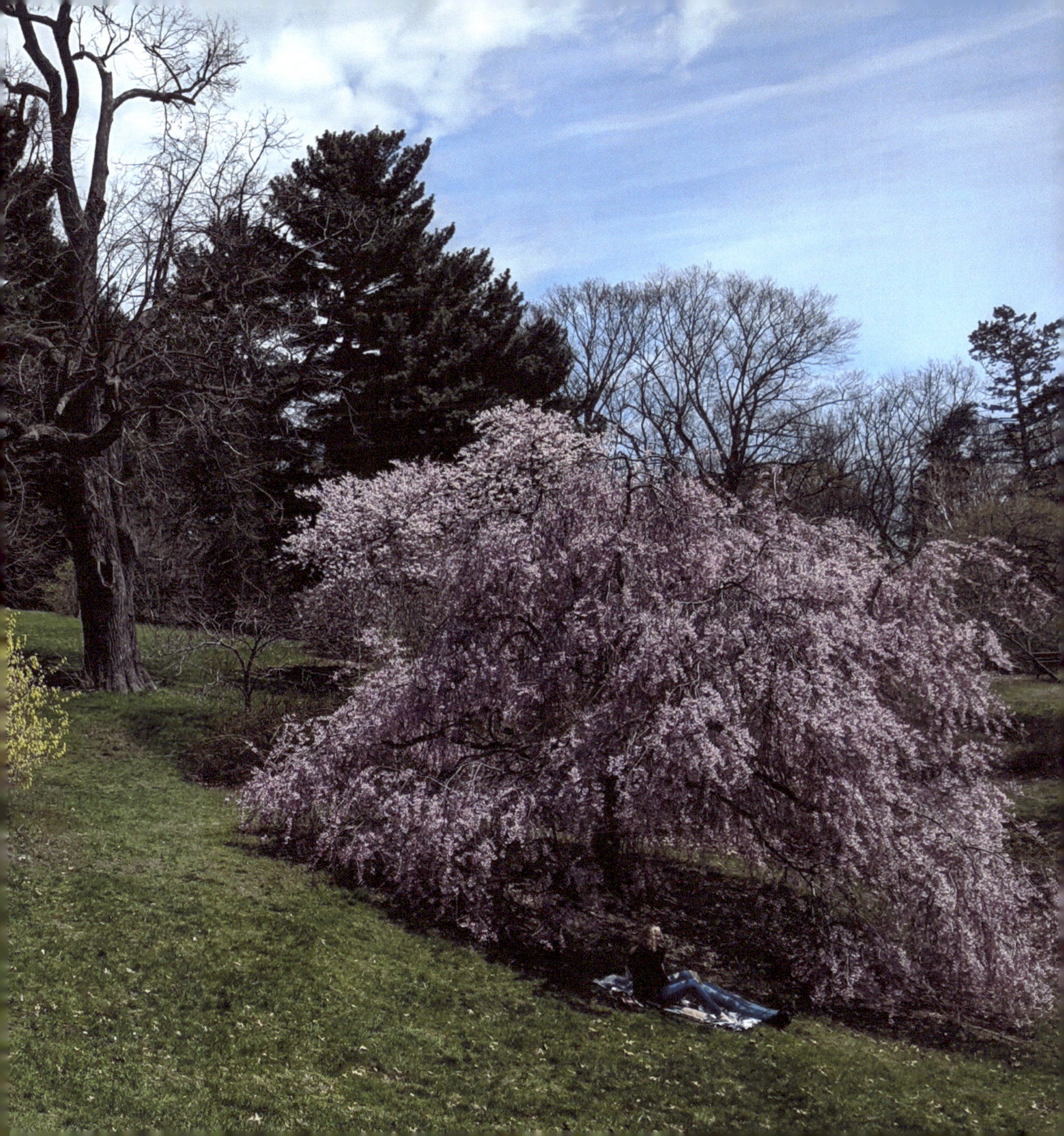

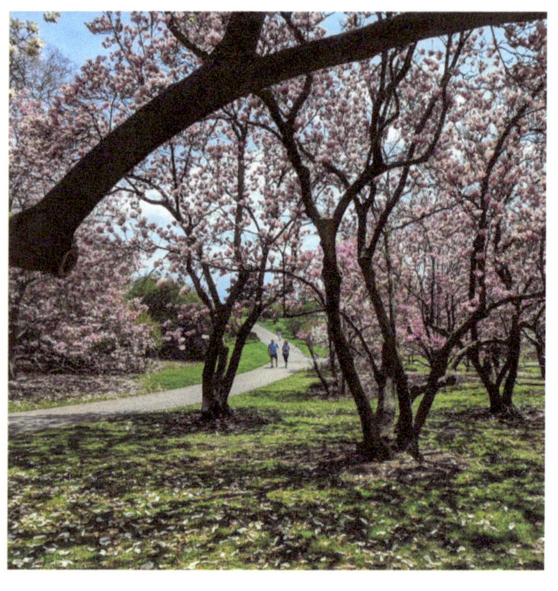
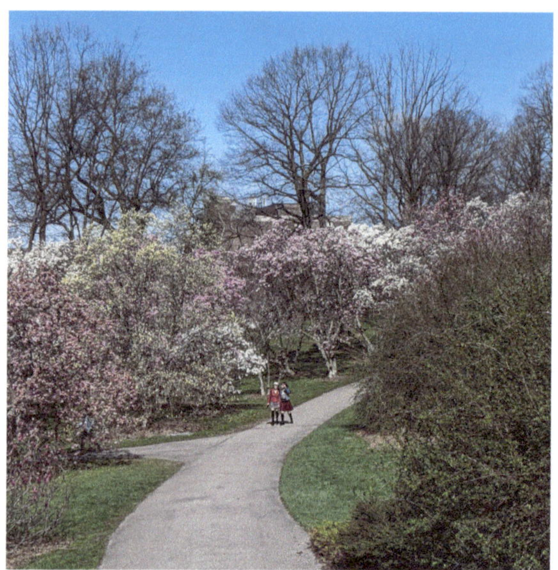
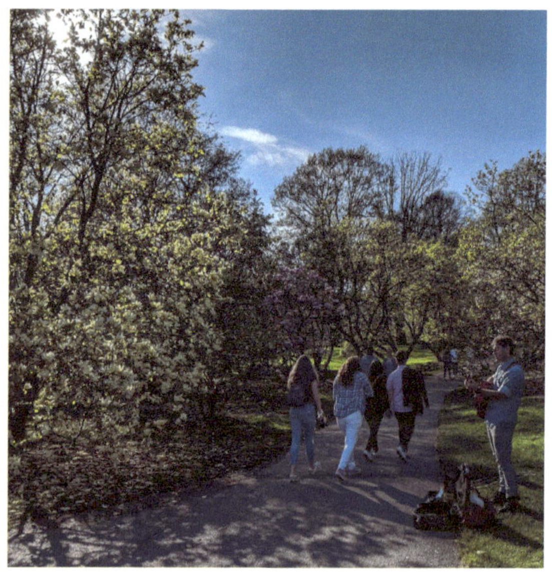
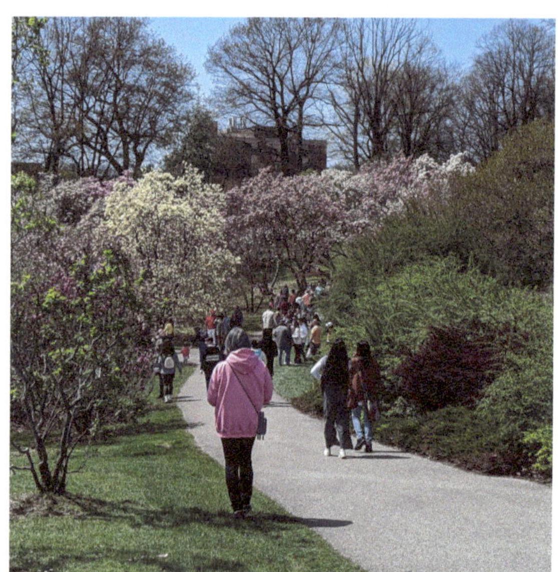

The Magnolia Collection

Before the lilacs awaken and the lawns turn fully green, Highland Park glows with magnolias. Their branches, still stark from winter, suddenly bear blossoms—large and luminous against leafless limbs.

From April into May, slopes near the conservatory and reservoir are brushed with ivory, lemon, blush, and deep rose. Their fragrance drifts through the cool air.

Highland's magnolia collection began in the early twentieth century and became part of the park's growing reputation for ornamental displays. Saucer, star, cucumber, and the later-blooming Little Girl magnolias line a gently sloping path, their blossoms unfolding in succession, stretching the season across weeks. As the petals fall, they gather like silk underfoot, marking the transition from winter's restraint to spring's promise.

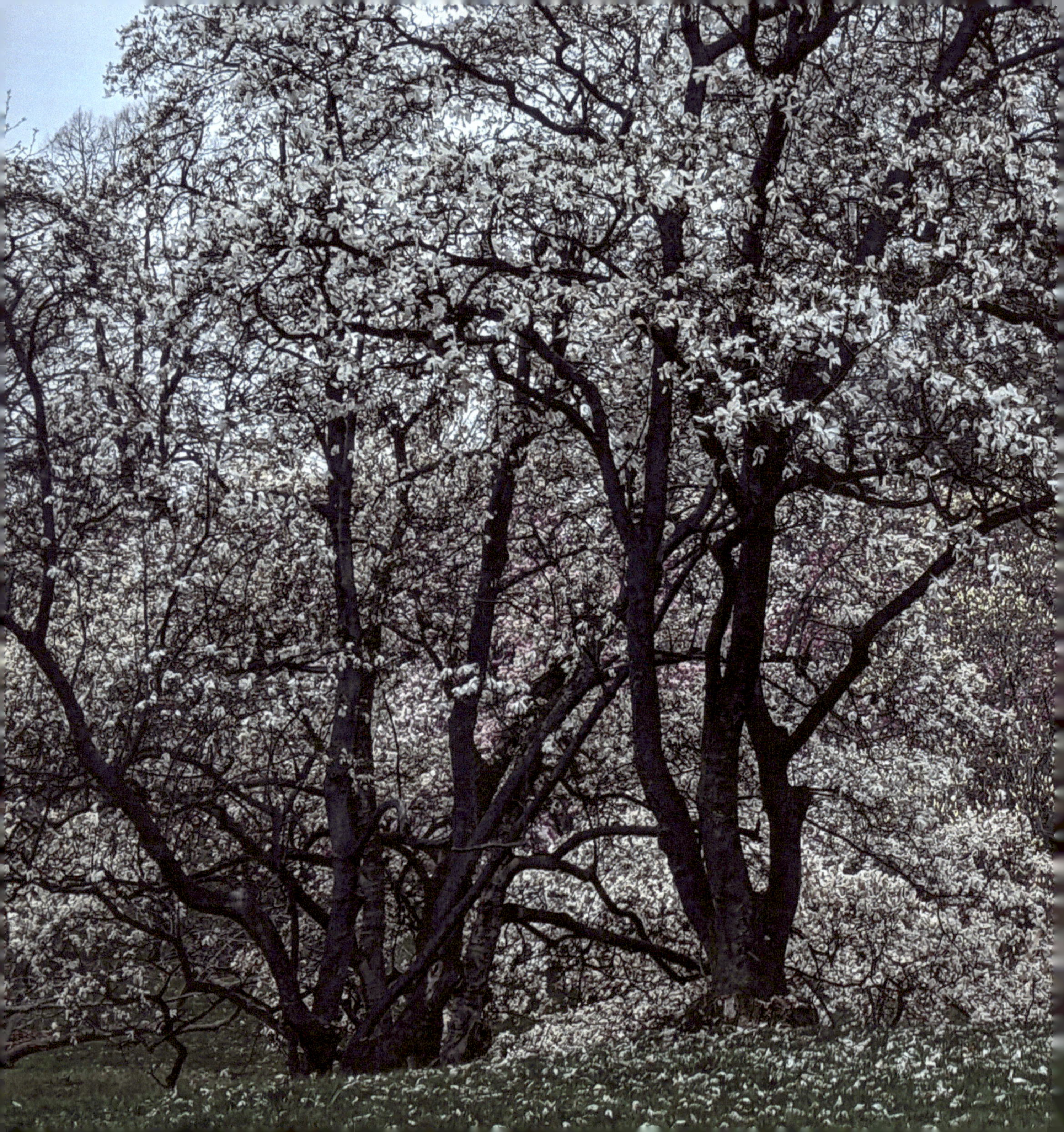

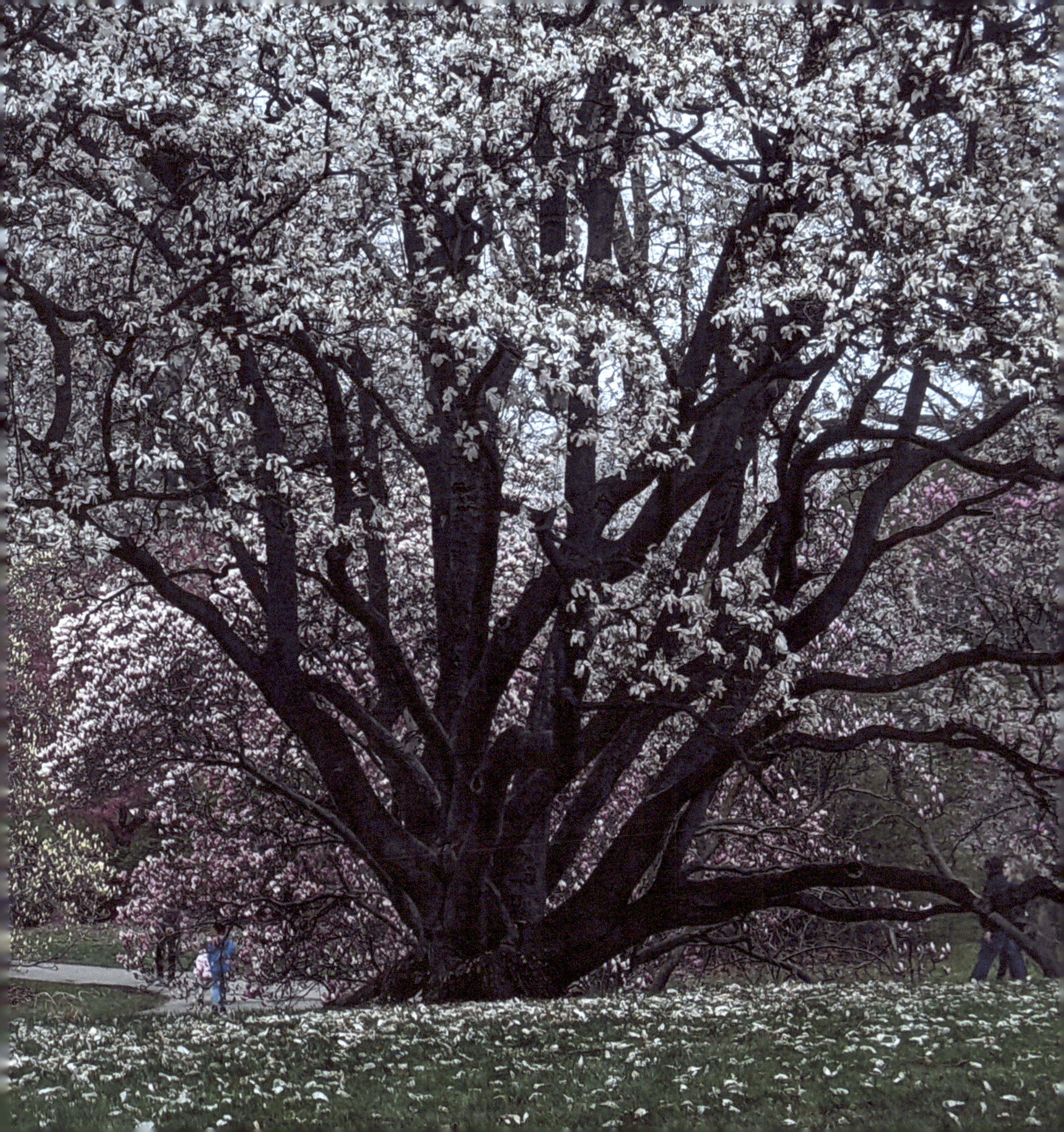

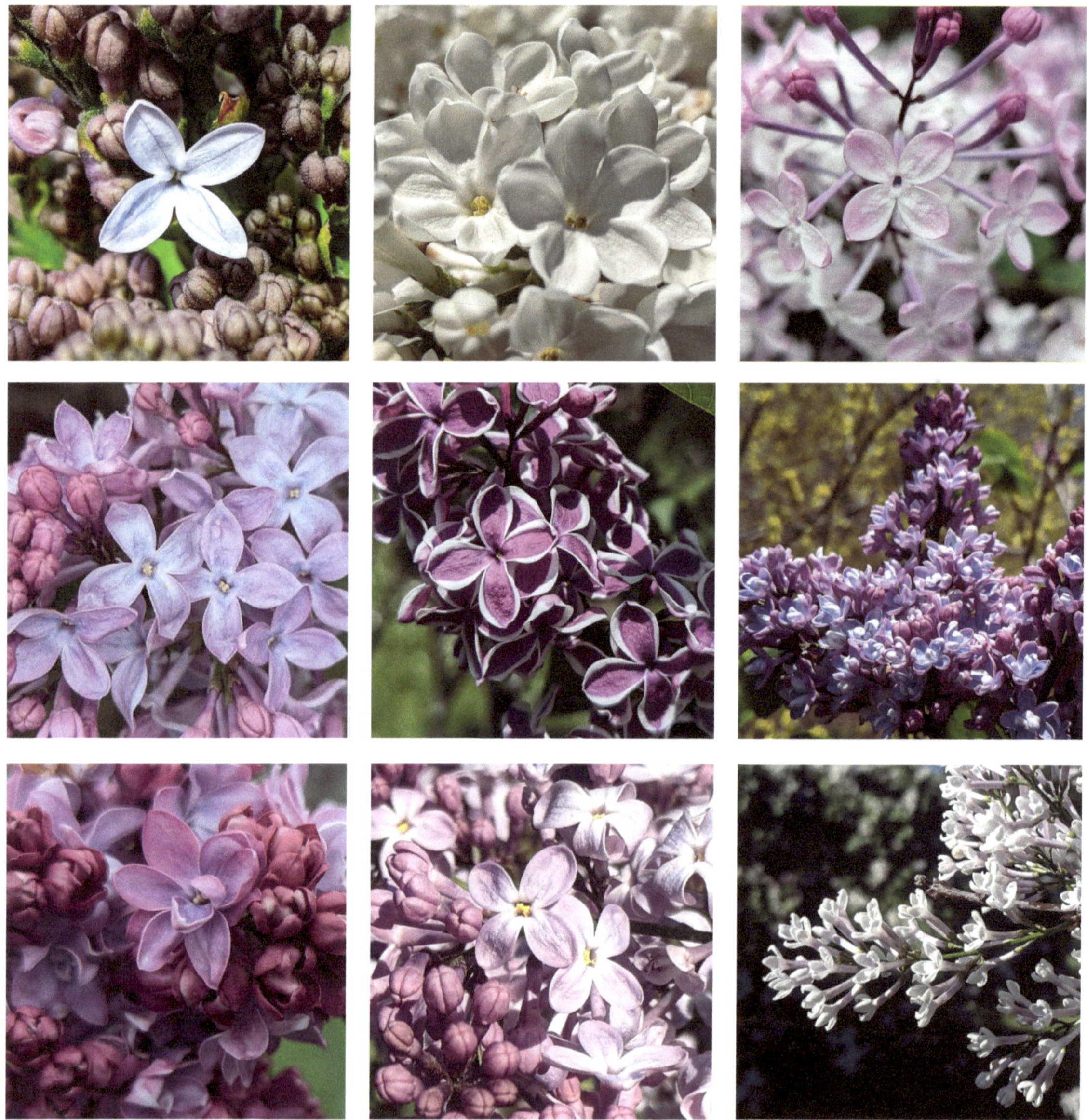

The Lilac Collection

Highland Park is home to one of the world's most significant lilac collections. More than 1,200 bushes, representing hundreds of varieties, line the park's glacial slopes and winding paths, an arrangement shaped by decades of cultivation and experimentation.

The park's lilacs bloom in sequence rather than all at once. Singles and doubles, pale whites and pinks, and deep purples and blues emerge in waves throughout May. Each variety has its own rhythm, extending the season and inviting return visits as the hillside changes from week to week. The scent remains persistently dense and deliciously heady.

Among them are historic French hybrids bred by Victor Lemoine in the late nineteenth century, including the luminous white 'Mme. Lemoine,' the velvety, wine-toned 'Charles Joly,' softer lavenders like 'Katherine Havemeyer,' and the nearly cobalt blooms of 'President Lincoln'—a sweep of color that shifts subtly as one moves along the hillside.

For those who pause to read the small metal tags that announce each shrub, the hillside becomes something of a scavenger hunt, each name an invitation to look closer.

Yet within this international collection, one variety belongs distinctly to Rochester.

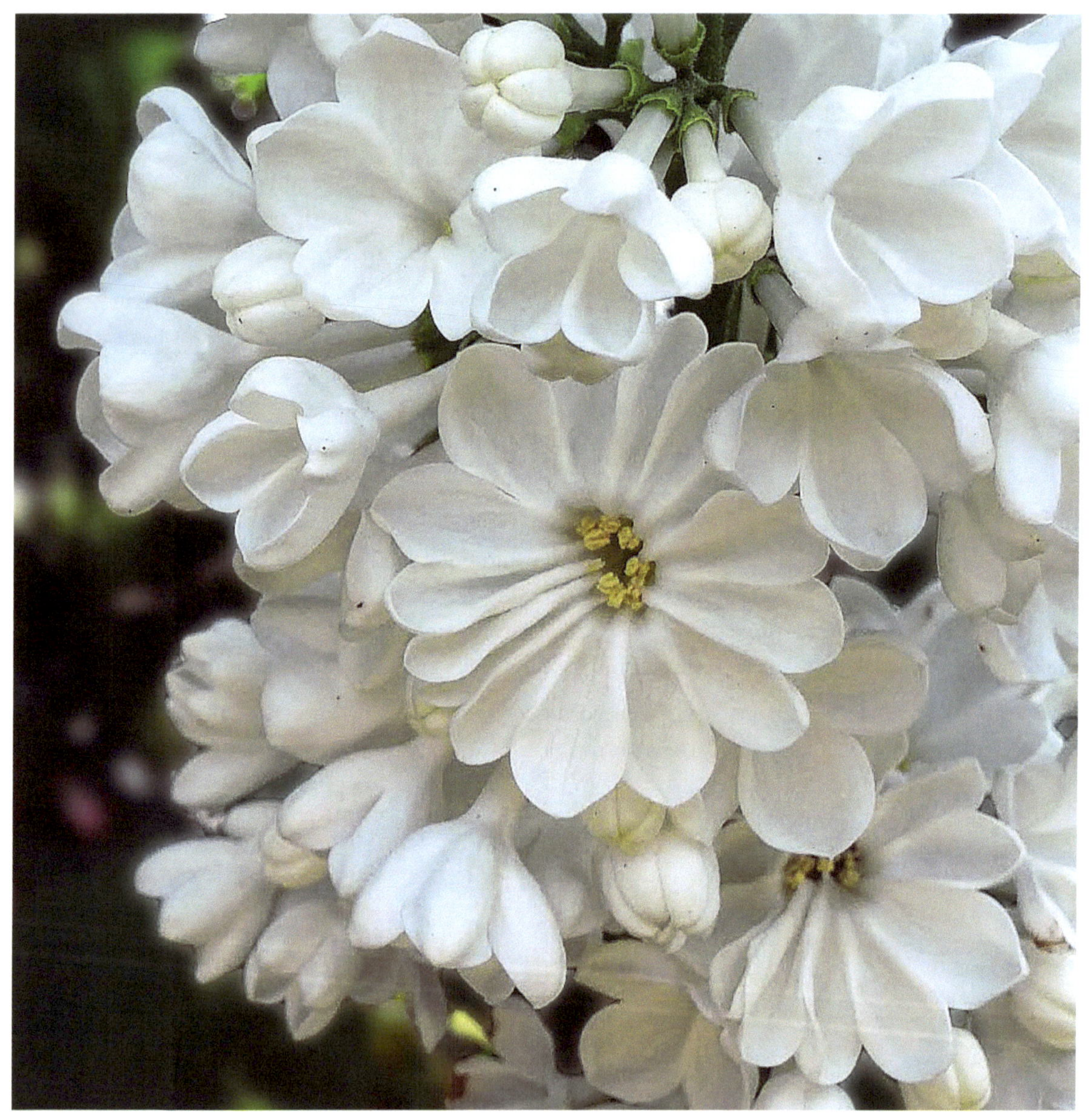

The 'Rochester' Lilac

Among Highland Park's many cultivars, one holds special local significance: the single white variety known as 'Rochester.' In the 1950s, Alvan Grant, Rochester's director of parks, and Richard Fenicchia, superintendent of horticulture, identified the plant as a chance seedling growing within the collection.

Introduced in 1963, 'Rochester' became the first recorded multipetaled lilac. Instead of the customary four-petaled floret, its blossoms frequently open with five or more petals, giving each cluster a subtly fuller, star-like form. In the 1970s, Fenicchia used this cultivar as a parent plant to develop additional hybrids known collectively as the Rochester strain, including 'Sesquicentennial' and 'Martha Stewart.'

The 'Rochester' lilac's five-petaled form has become a civic symbol. Today, the City of Rochester's mark reflects the city's dual identity: the Flour City, represented by a stylized water wheel, and the Flower City, symbolized by the lilac itself—now recognized as Rochester's official flower.

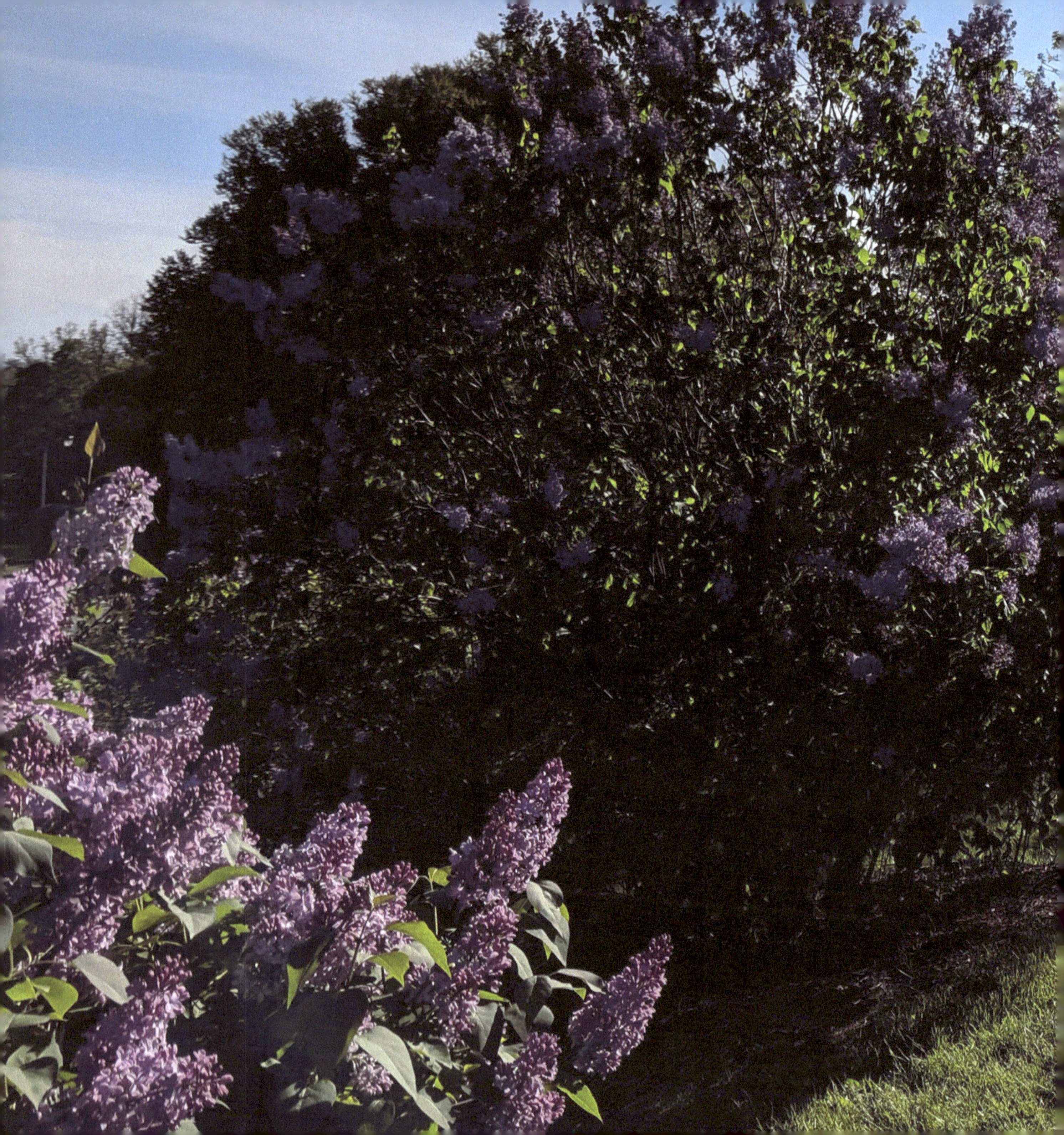

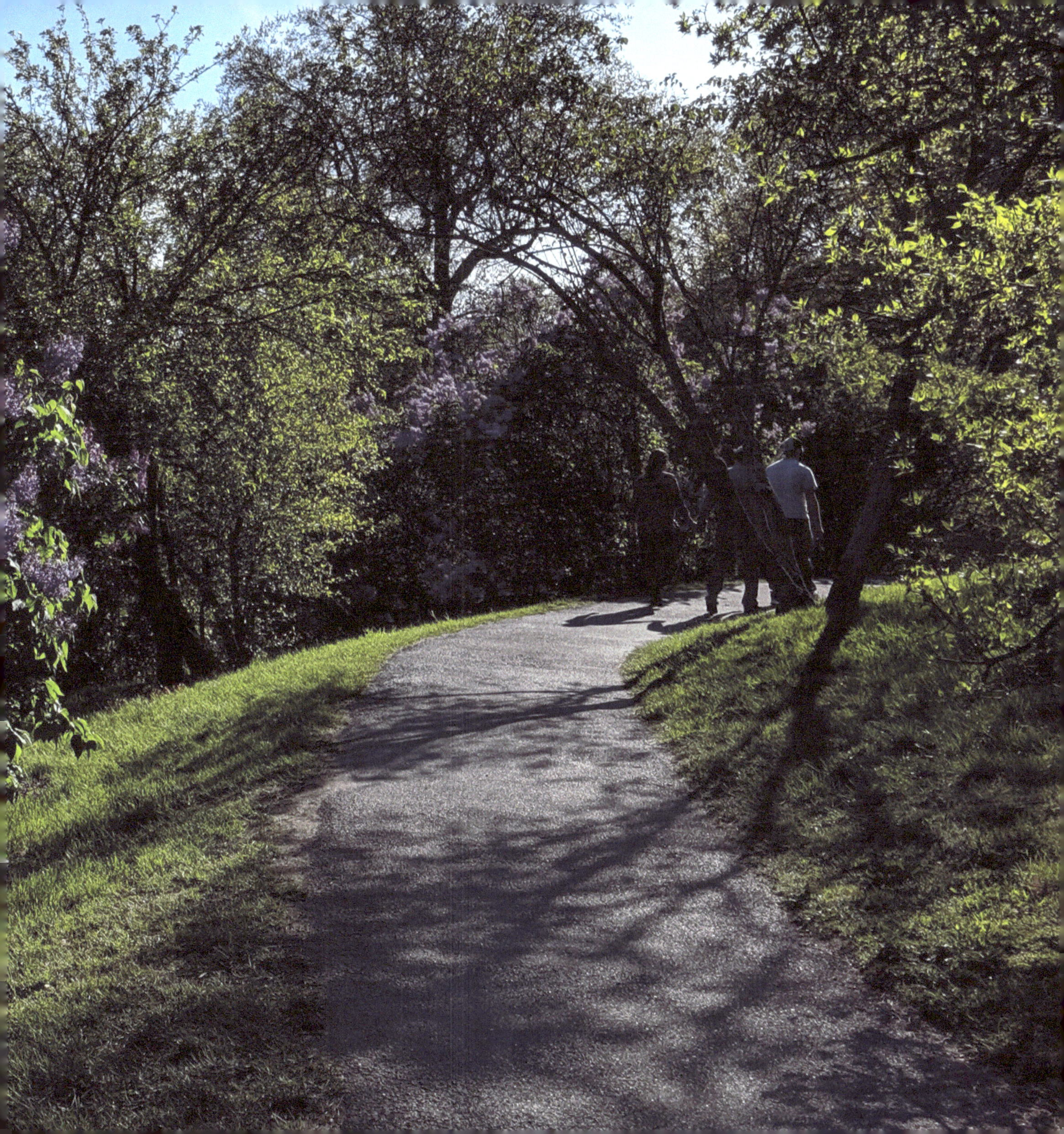

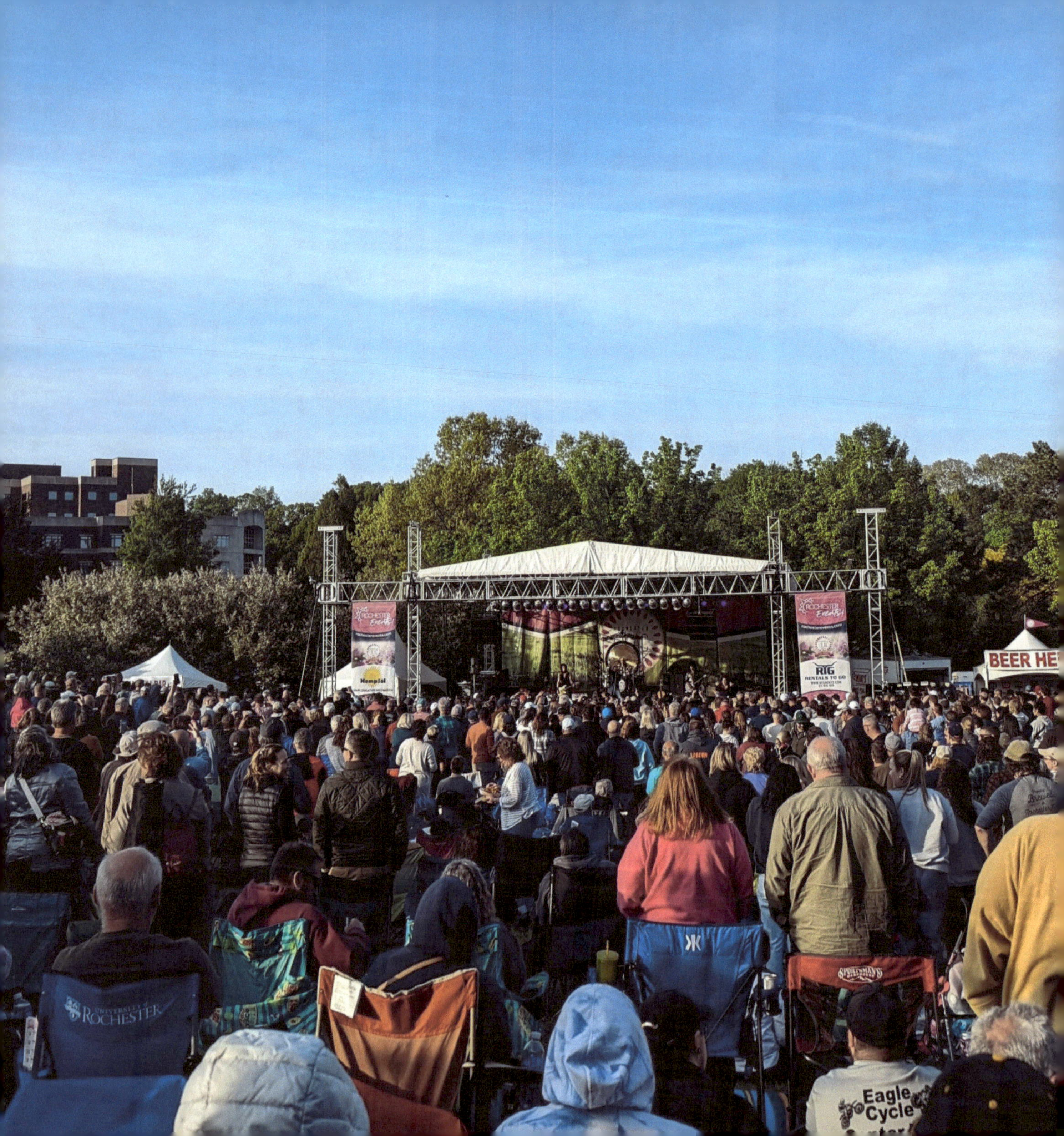

ROCHESTER Events
Hempjal
RIG
RENTALS TO GO
ROCHESTER Events
RIG
BEER HE
UNIVERSITY of ROCHESTER
Eagle
Cycle

The Lilac Festival

Each May, the two-week Lilac Festival transforms Highland Park into a shared spring celebration, uniting fragrance, community, and tradition.

The ritual began in the late nineteenth century, when horticulturist John Dunbar expanded Highland's lilac plantings. By 1898, the first informal "Lilac Sunday" drew 3,000 visitors to walk the slopes during peak bloom. That casual stroll soon evolved; by 1908, the crowds had swelled to 25,000.

Today, the festival draws more than 500,000 visitors annually. It fills the park with movement and sound—from concerts and art shows to parades and picnics. Families return to familiar paths, and new memories layer over old ones. Amid the activity lies a constant truth: this beauty belongs to everyone. Sharing it is part of what makes the season complete.

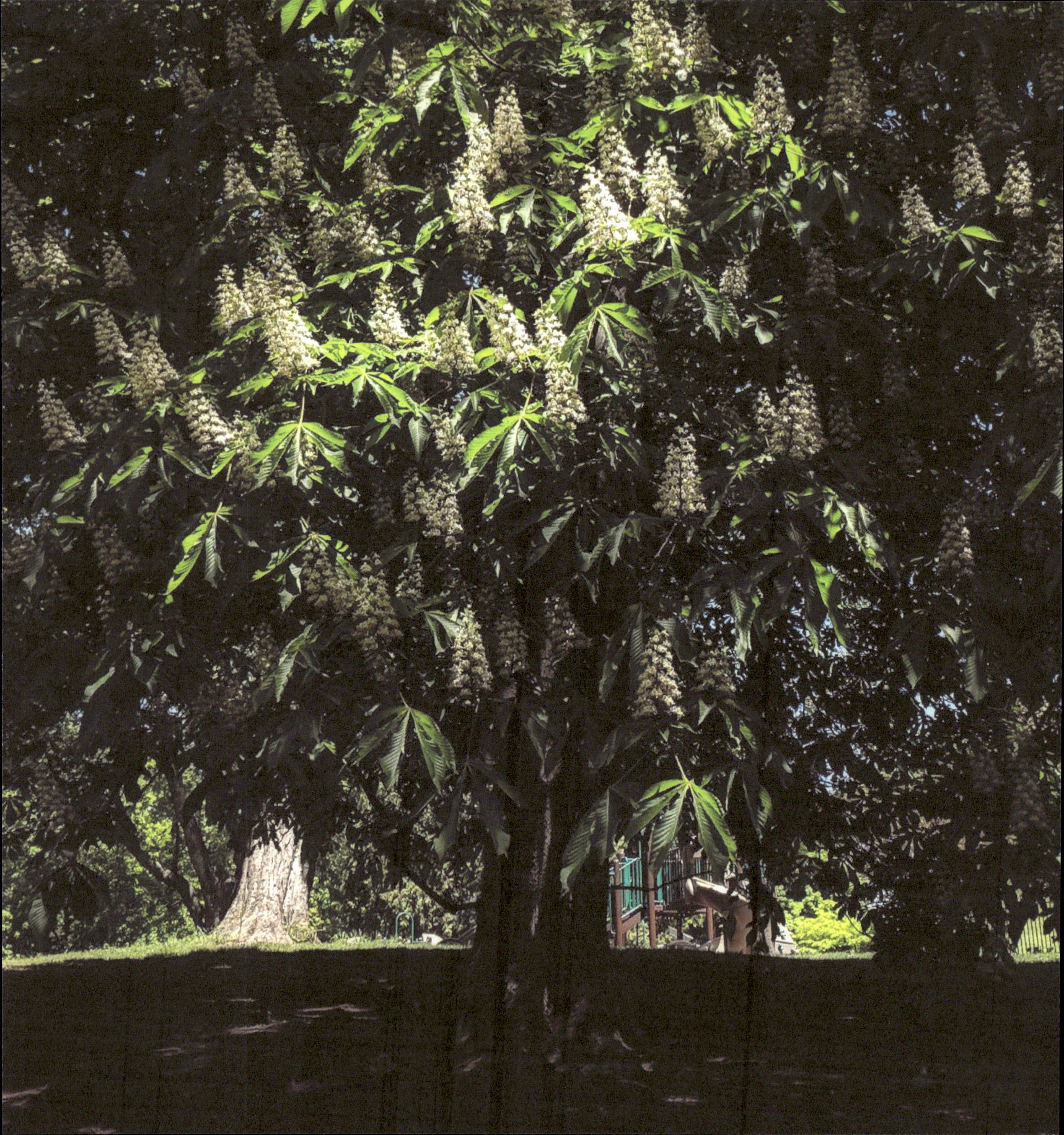

Horse Chestnuts & Buckeyes

West of the reservoir, a shaded walkway passes through one of Highland Park's most distinctive tree groupings: a grove of horse chestnuts and buckeyes. The collection includes more than thirty species and hybrids, many of which were initially sourced from Ellwanger & Barry's Mount Hope Nurseries.

Although their polished brown seeds are often called chestnuts, these trees are unrelated to the edible sweet chestnut. The resemblance—smooth mahogany shells marked with a pale "eye"—is coincidental.

Horse chestnuts, native to southeastern Europe, form broad architectural canopies and bear upright clusters of white flowers brushed with yellow or red. Buckeyes, native to North America, offer a looser silhouette and softer green foliage. Together, they create a corridor that feels both historic and seasonal—luminous with bloom in May, cool and shaded in summer, and scattered each autumn with glossy seeds that signal the turning year.

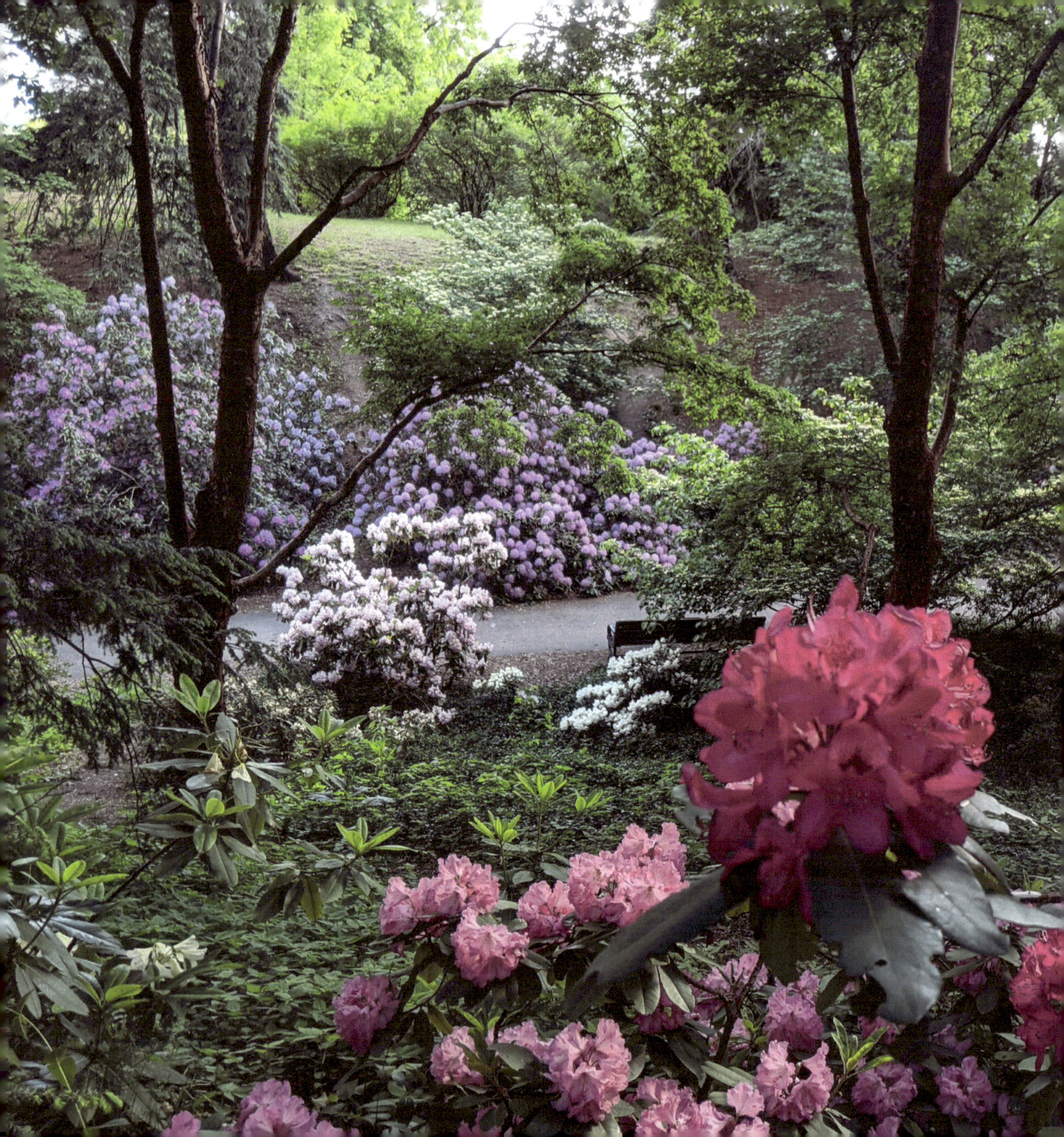

Rhododendron Valley

Between the pinetum and the azalea slopes lies one of Highland Park's most immersive paths: Rhododendron Valley. In late May and early June, it becomes a corridor of color—pinks, purples, corals, and creams unfurling along a gently winding trail, where rhododendrons and azaleas bloom side by side.

The air feels softer here. Petals catch the light. Shrubs rise and spill at varying heights, some towering overhead, others low and dense, blurring the boundary between woodland and garden.

Olmsted valued contrast—open lawns followed by enclosed spaces, broad views balanced by intimacy—and Rhododendron Valley embodies that rhythm. The path narrows just enough to feel sheltered. For a moment, the landscape folds around you, and the rest of the park recedes.

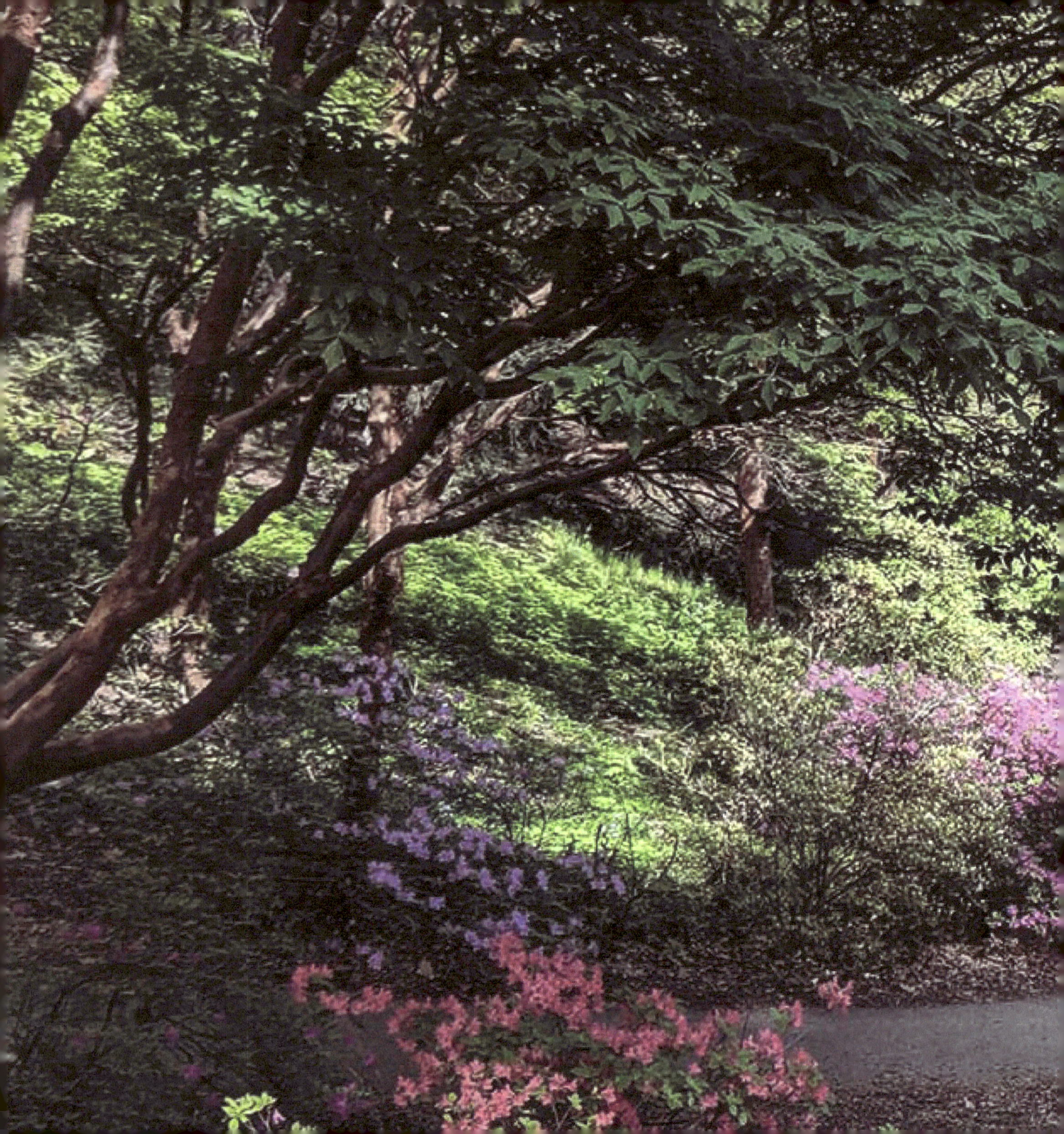

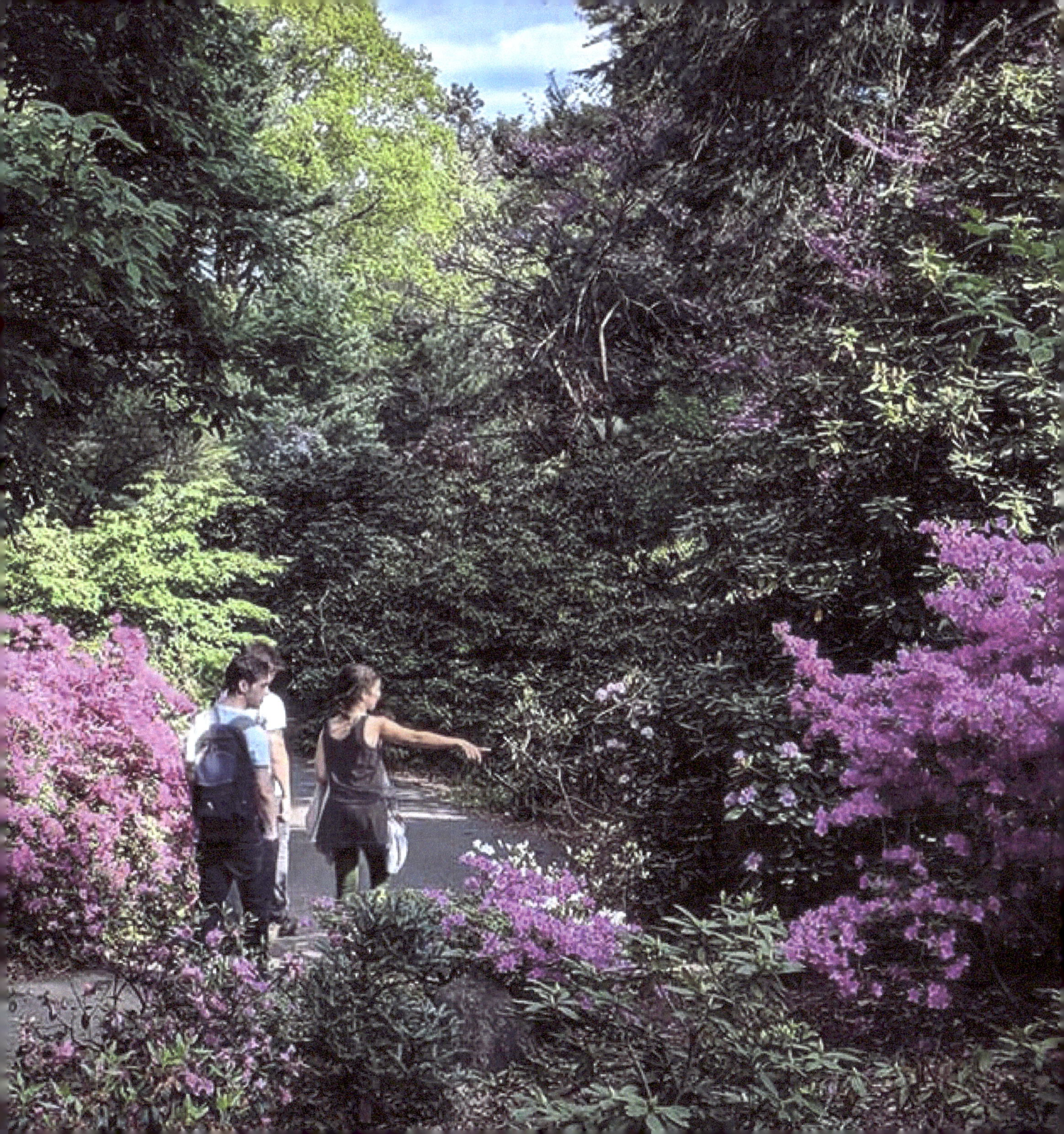

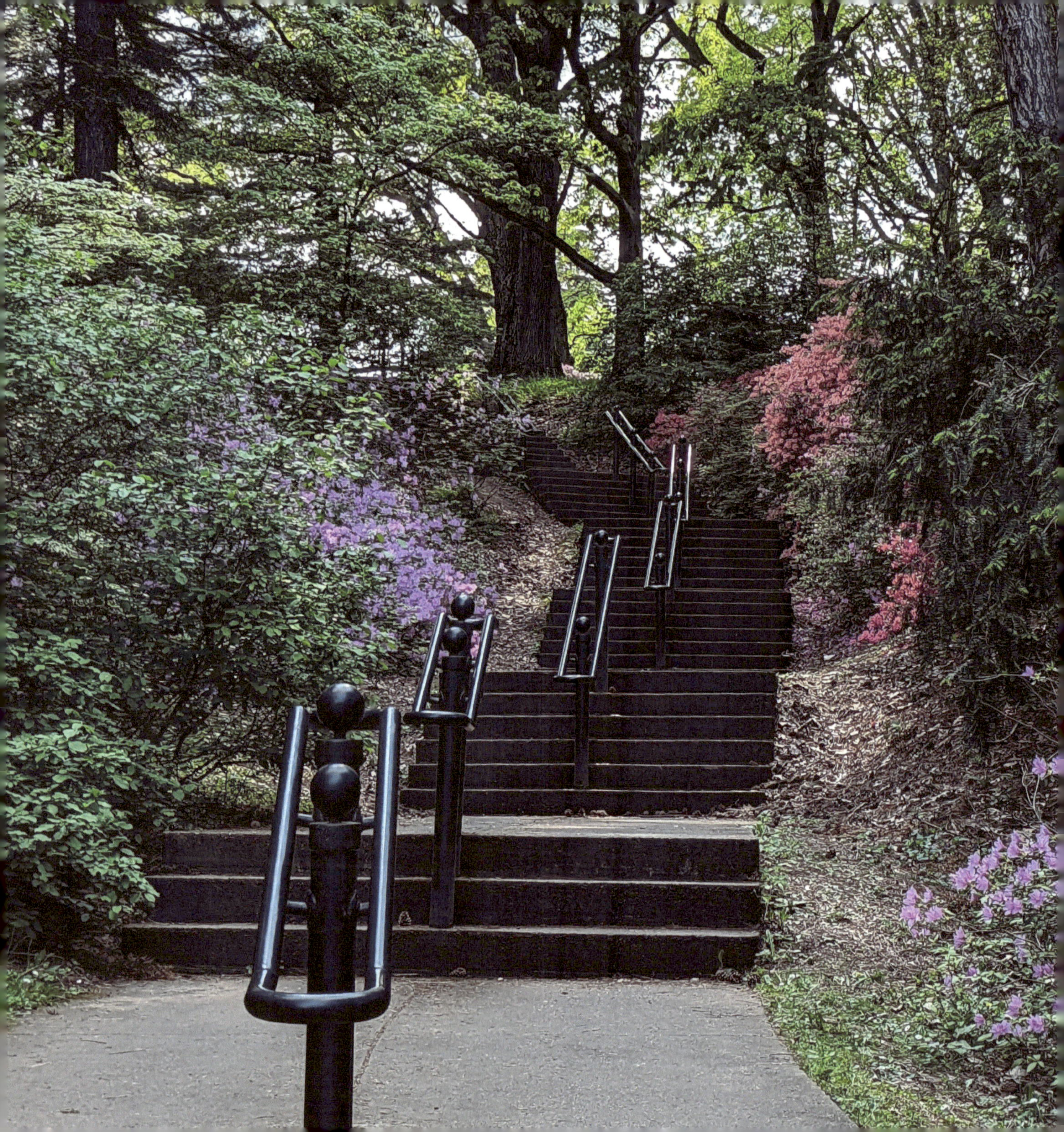

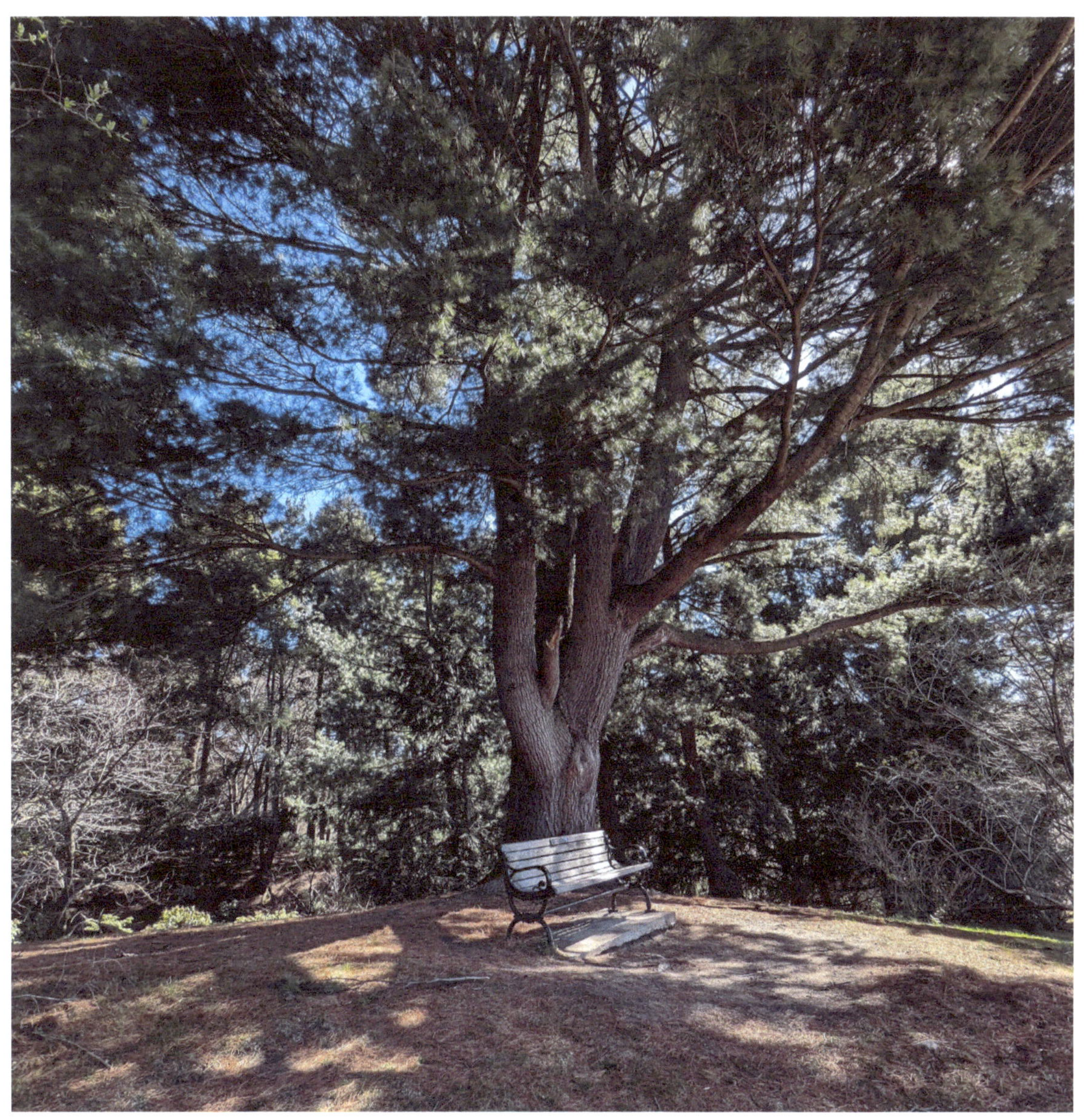

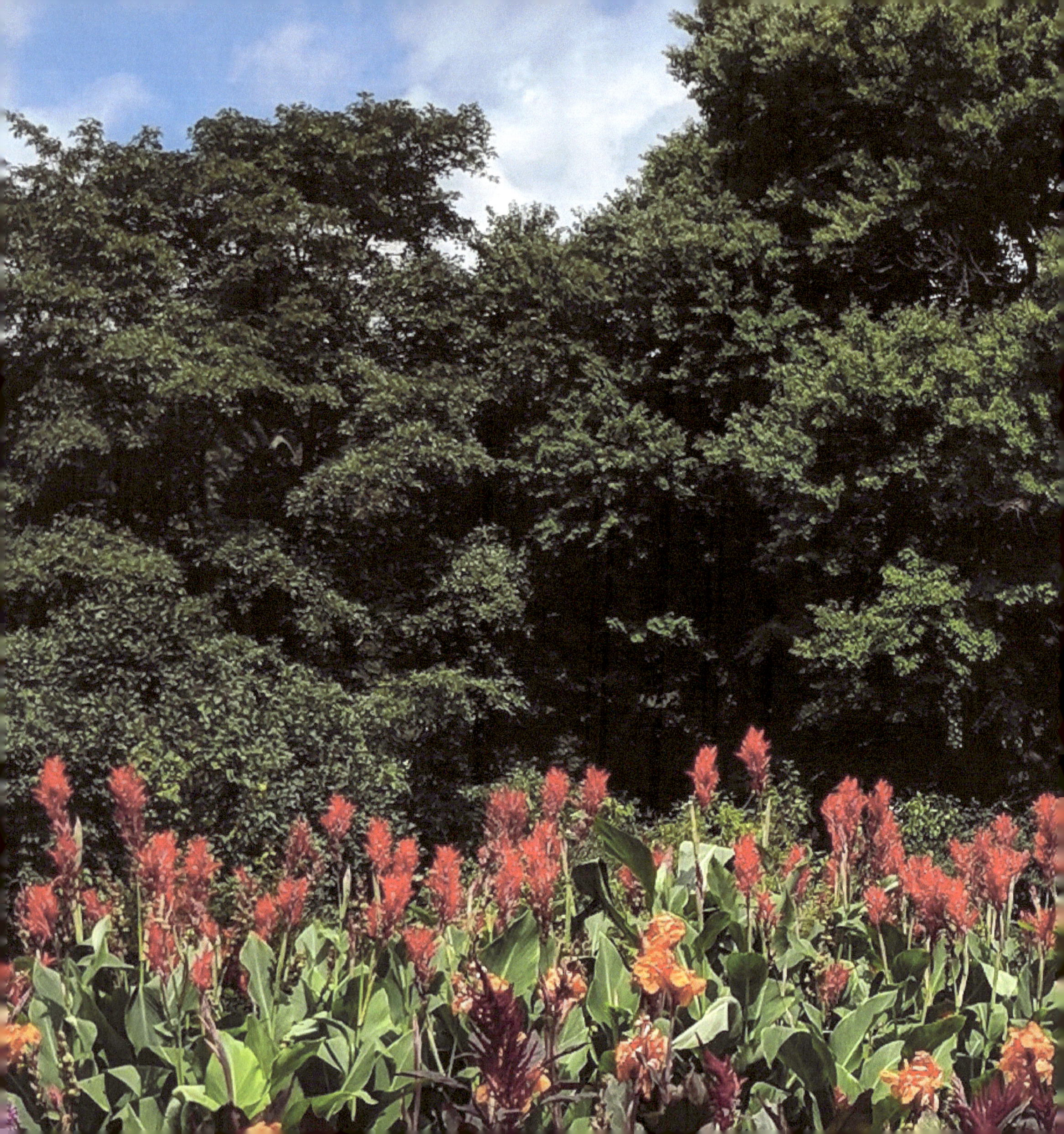

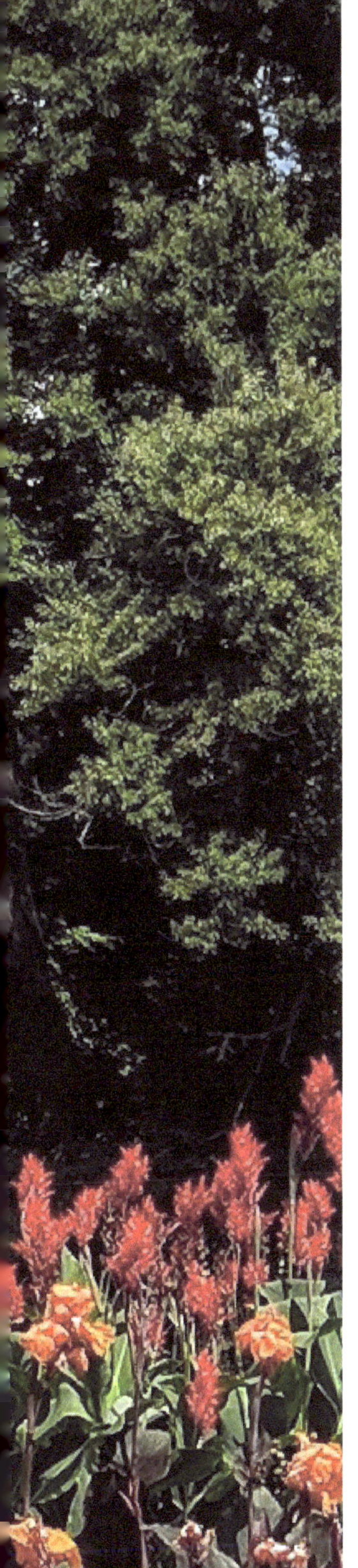

Summer

Summer settles into Highland Park steadily, as shade expands and growth thickens, enclosing the landscape. This is a season defined less by change than by continuity, when the park holds its shape and offers relief from heat.

In the pinetum, conifer canopies moderate both temperature and sound, long paths remain cool even at midday, and the air carries the scent of resin. Ferns fill the understory, and birds move through the trees. Olmsted's design here favors refuge—shelter without enclosure, quiet without isolation.

Elsewhere, gardens fill in rather than bloom all at once. Annual beds grow dense and textured, the conservatory remains active inside and out, and visitors settle onto benches, lawns, and familiar overlooks.

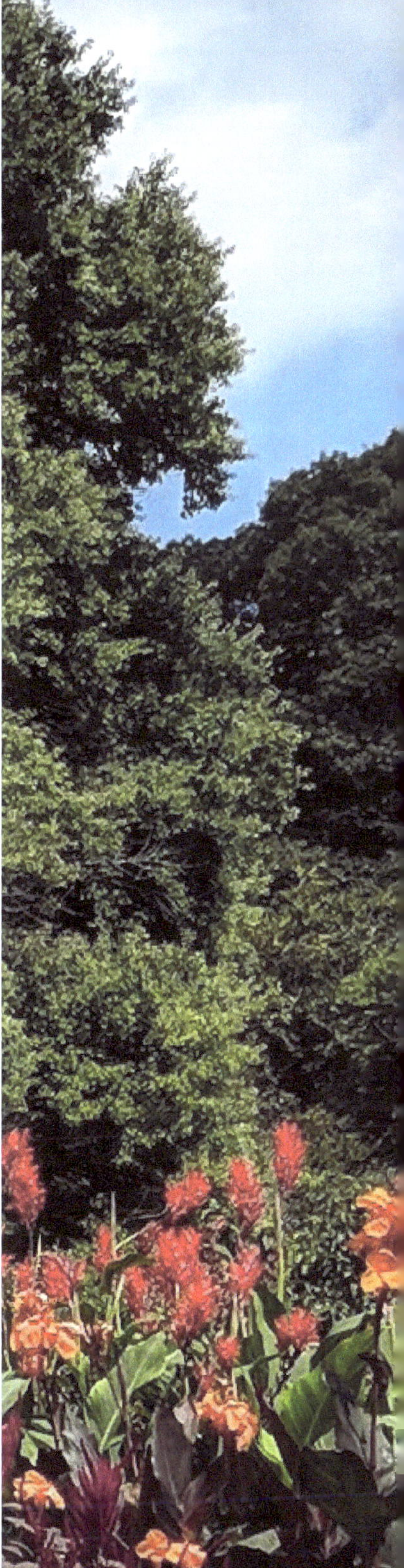

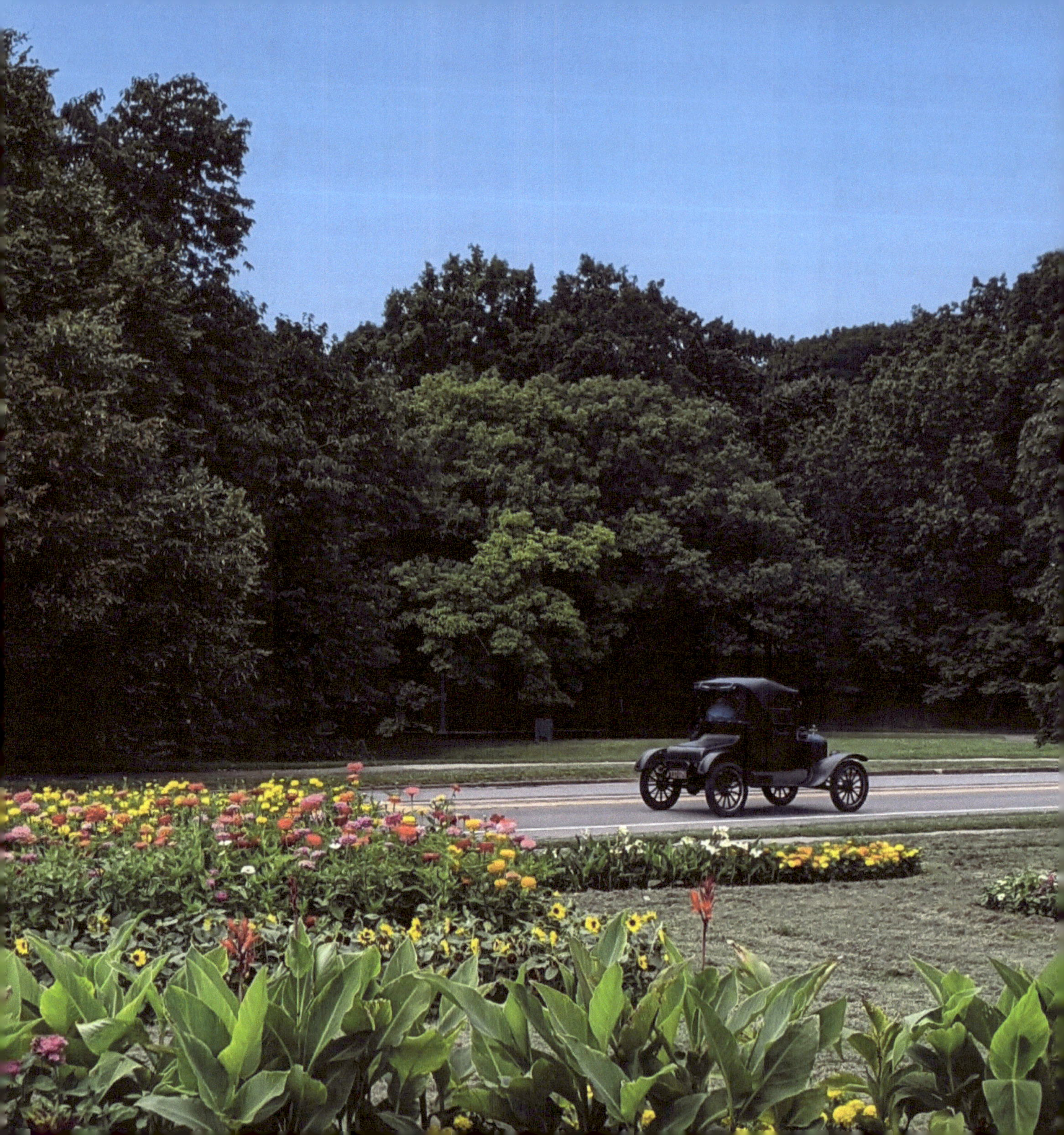

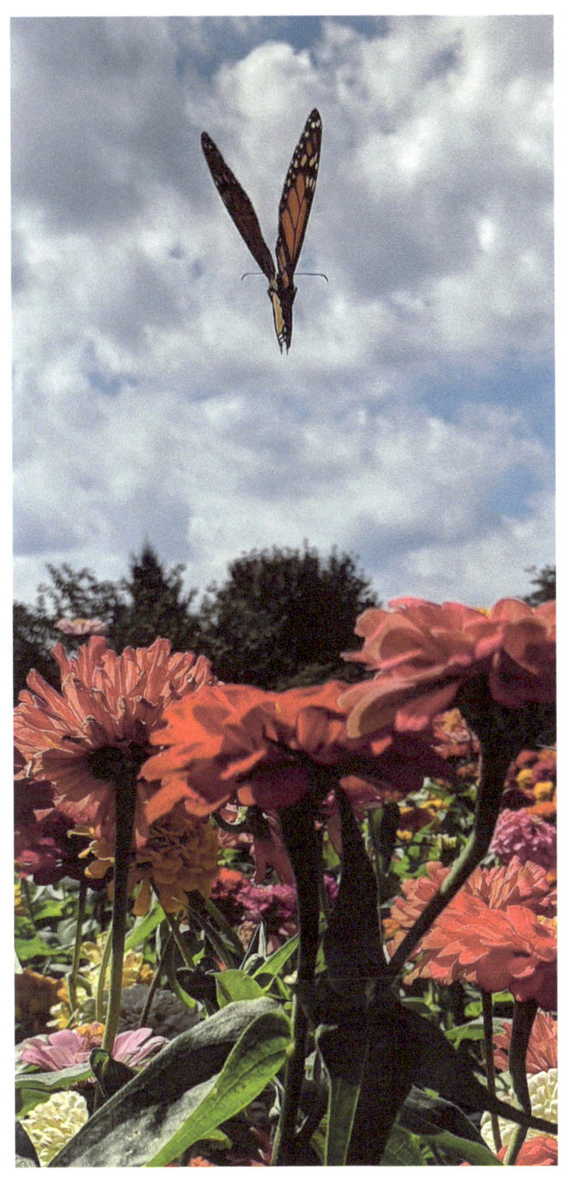
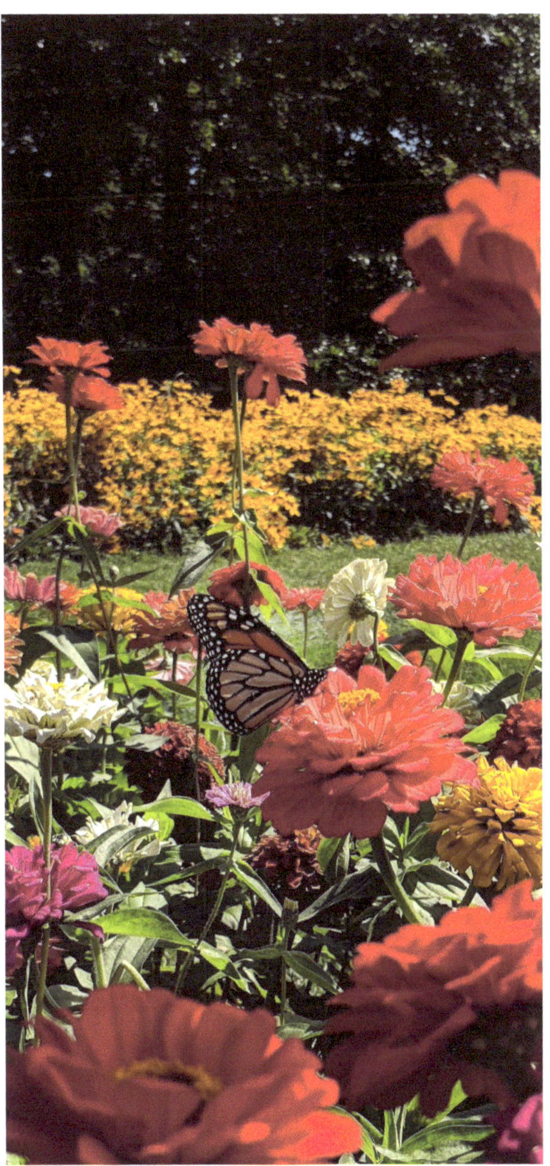

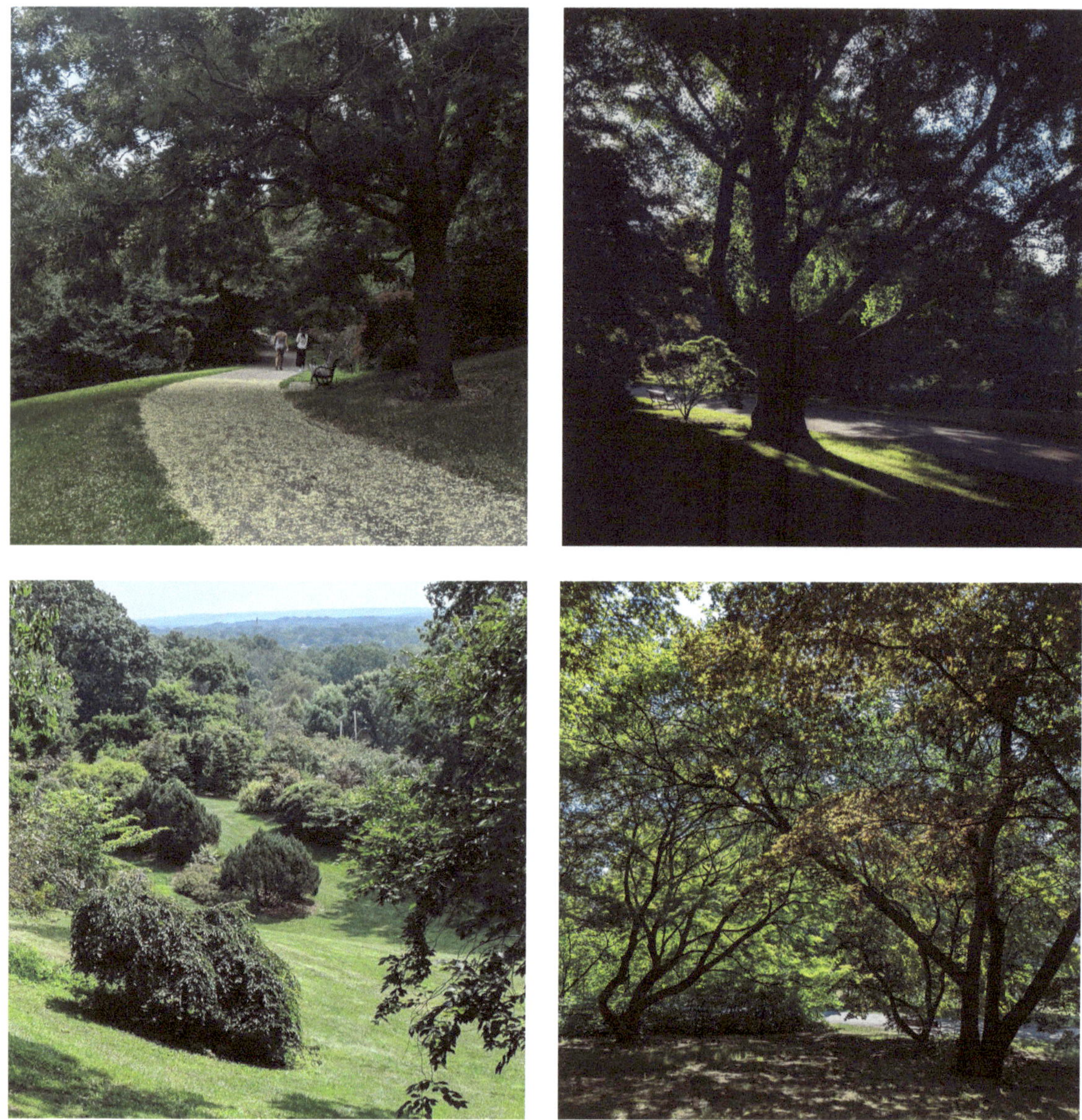

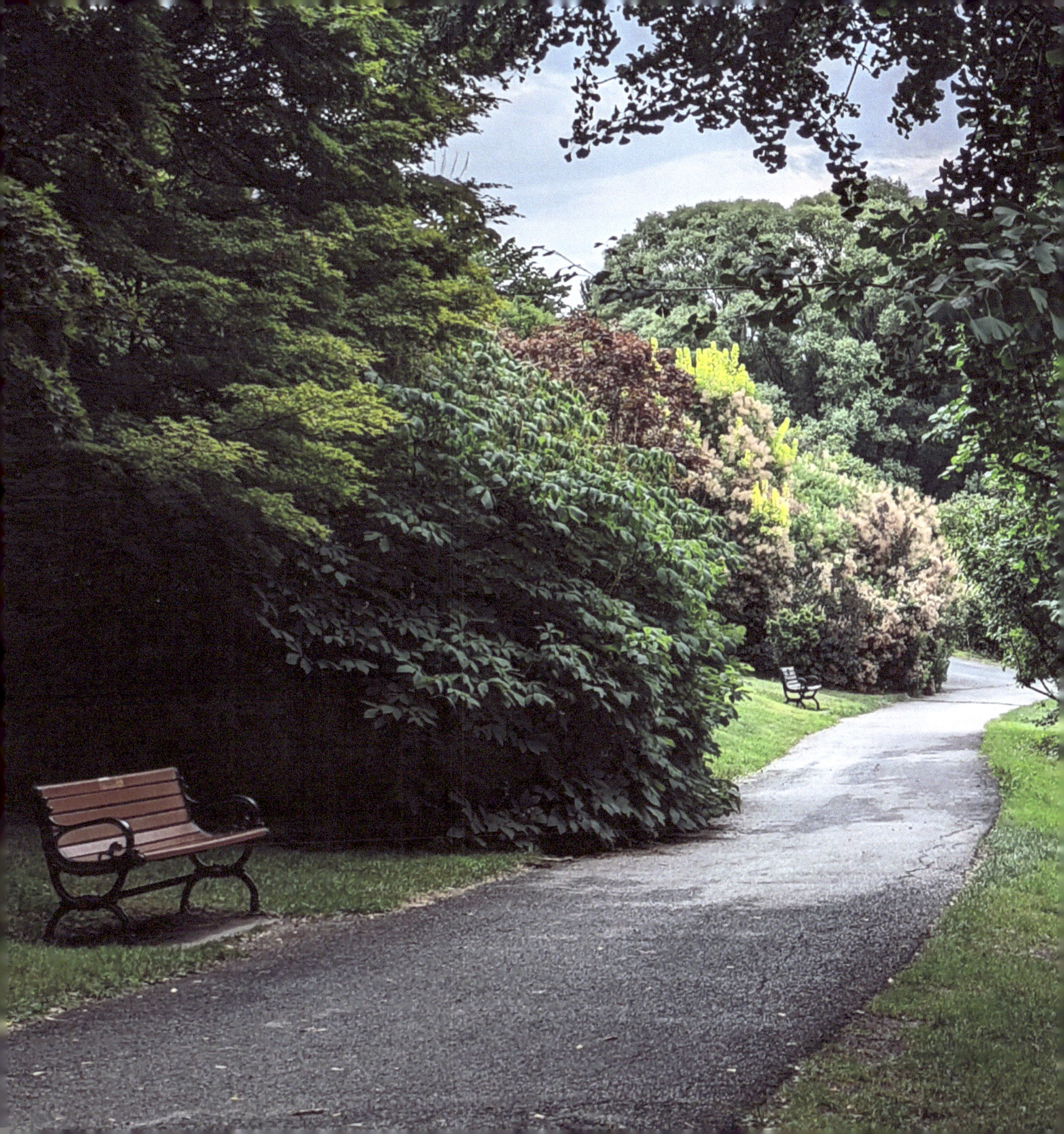

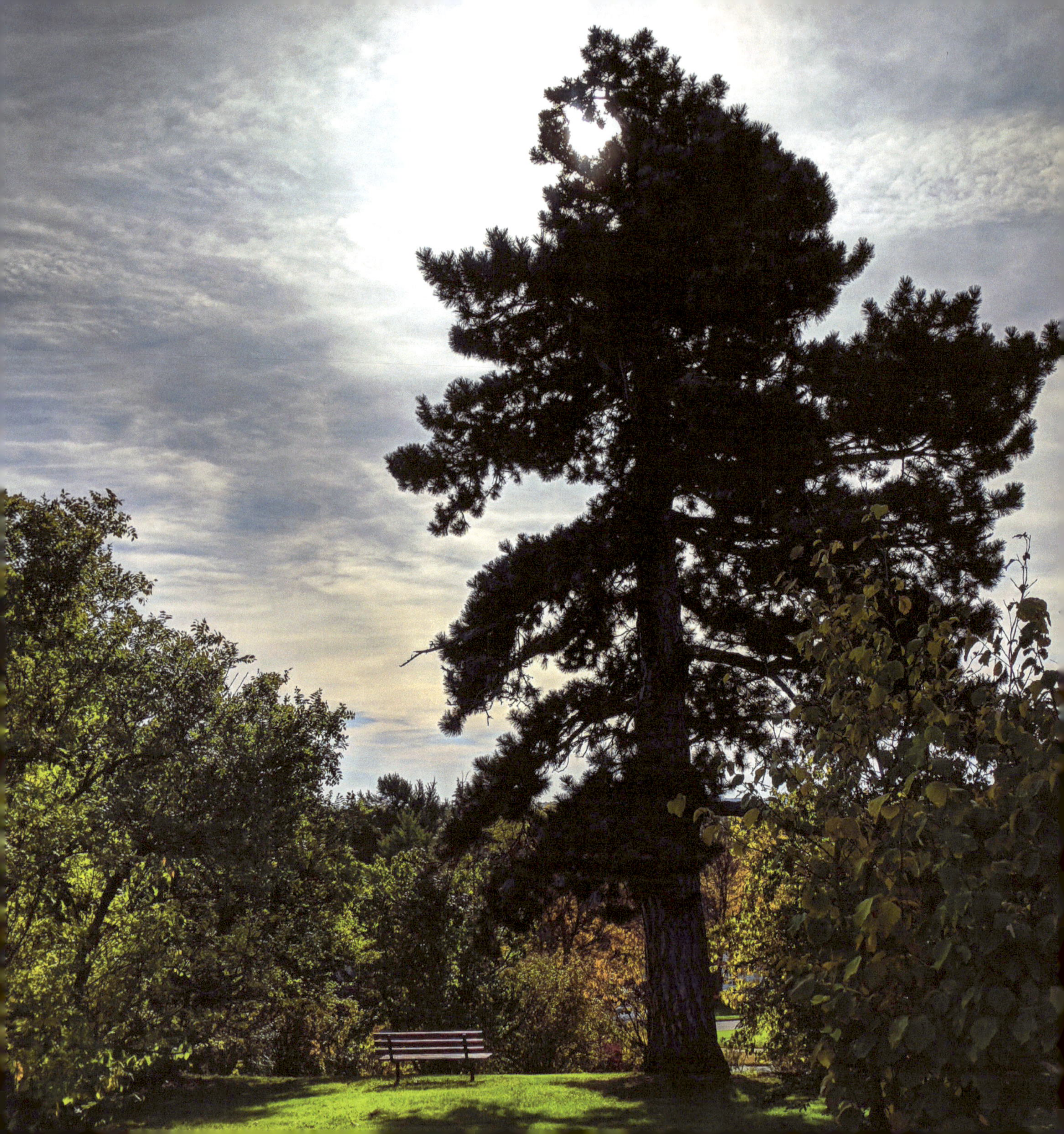

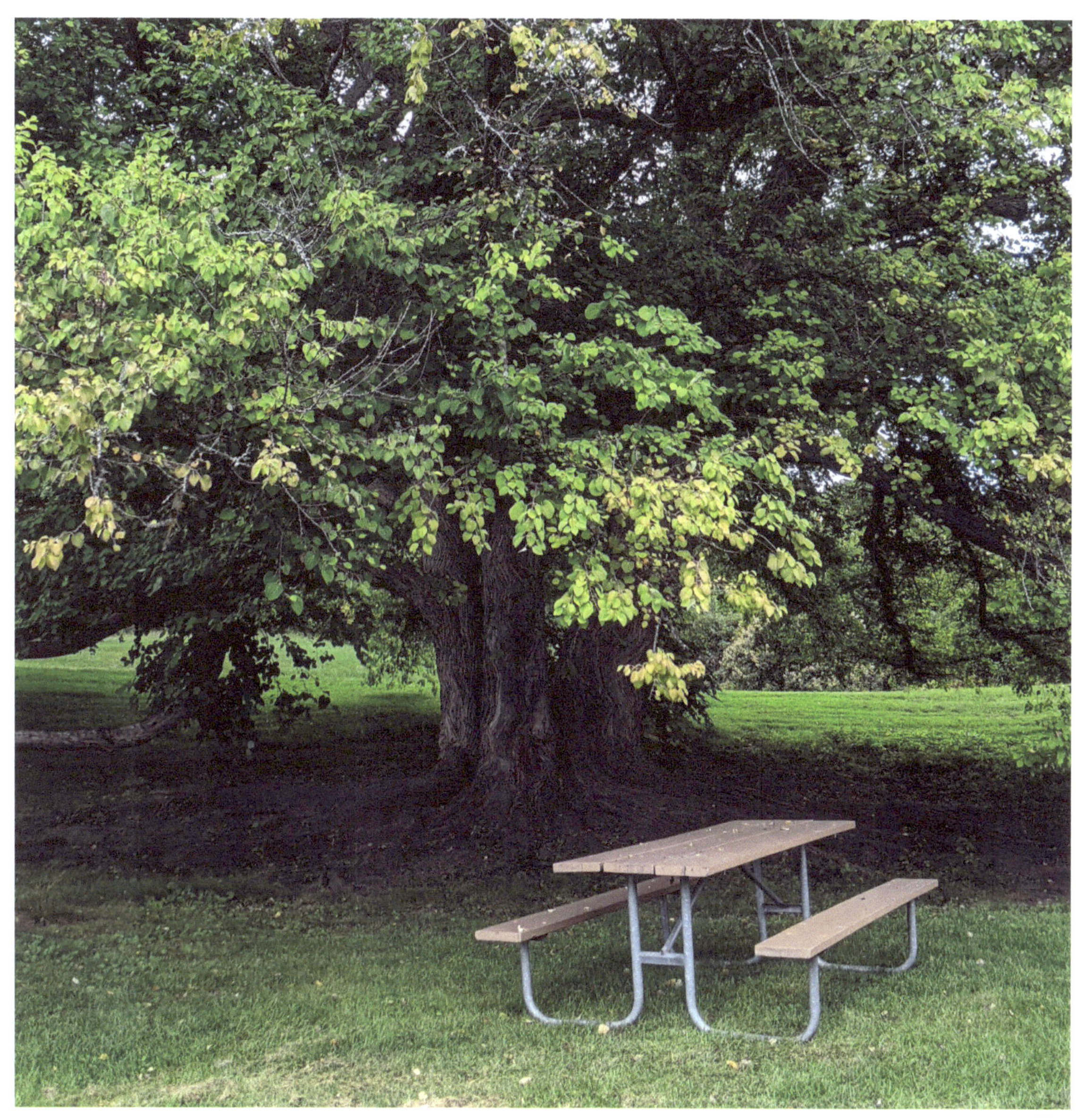

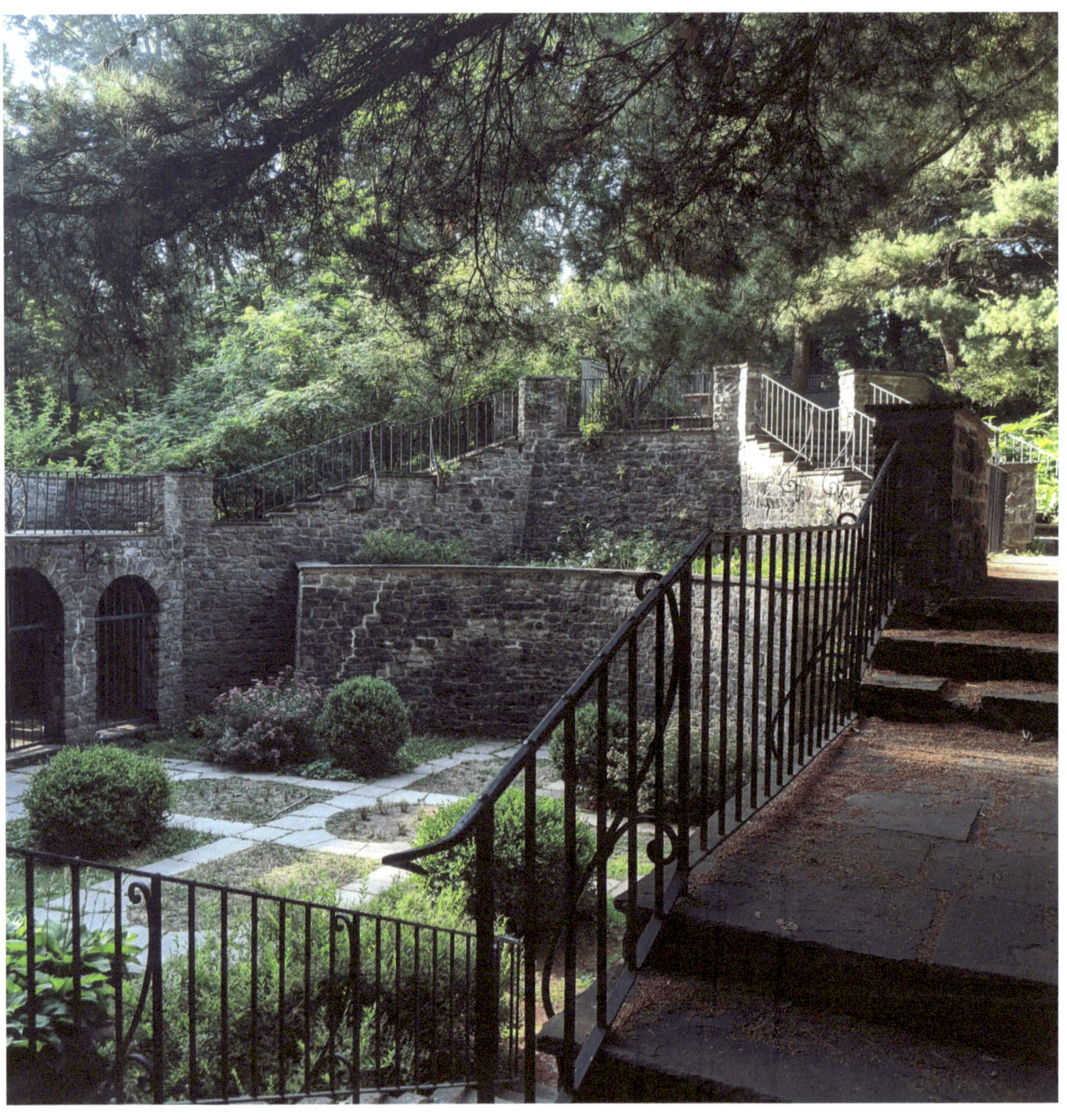

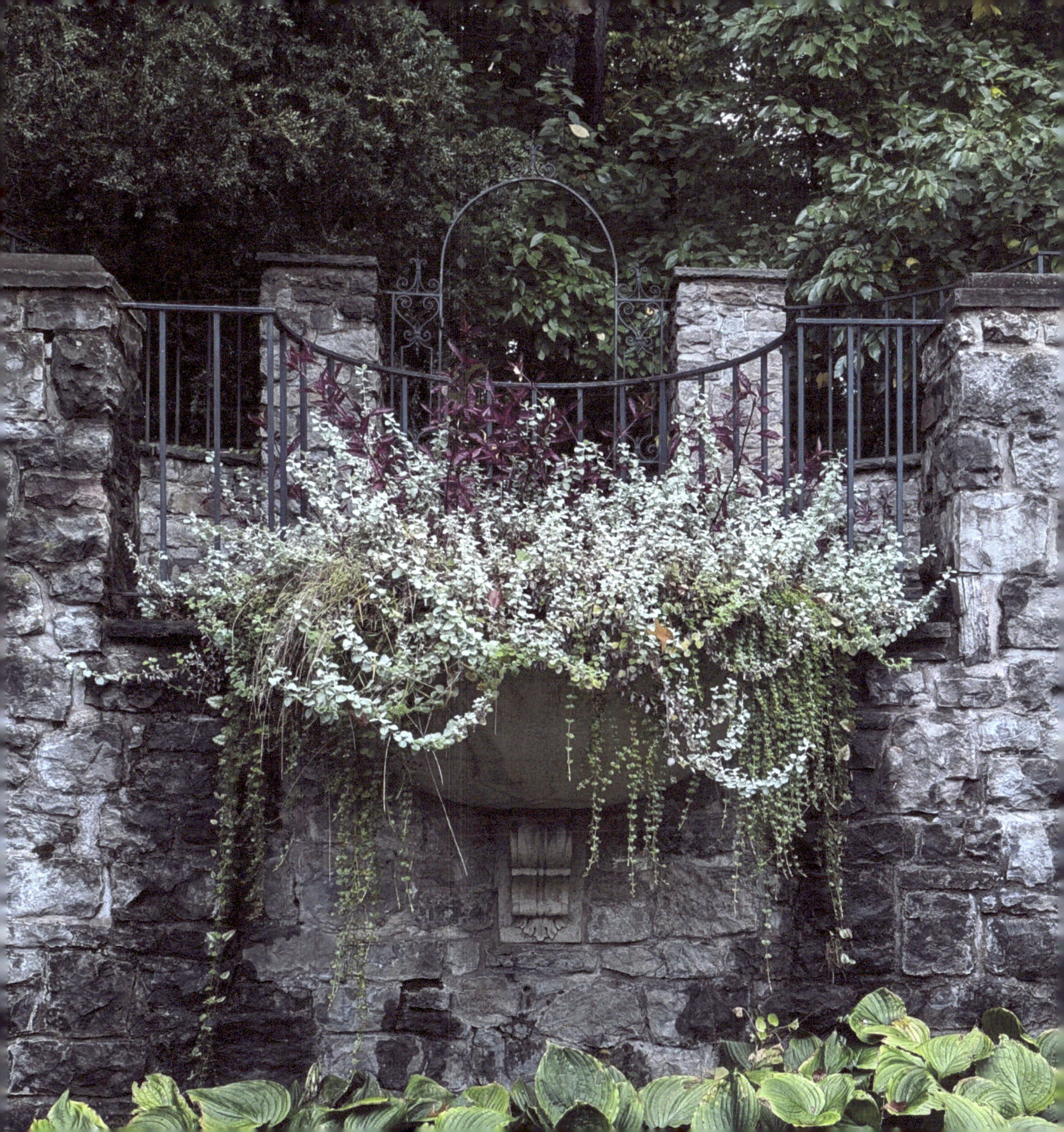

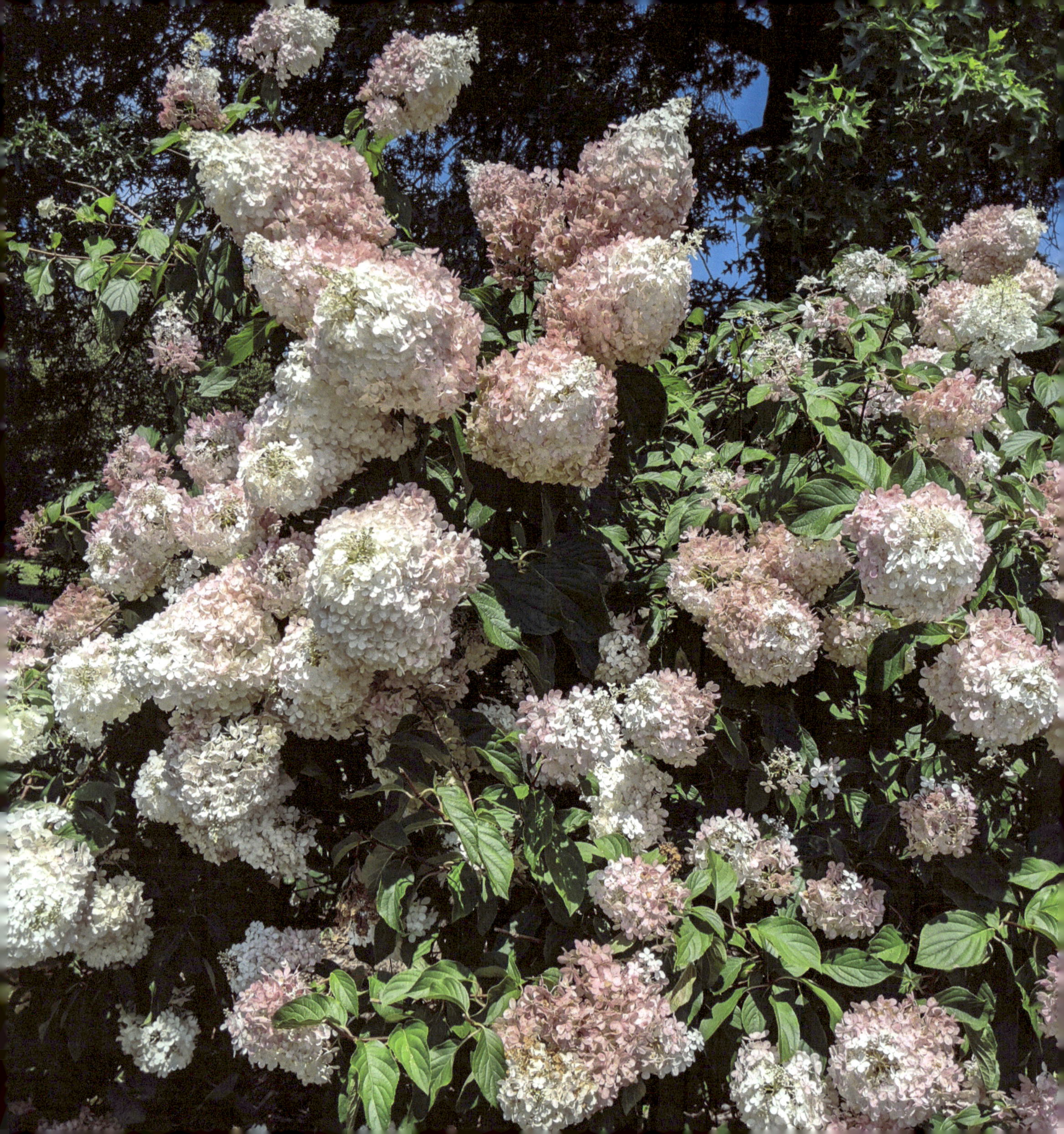

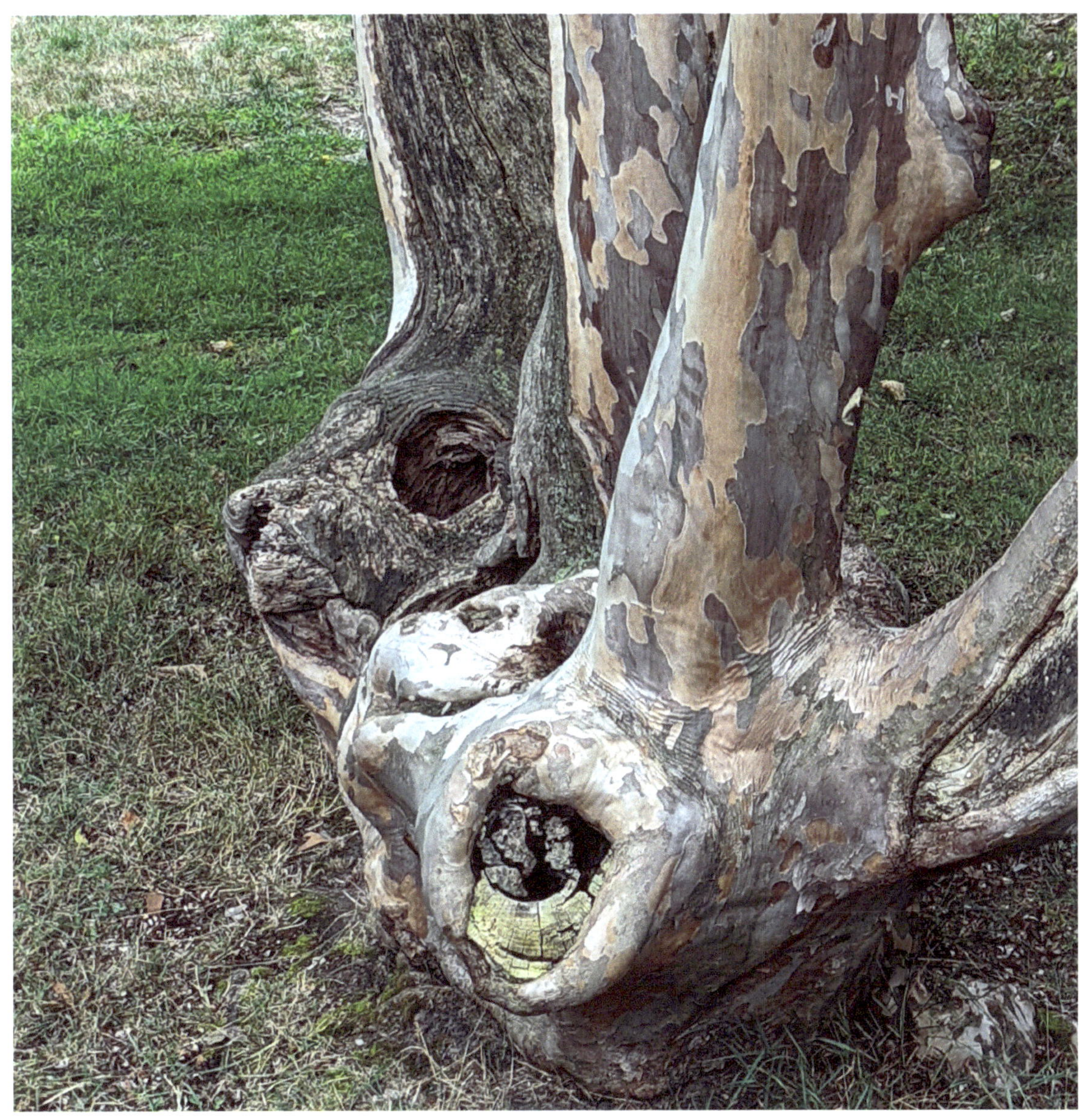

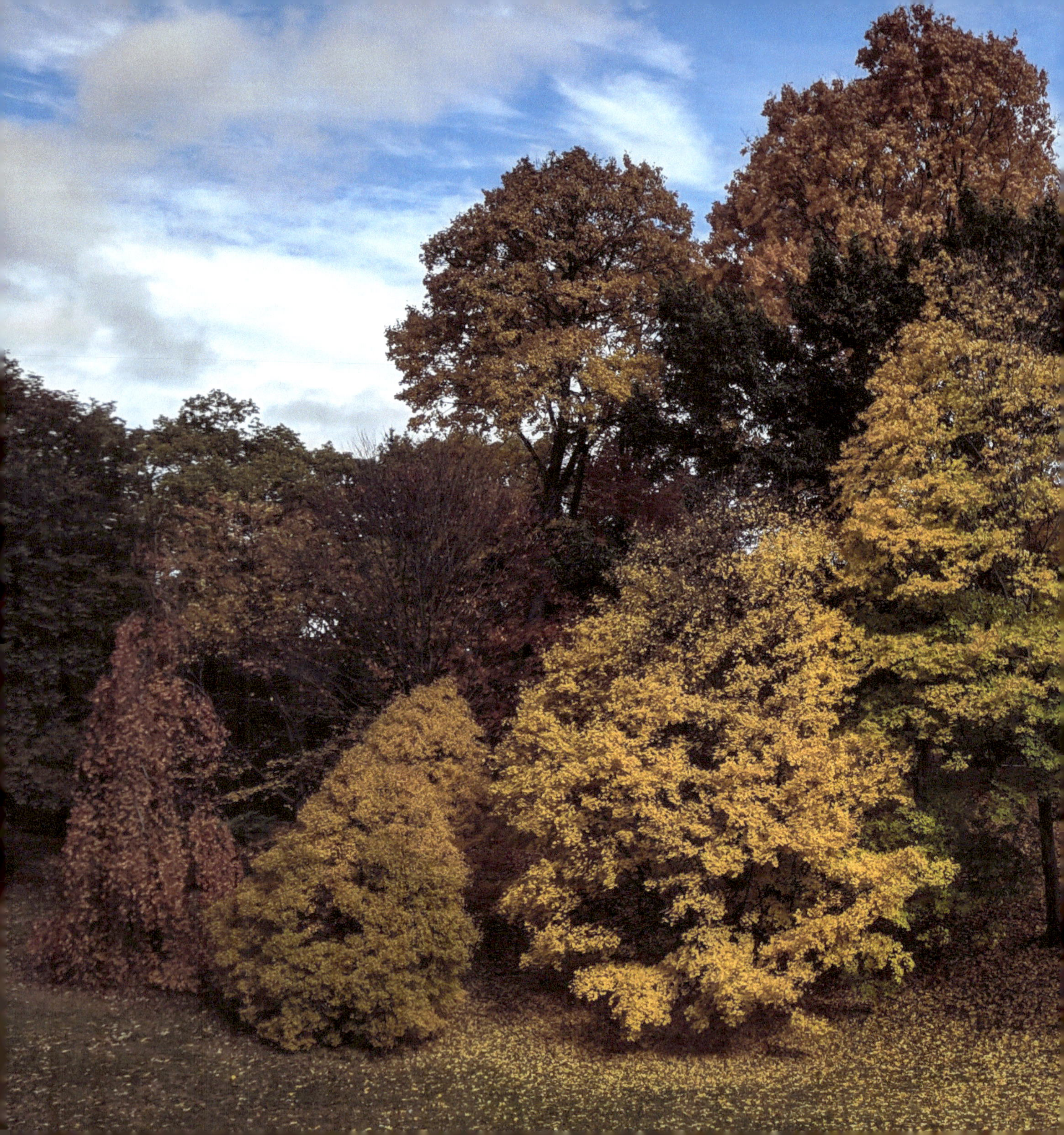

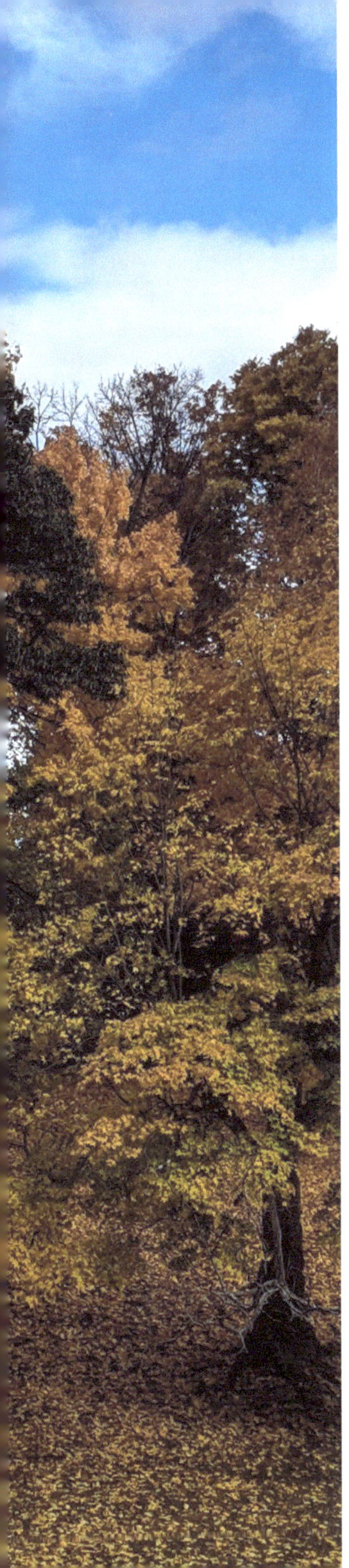

Autumn

In autumn, Highland Park reaches its final act. Change comes tree by tree, slope by slope, as color intensifies and light sharpens with the shortening days. What has been building all season arrives with clarity and force.

Japanese maples turn deep red and purple. Ginkgo leaves turn yellow at once, then fall, collecting beneath exposed branches. After rain, the ground smells of leaves and damp soil. Footsteps soften along paths layered with fallen foliage.

This is where Olmsted's design asserts itself. As canopies thin, long views open and contours reappear. The park reveals its structure at the height of color, delivering a dramatic conclusion before winter strips the landscape to its bones.

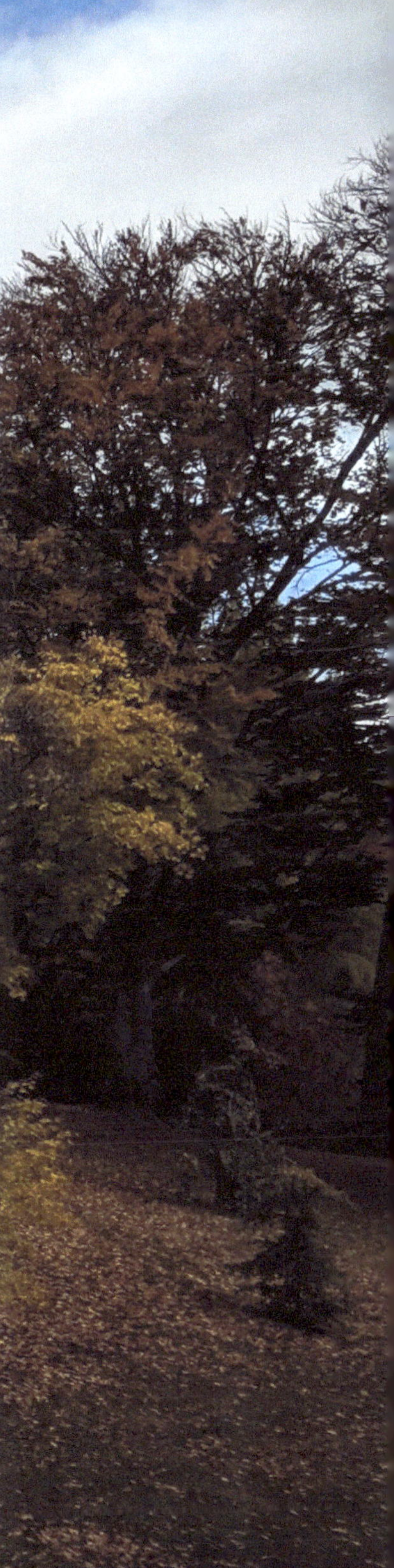

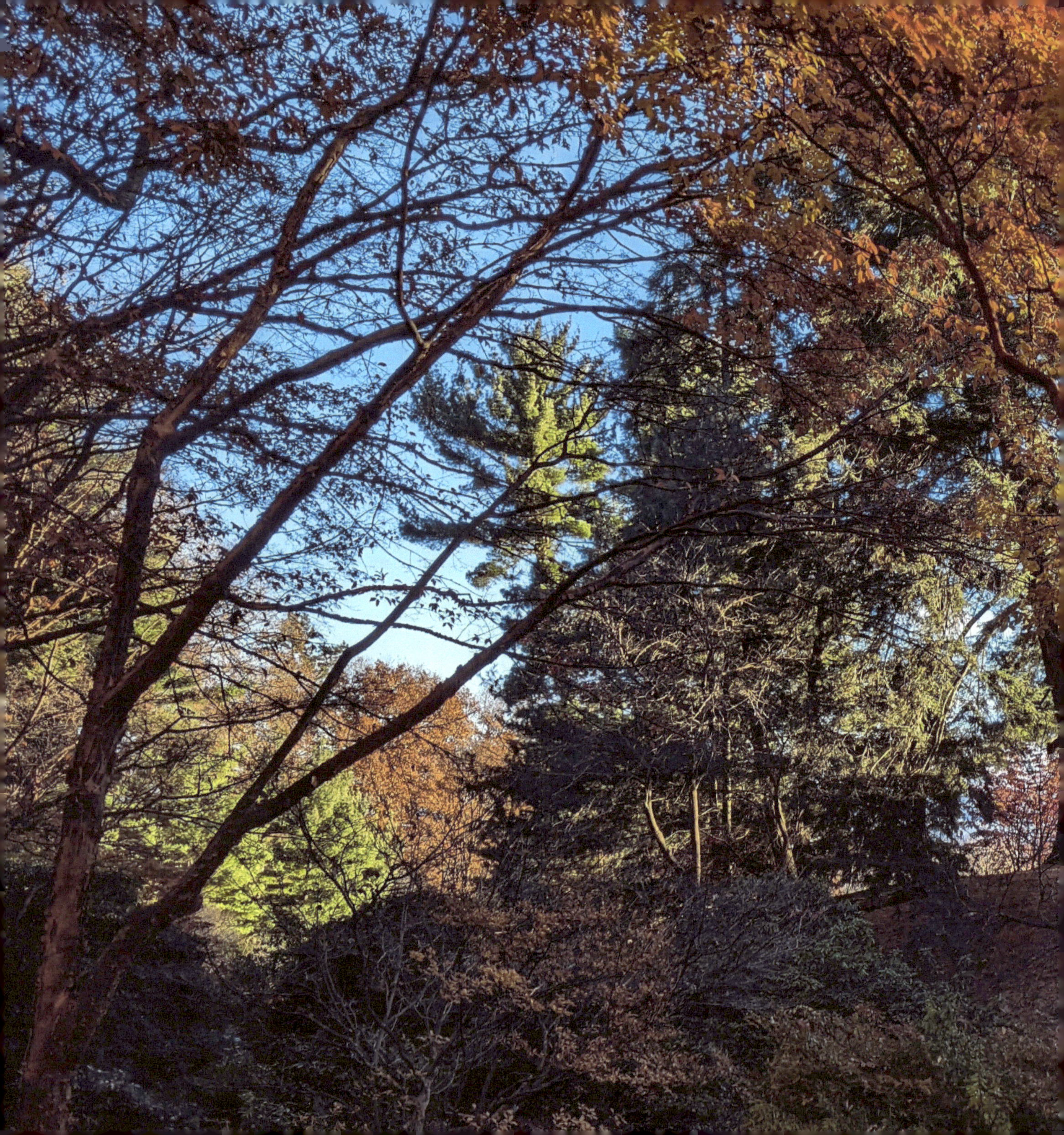

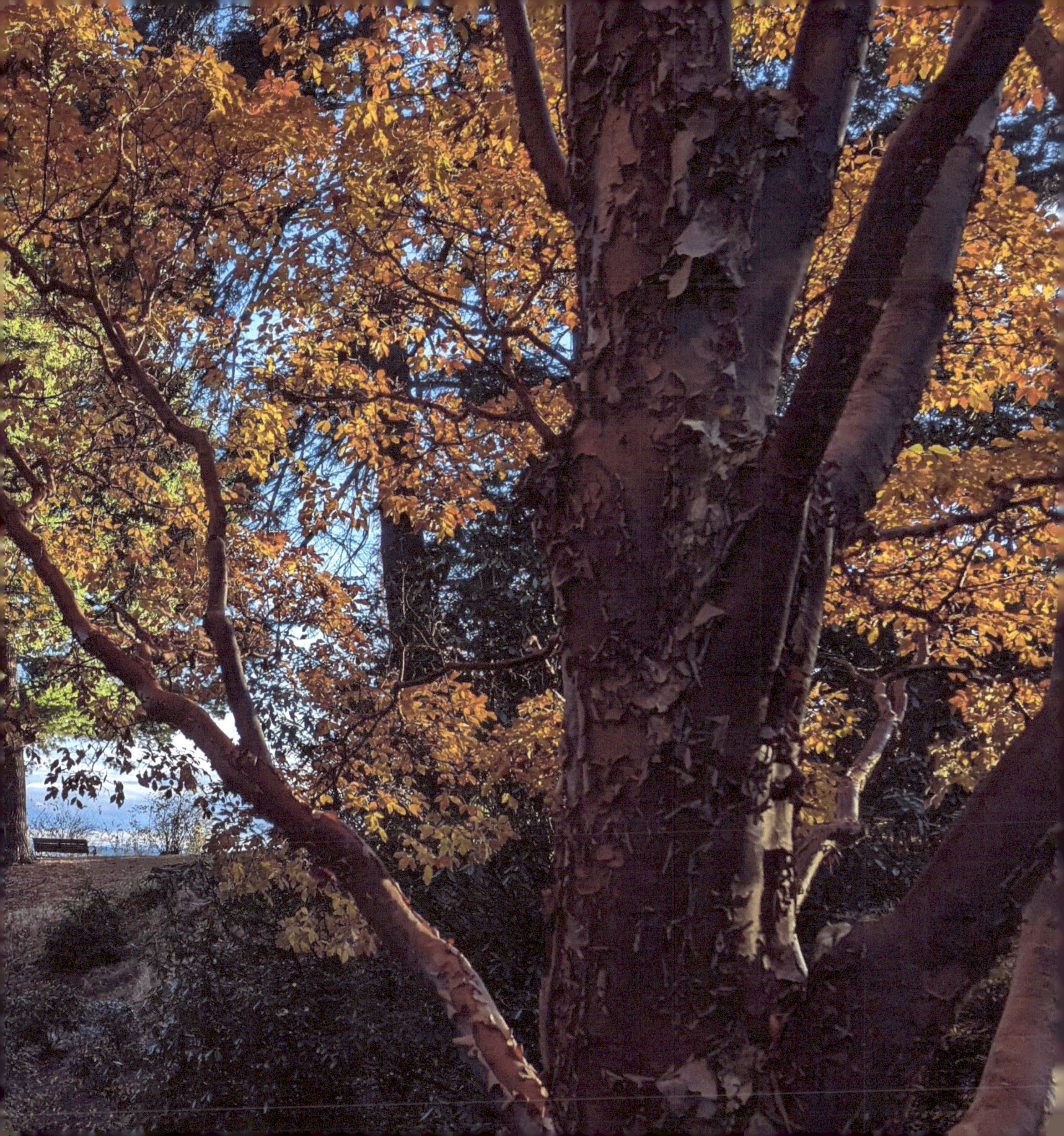

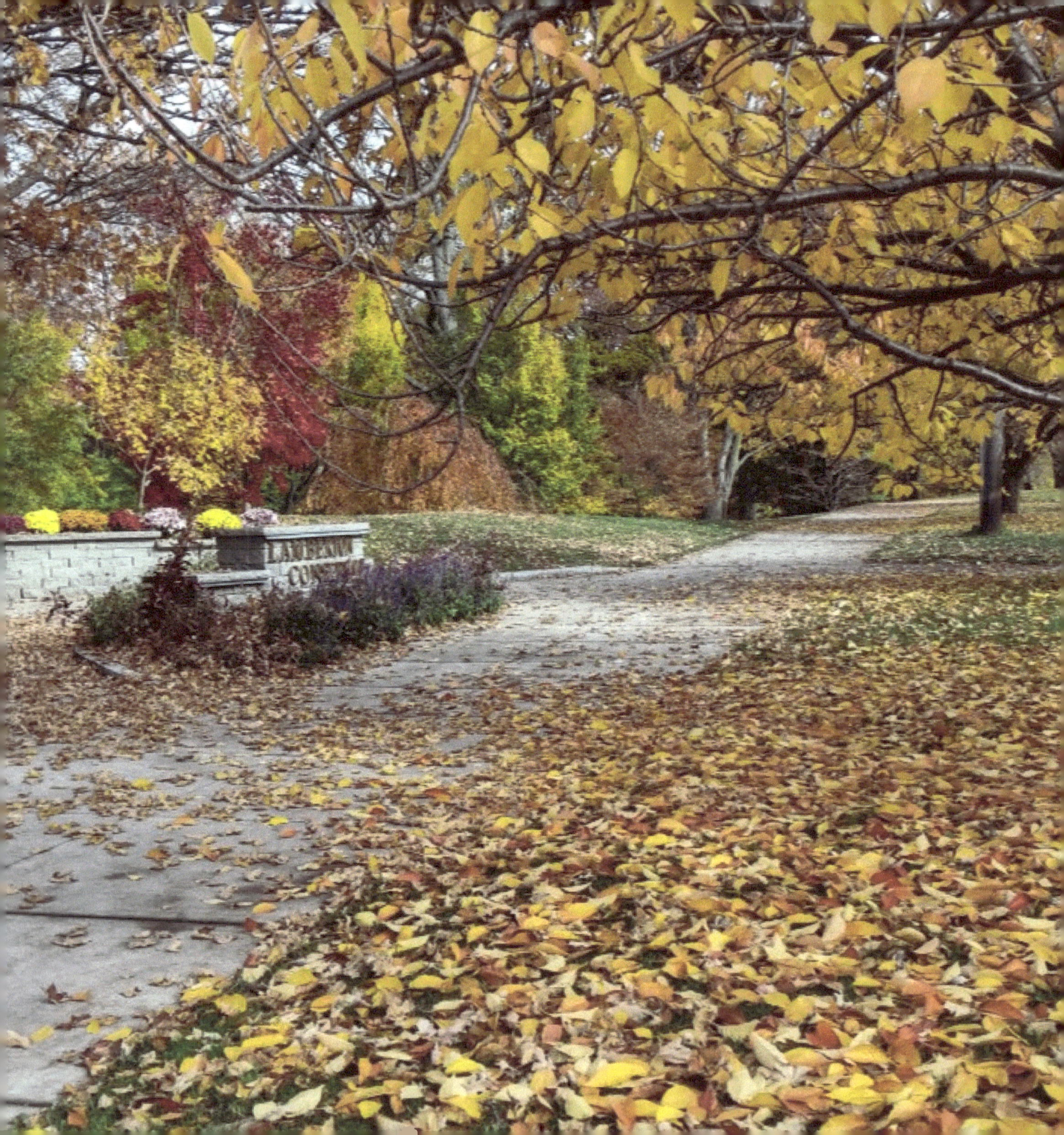
LAURENTIAN
CONSE...

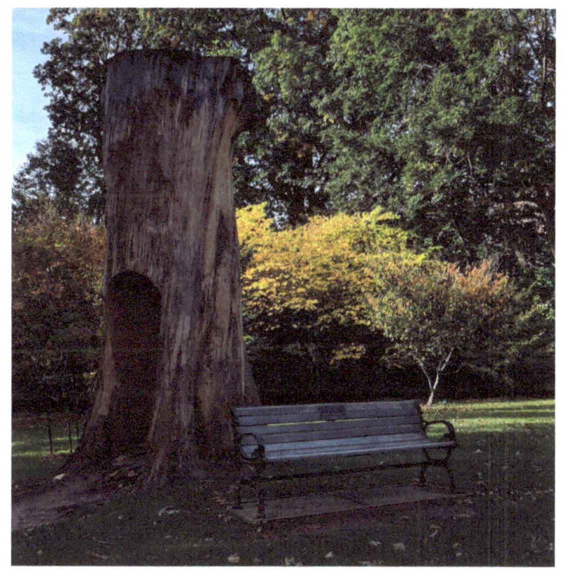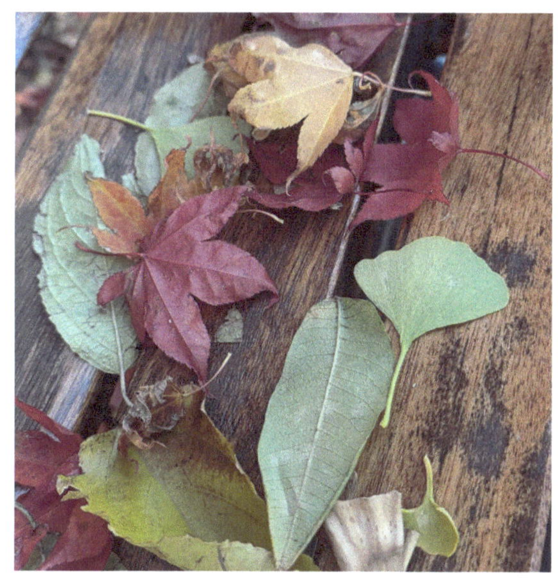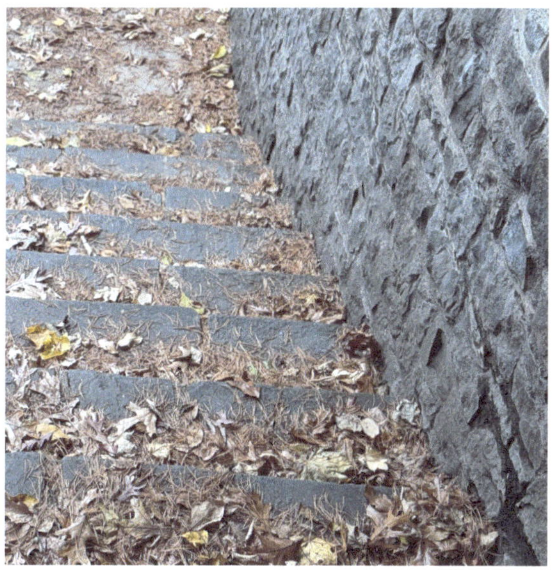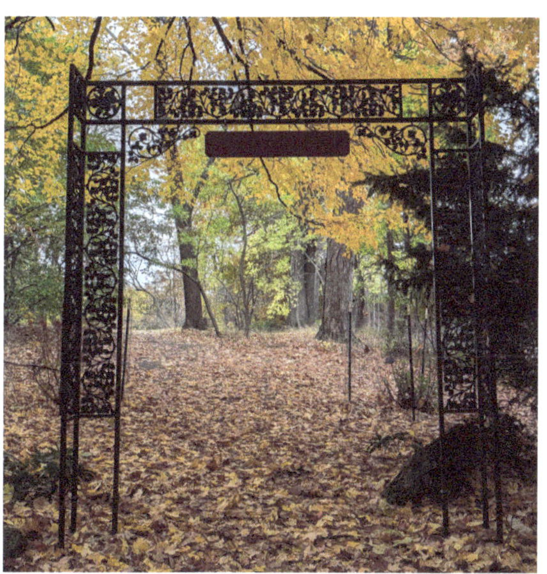

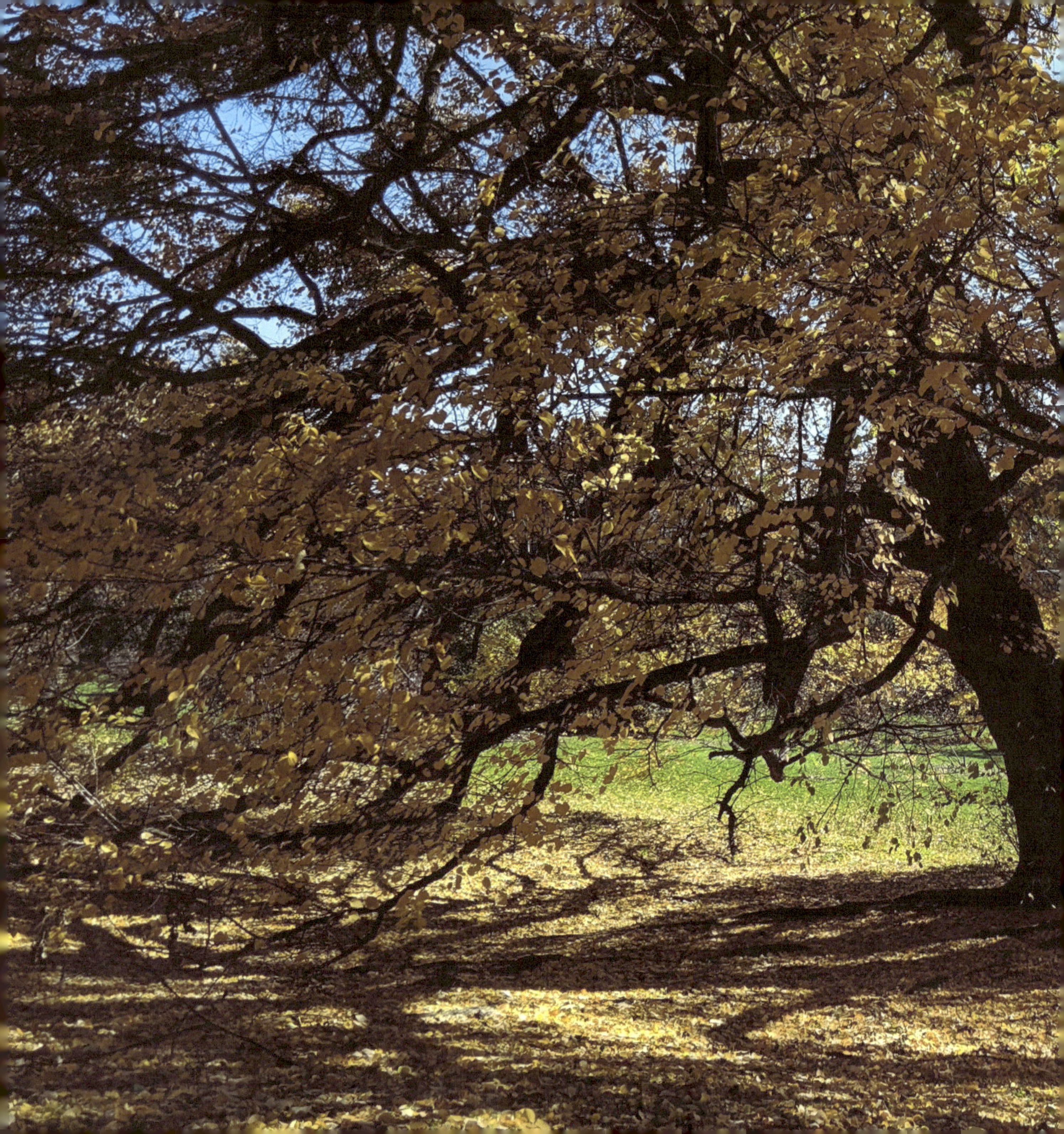

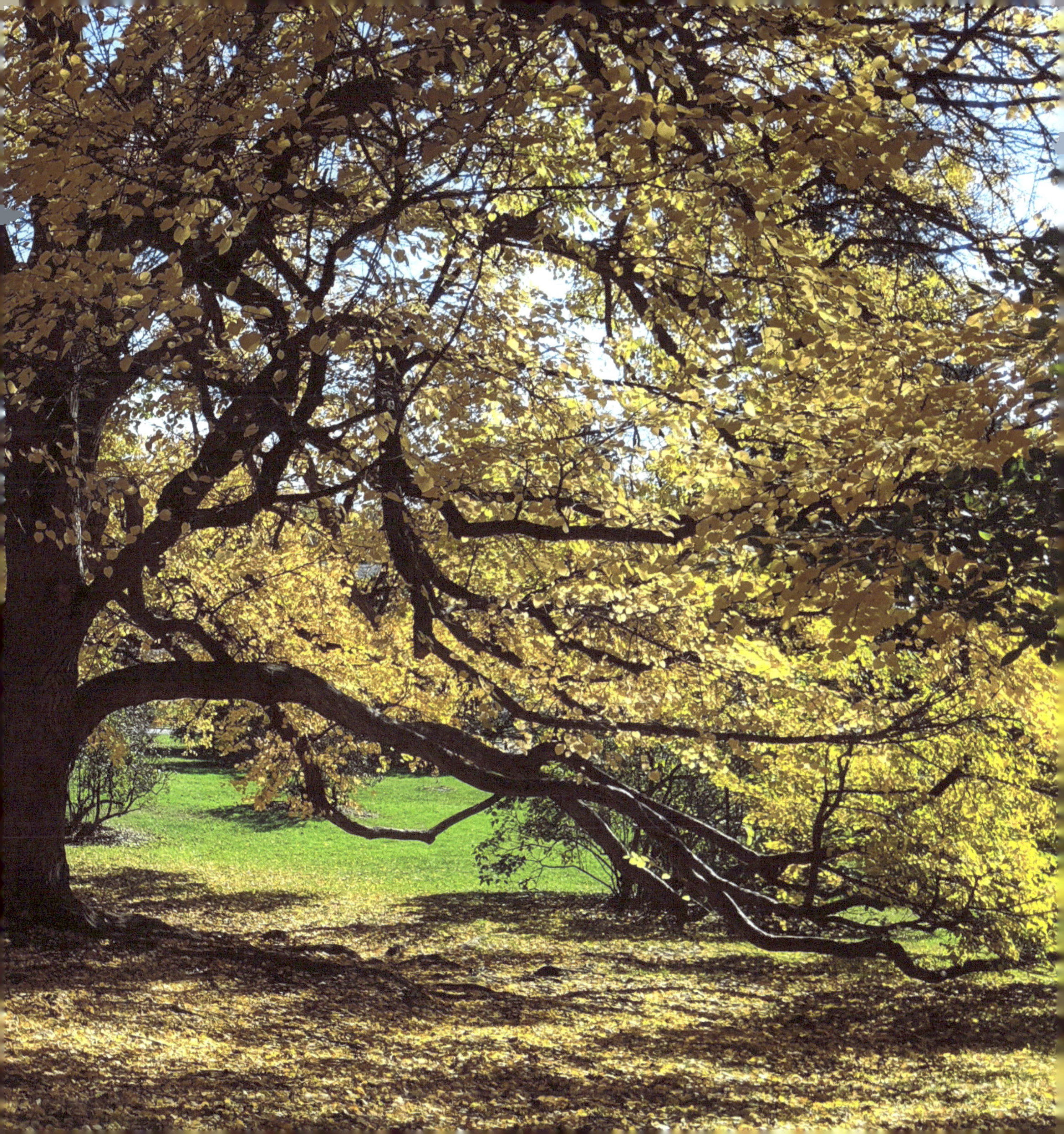

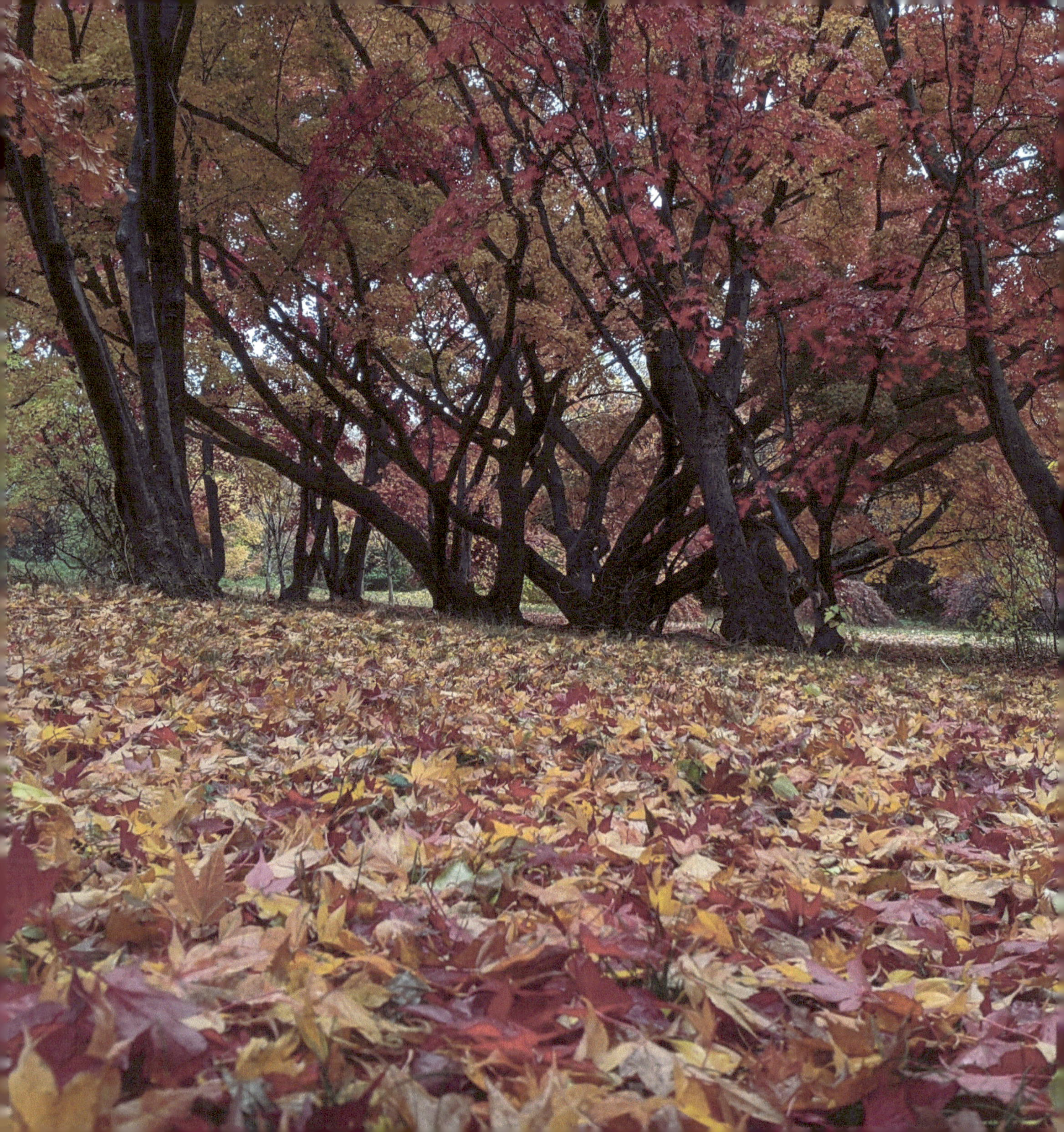

Japanese Maples

Below the reservoir, a south-facing slope holds one of Highland Park's most carefully composed collections. Japanese maples here are selected for both form and color: upright trees with strong branching, cascading weeping forms, and finely cut leaves that capture even subtle changes in light.

Through the seasons, the hillside shifts. Spring and summer remain predominantly green, emphasizing structure and habit. In autumn, the slope ignites with reds, oranges, and golds layered against a gray sky.

The warm exposure and varied growth habits heighten the effect as light moves across the canopy. By fall, the composition feels intentional and complete, as though the landscape has been quietly building toward this moment all year.

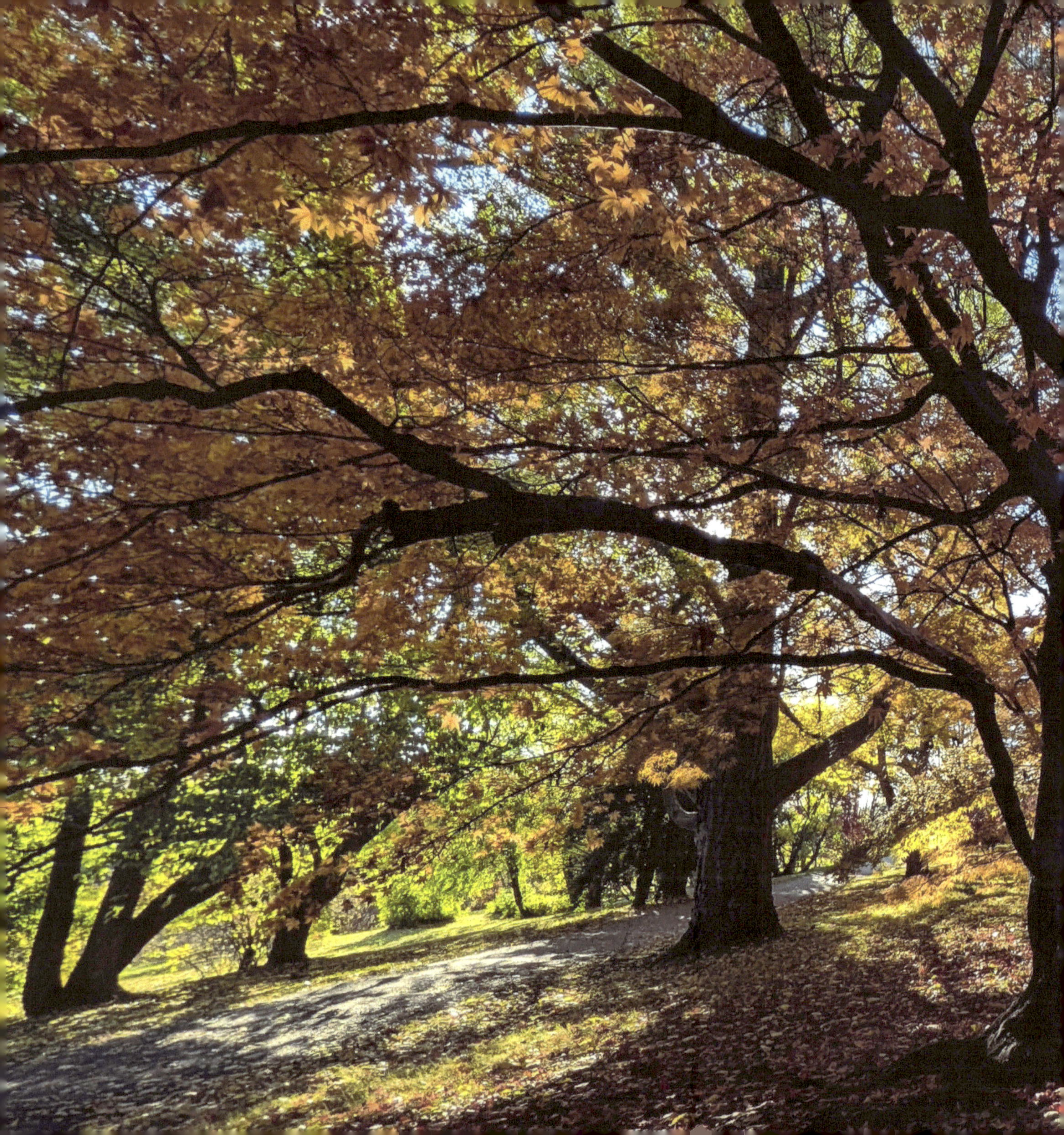

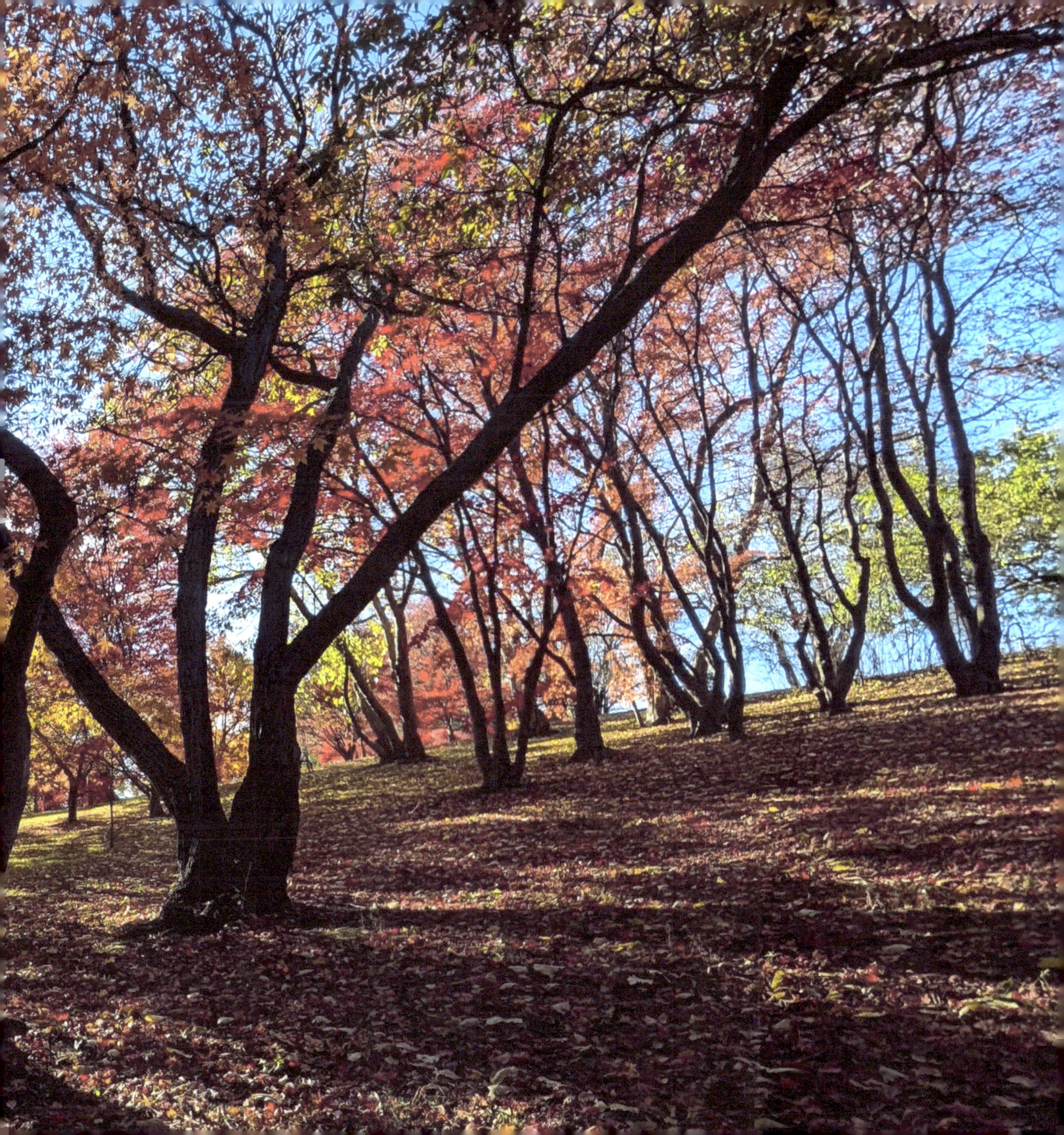

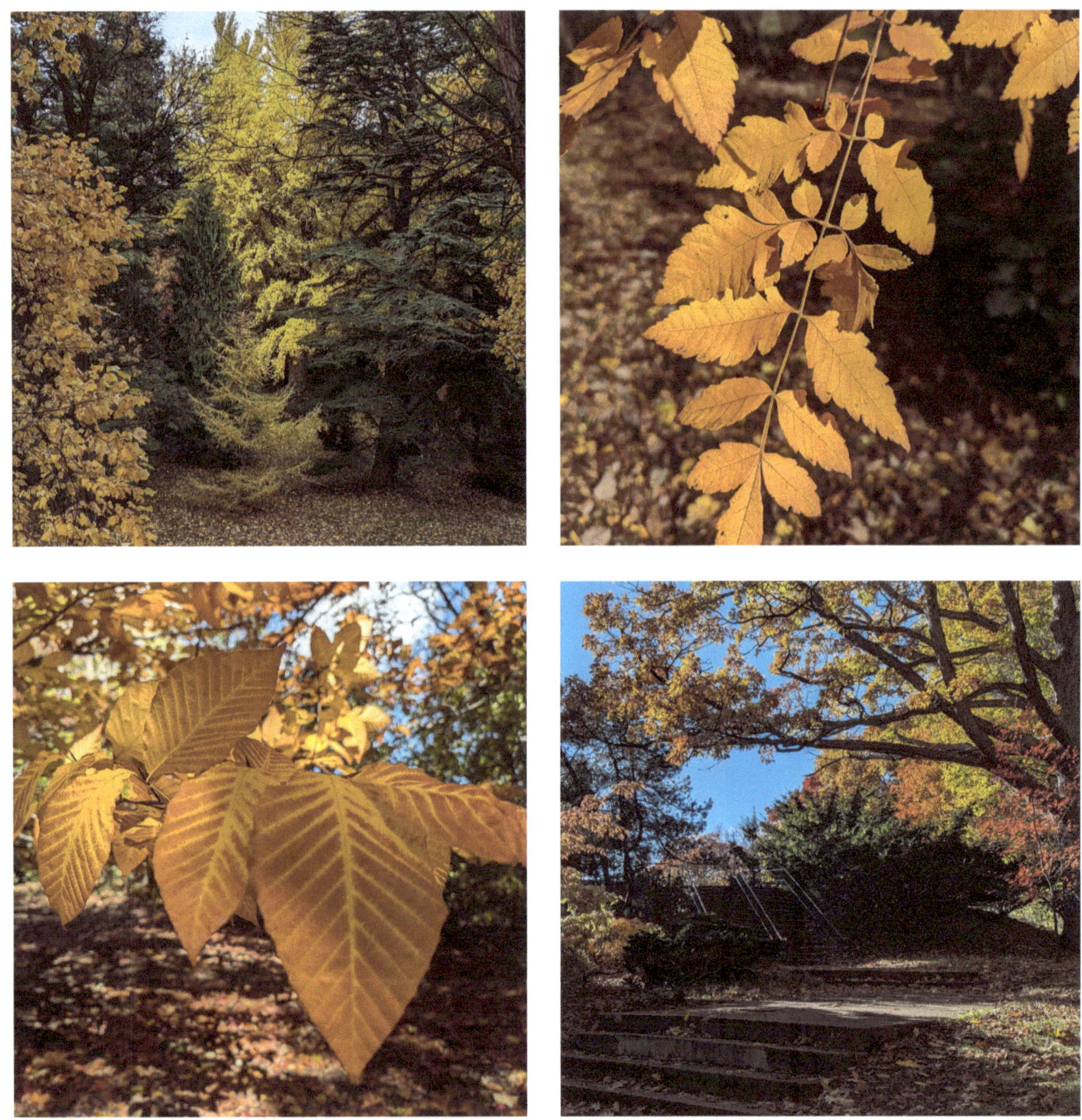

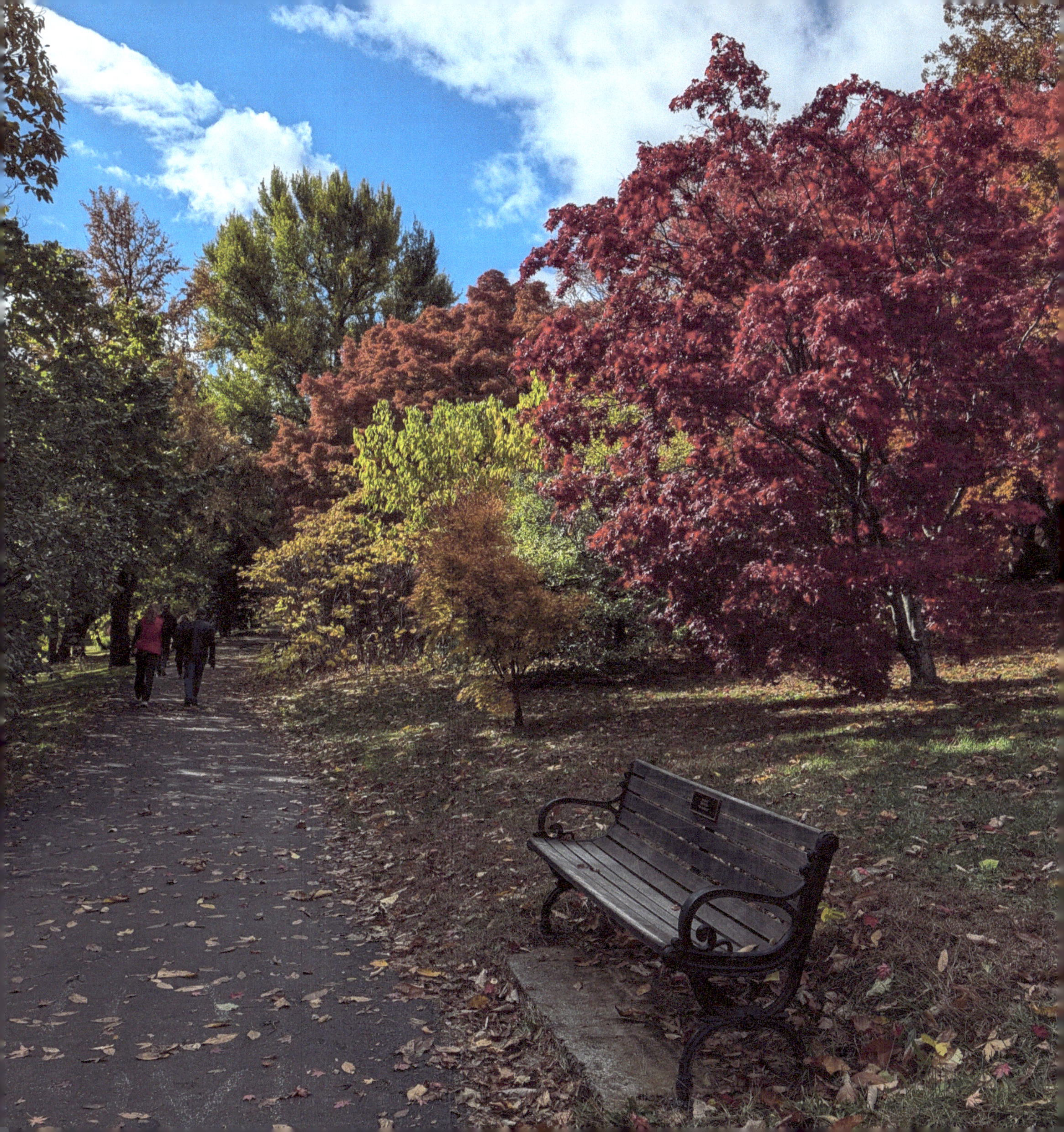

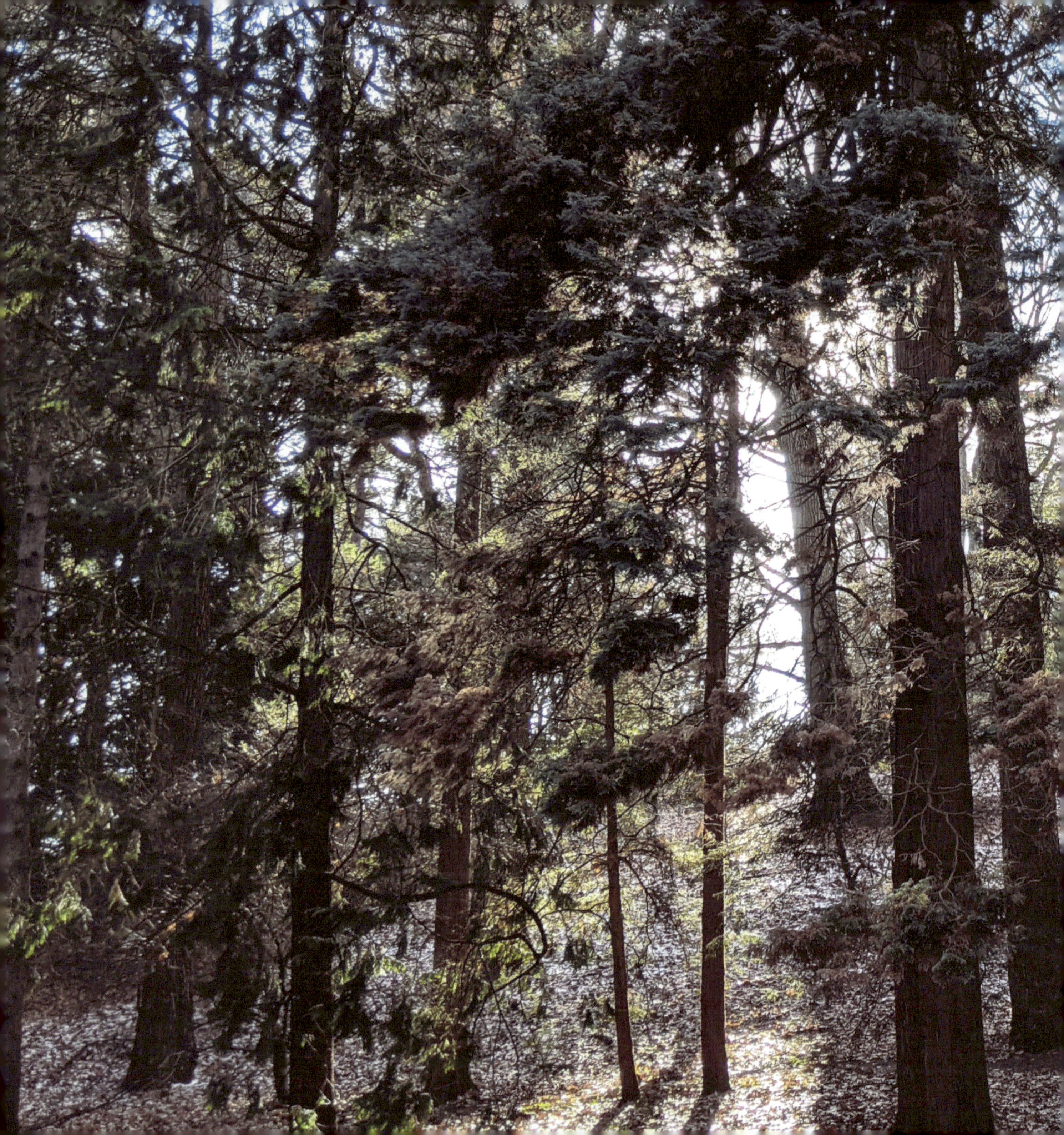

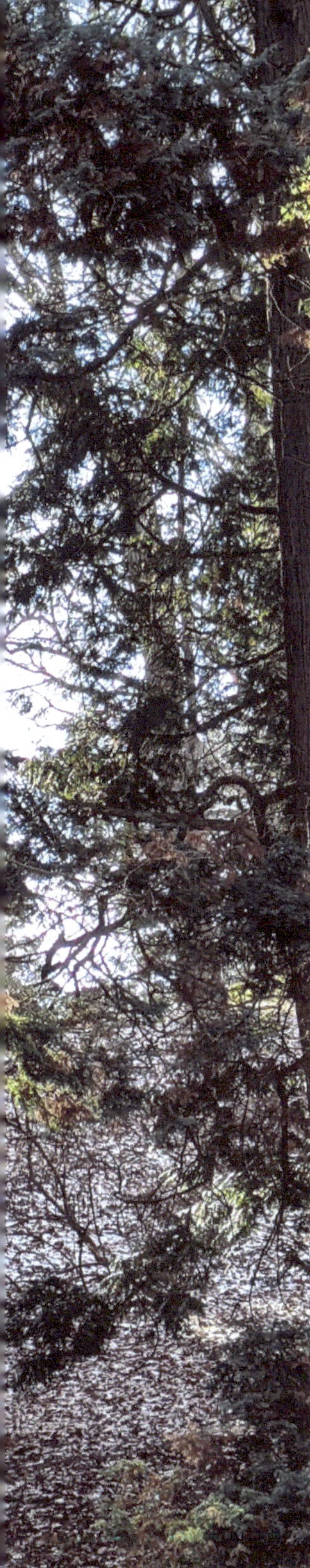

Winter

In winter, Highland Park reveals its structure as leaves fall and branches trace the air like ink on paper. Stone steps, benches, and balustrades emerge from behind summer's green veil, making the park's underlying form visible.

Snow softens edges even as it sharpens intention. Paths curve gently, ridges draw the eye, and a single tree can become a focal point, guiding attention through a quieter, more deliberate landscape.

Winter reveals not what is missing but what endures. In the absence of color and bloom, the park's structure and purpose become unmistakable.

Highland Park becomes a sculpture in winter: spare, balanced, and deeply expressive. In that clarity, the landscape offers not distraction but understanding.

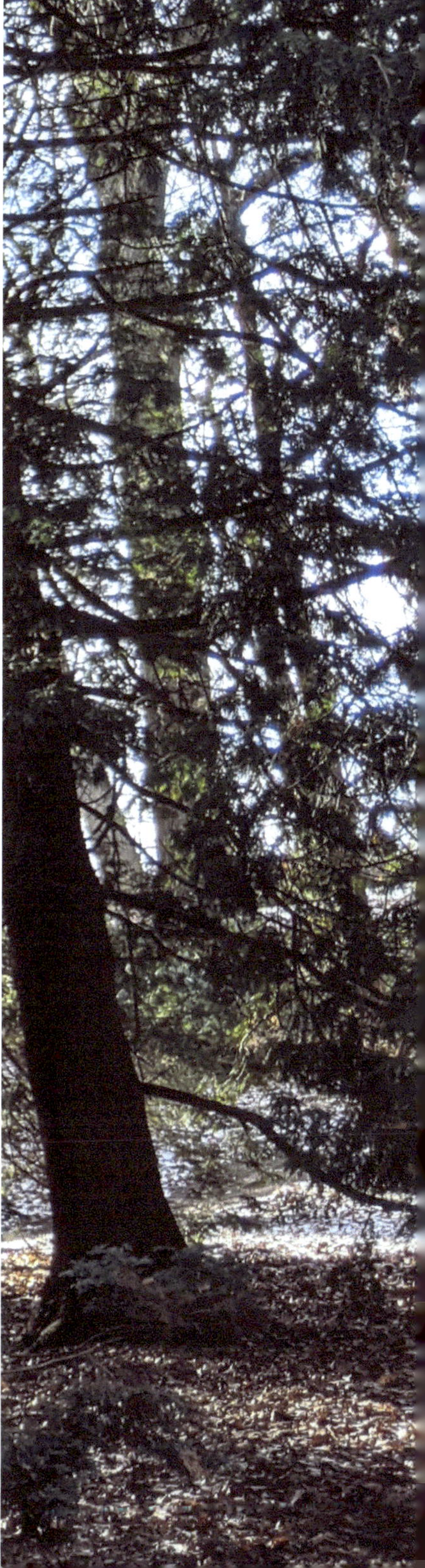

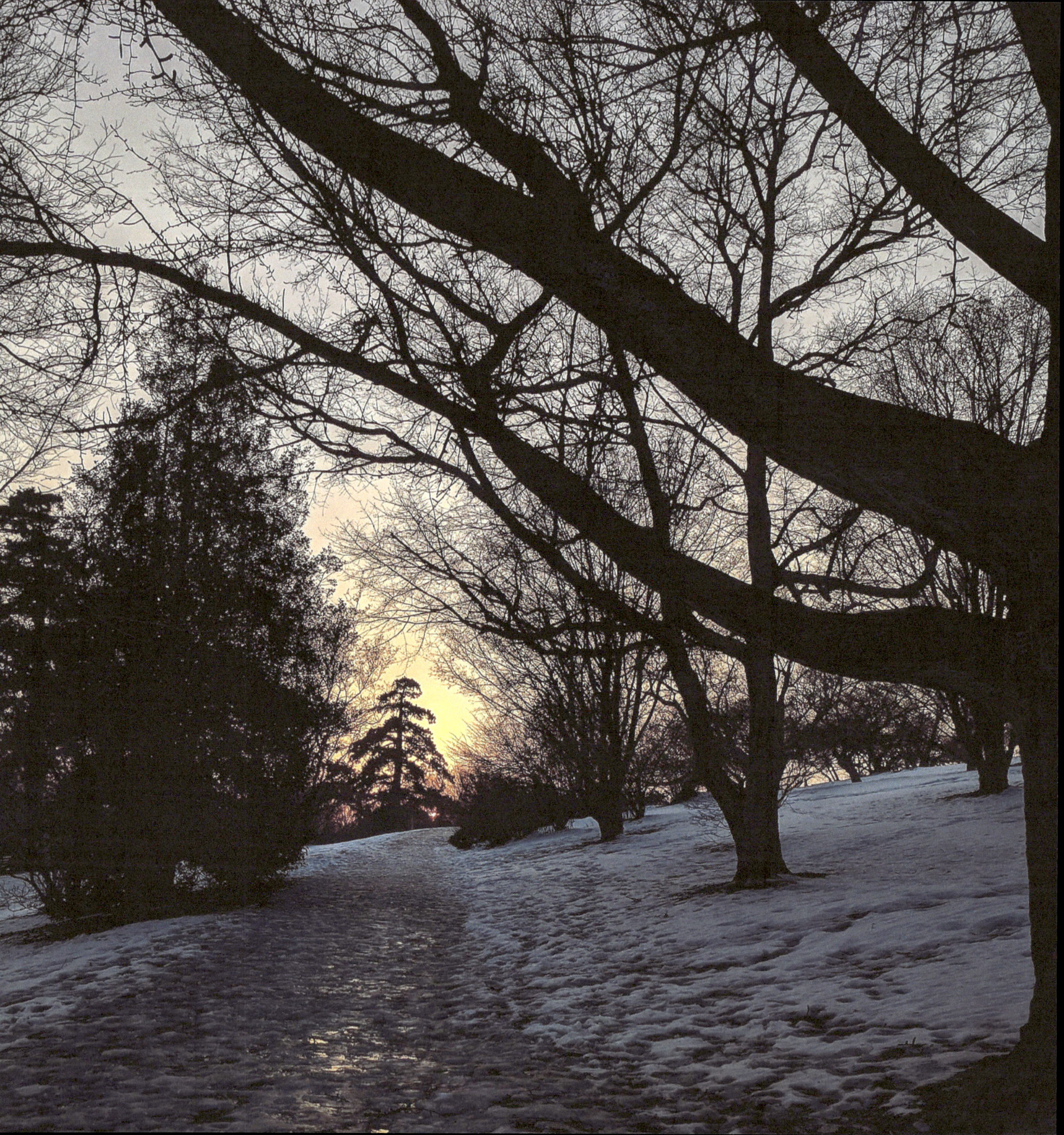

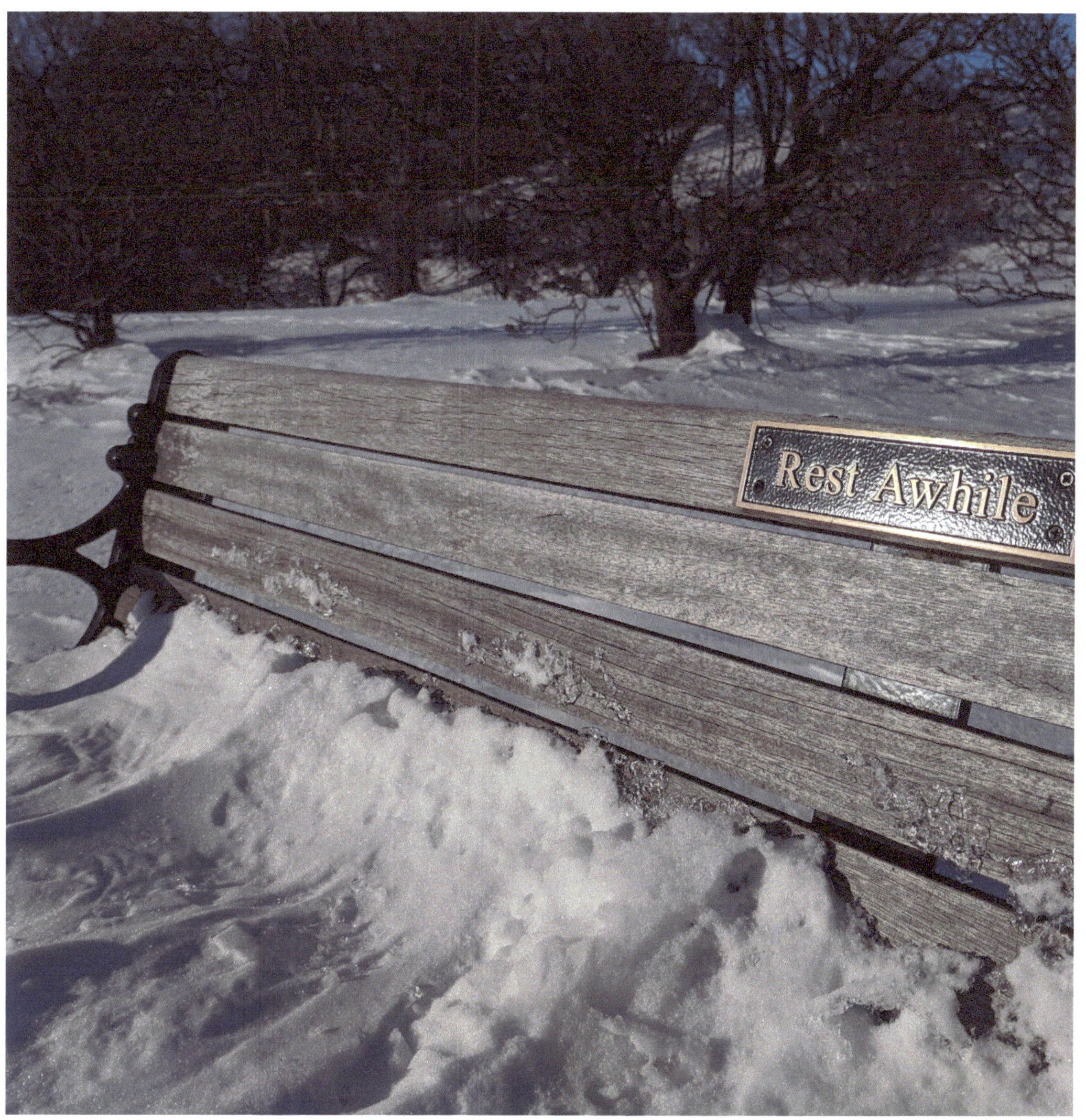
Rest Awhile

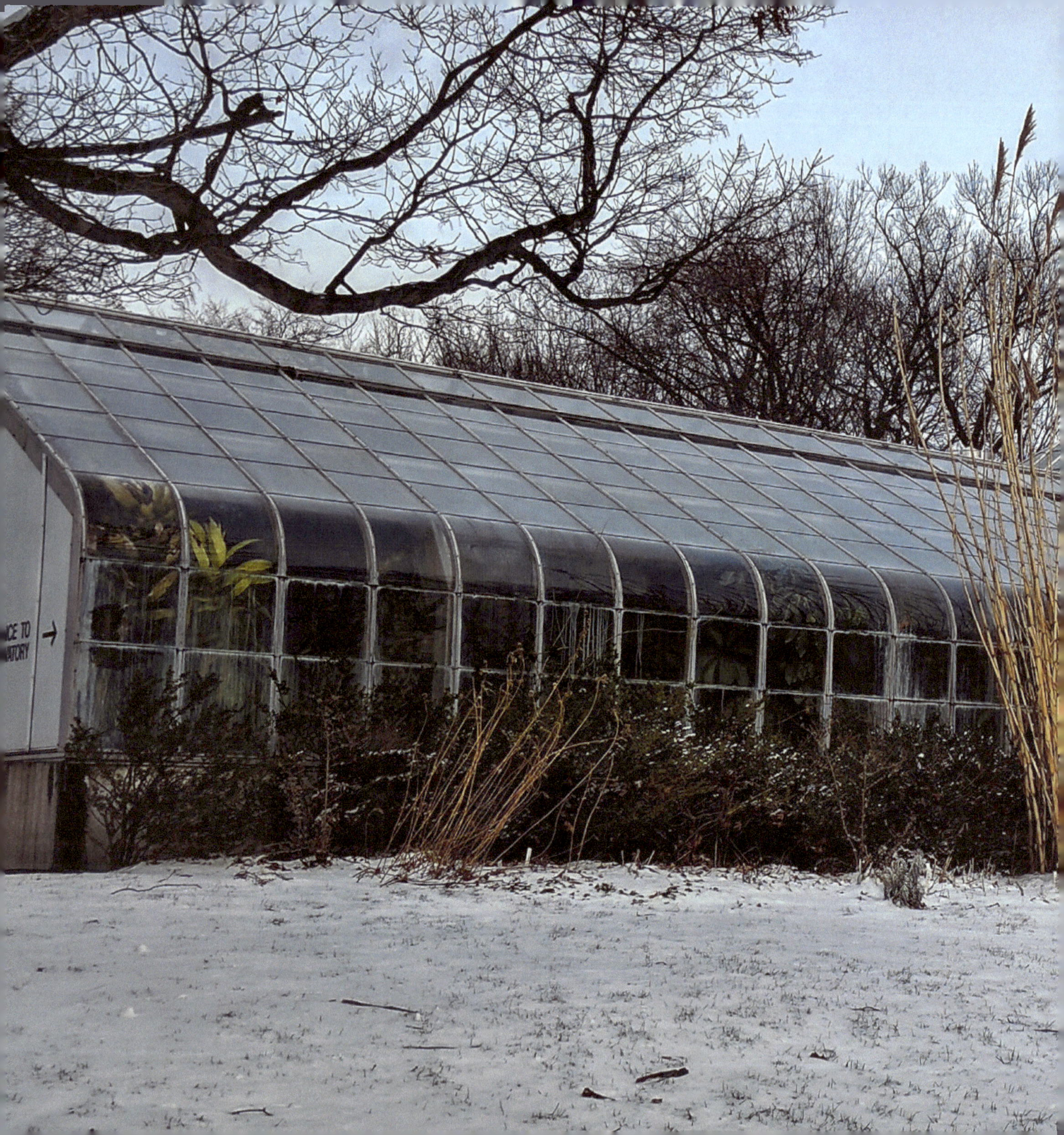
NCE TO
ATORY →

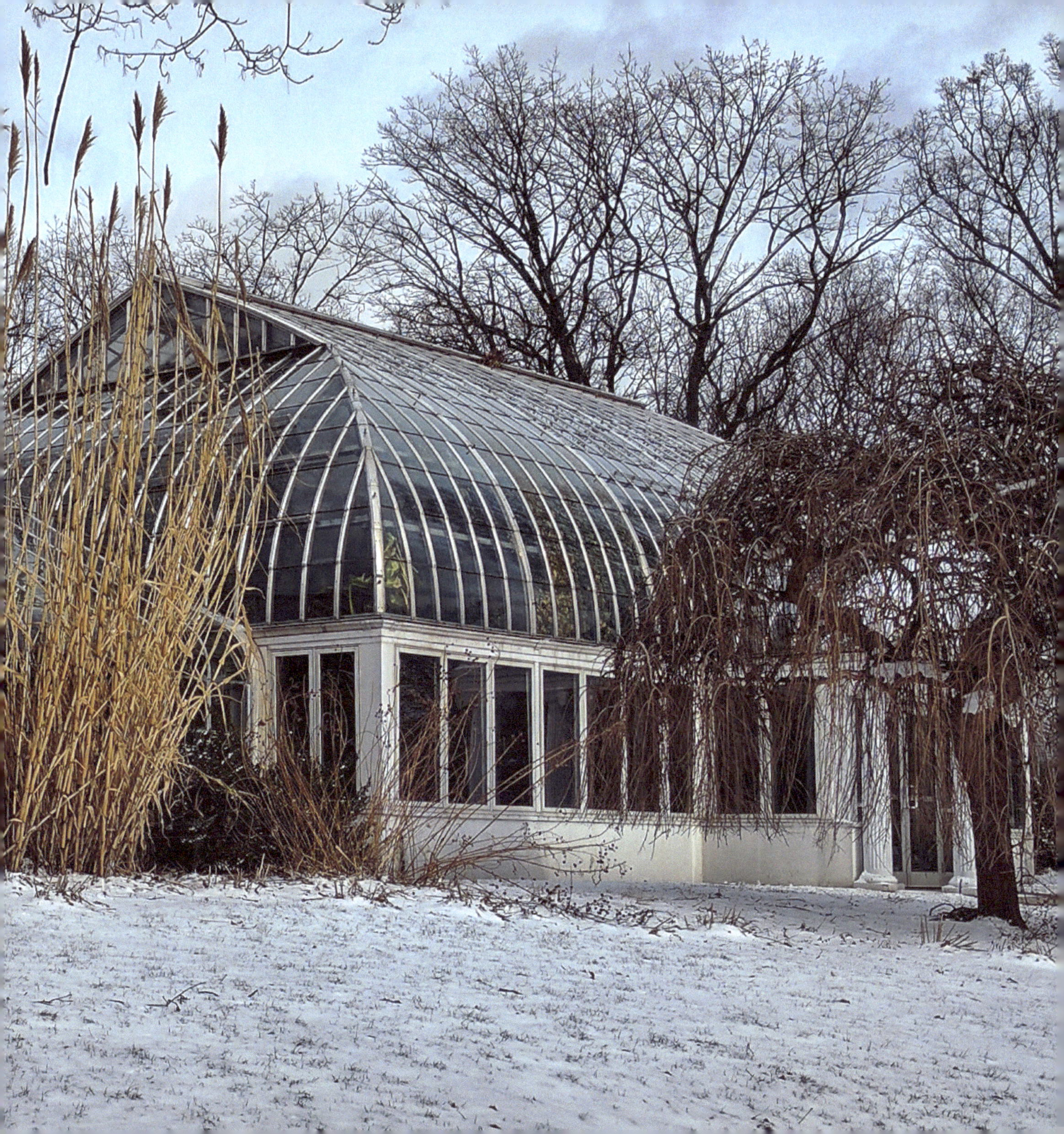

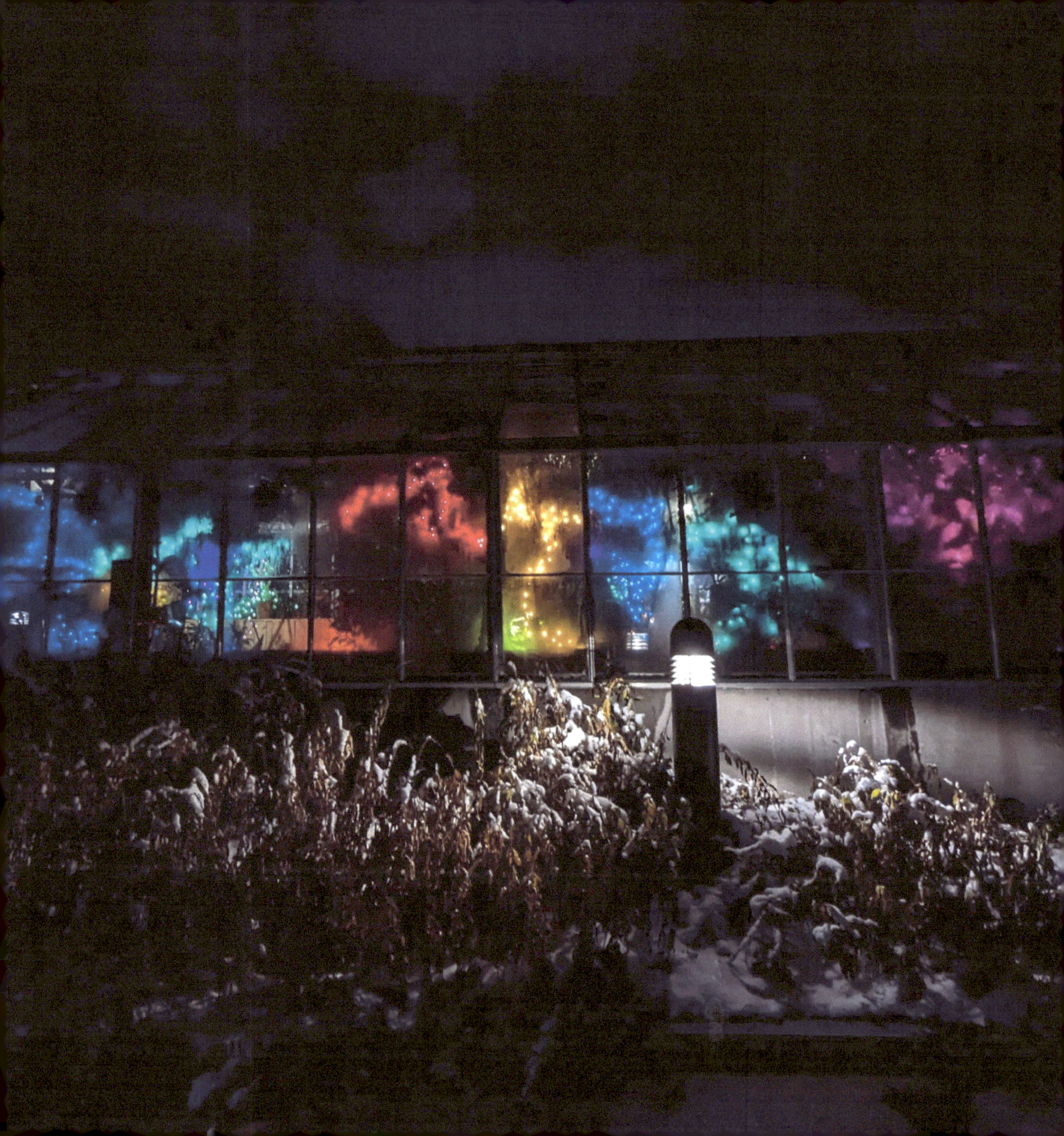

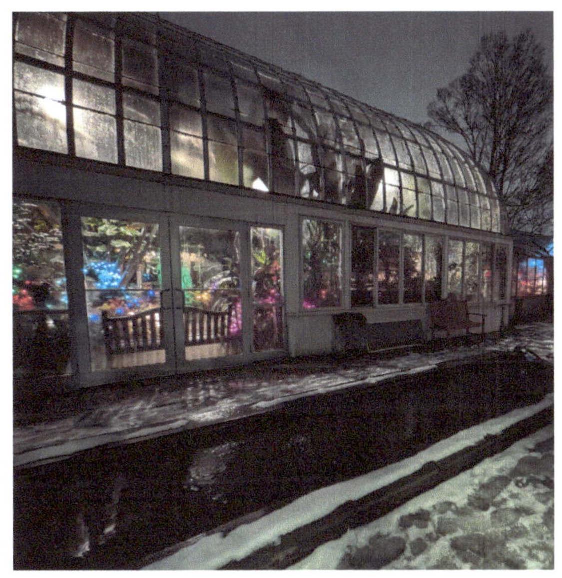
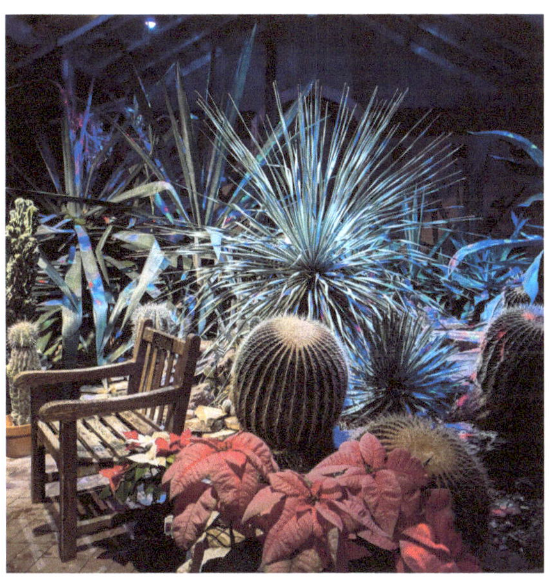
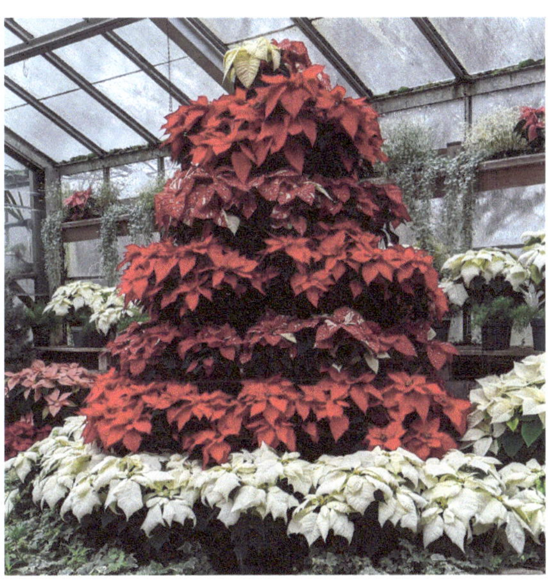
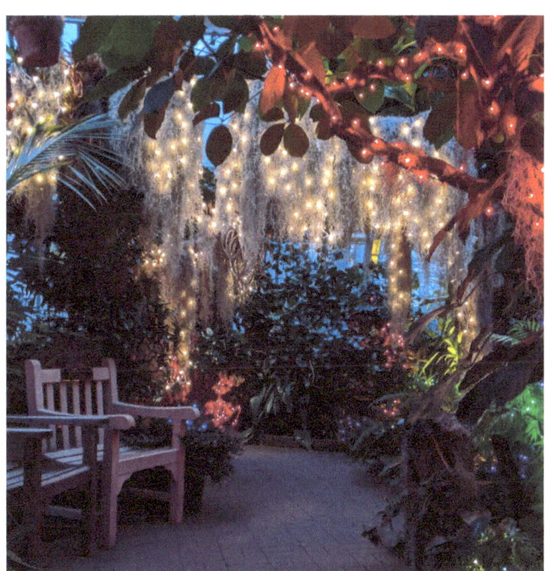

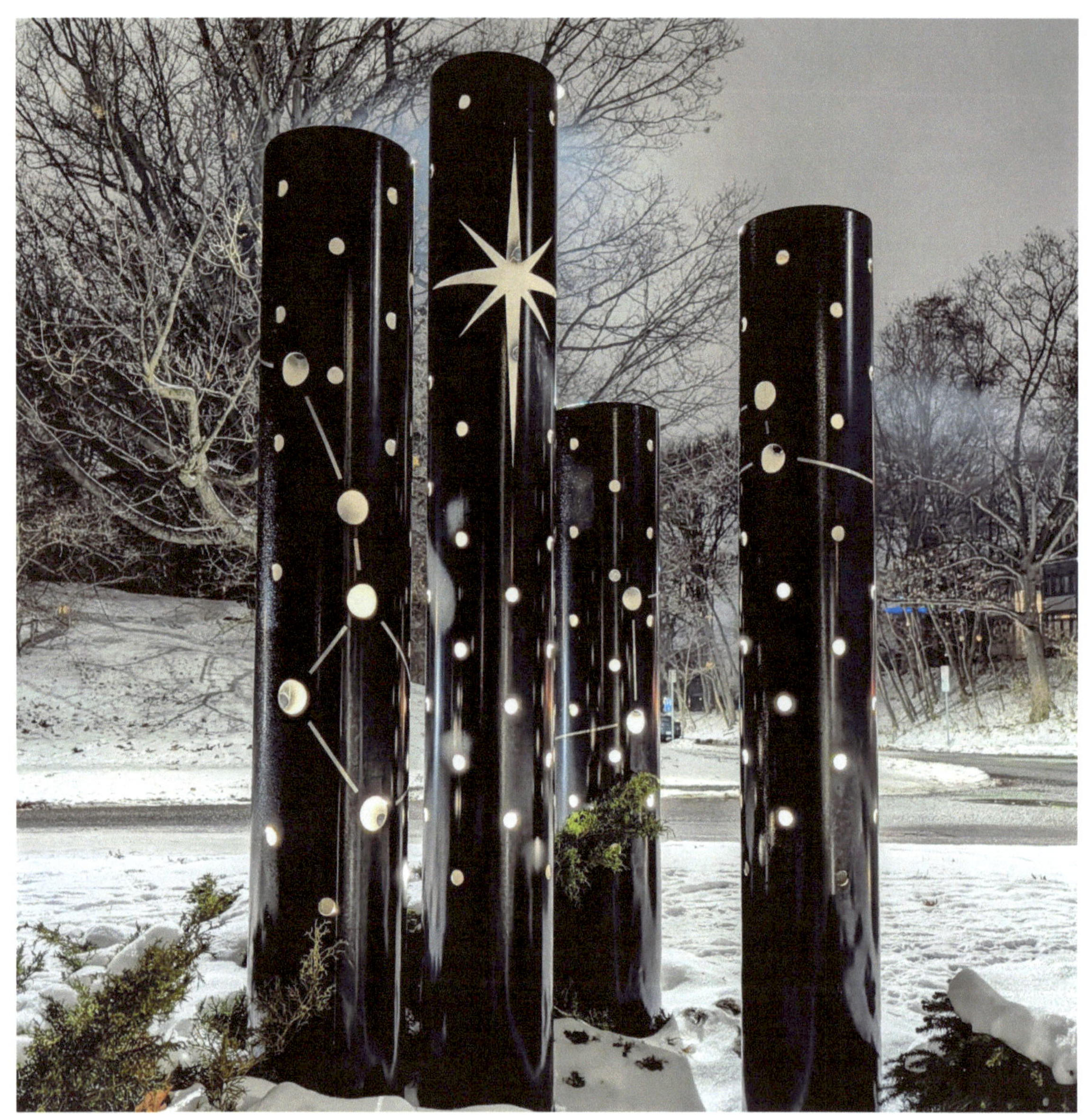

Above: The North Star sculpture in Frederick Douglass Memorial Plaza

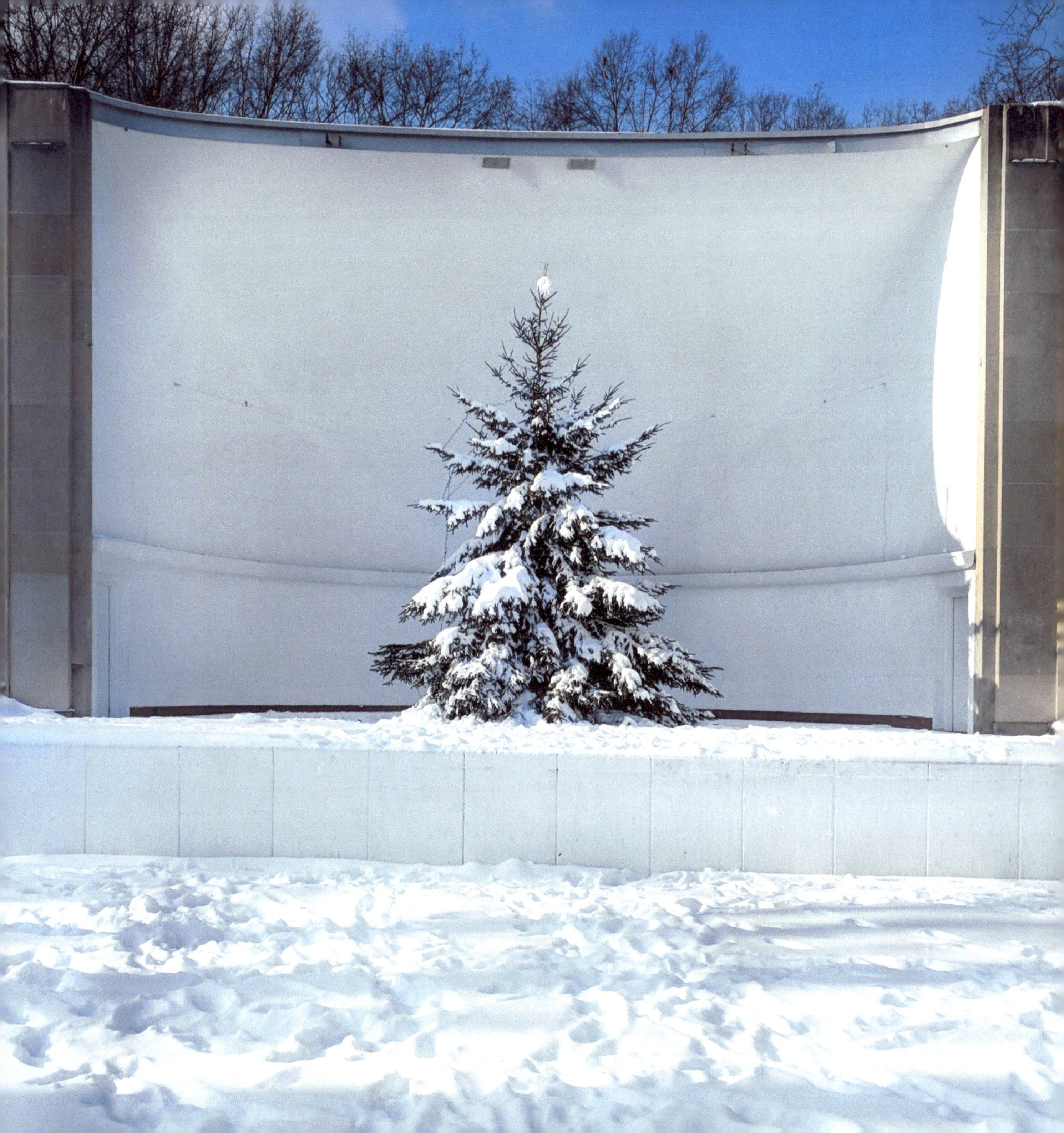

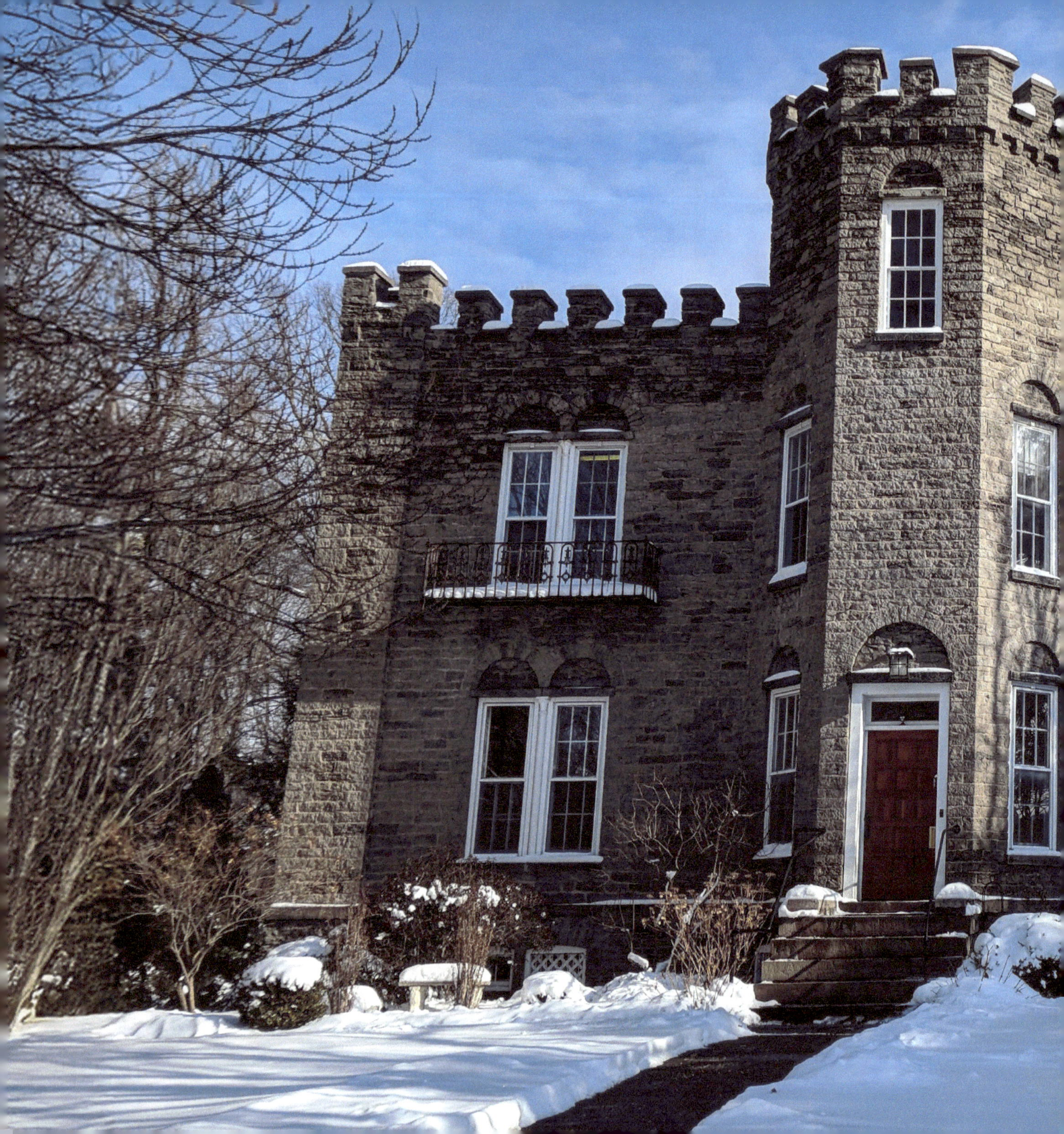

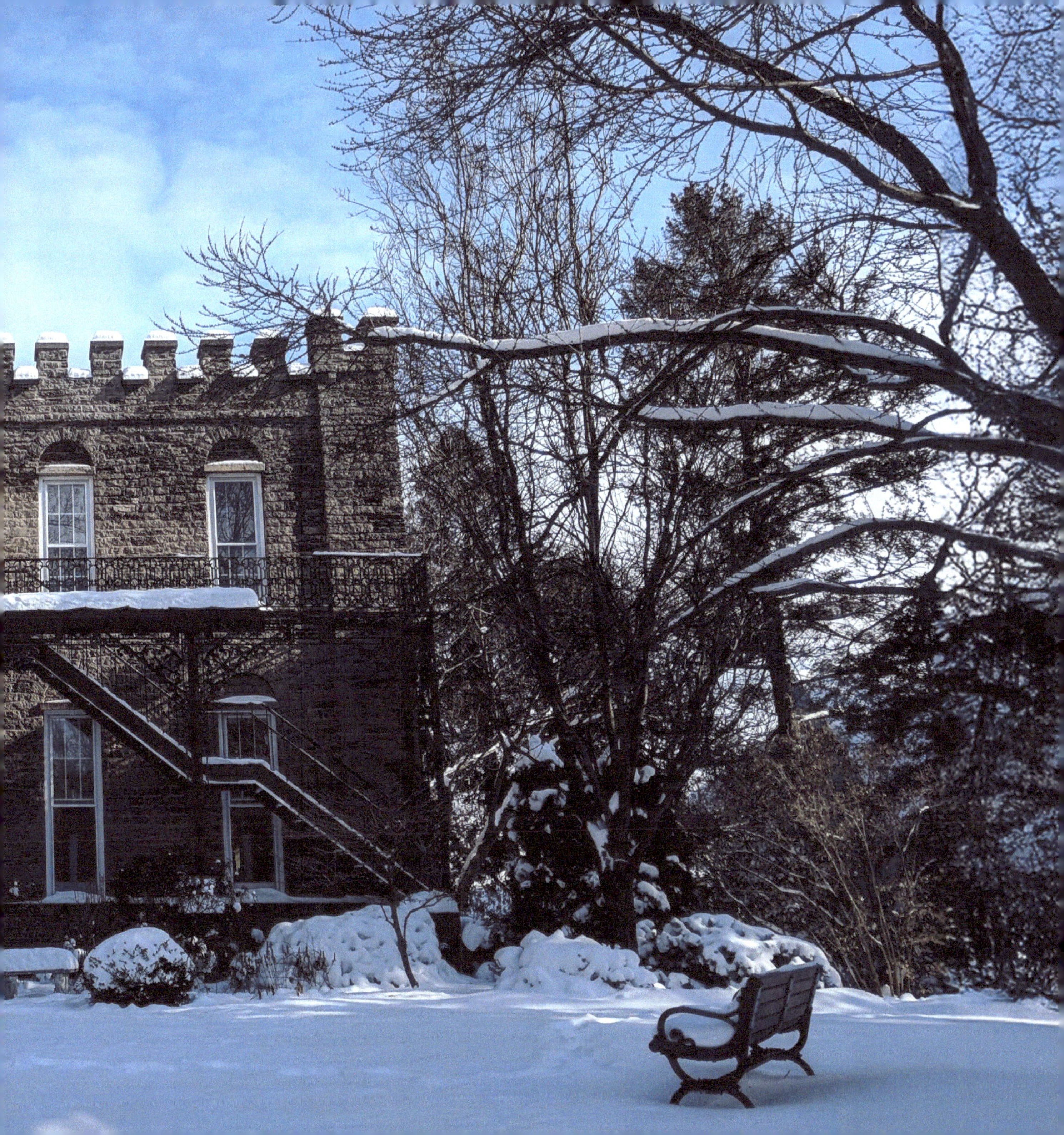

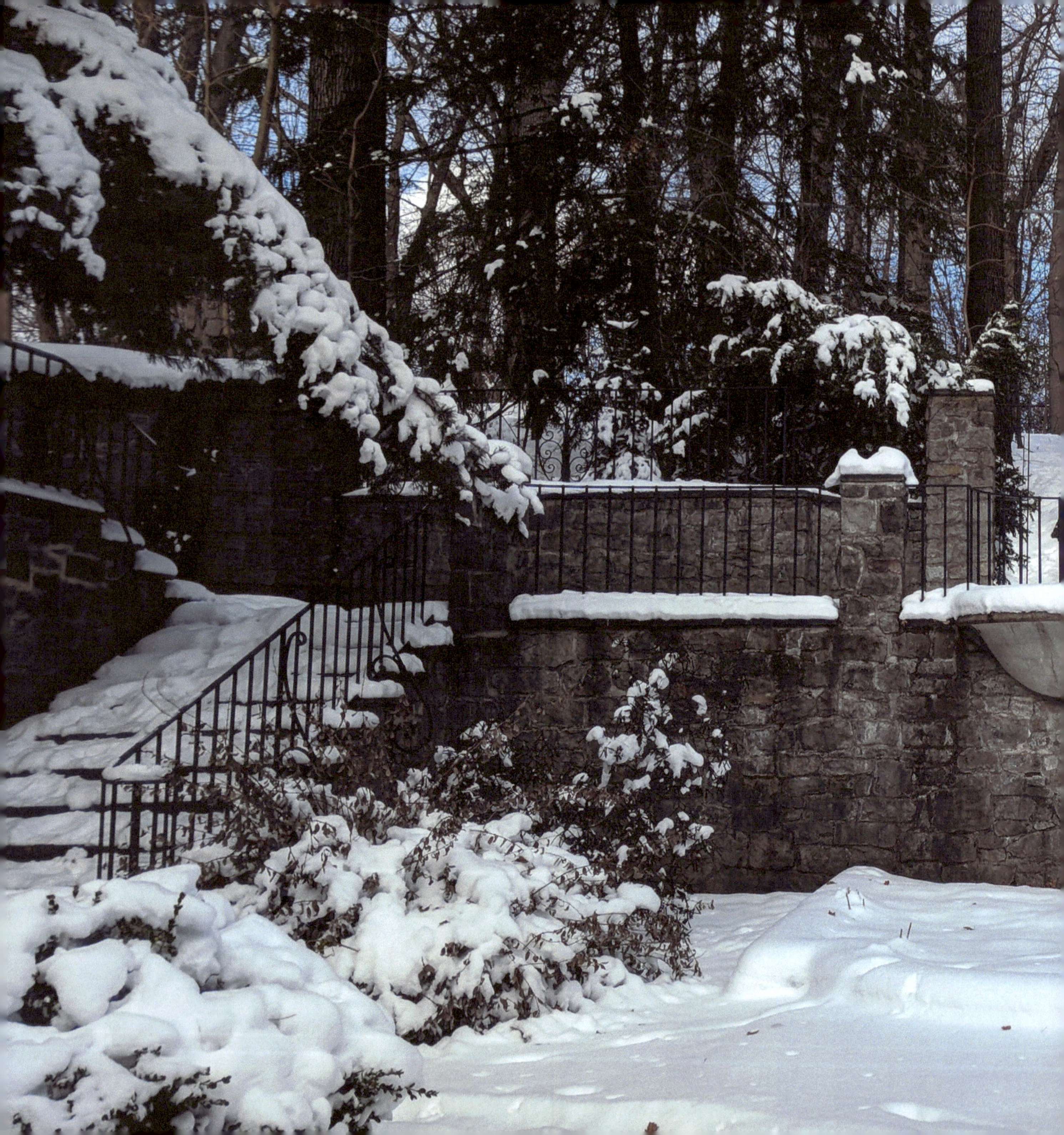

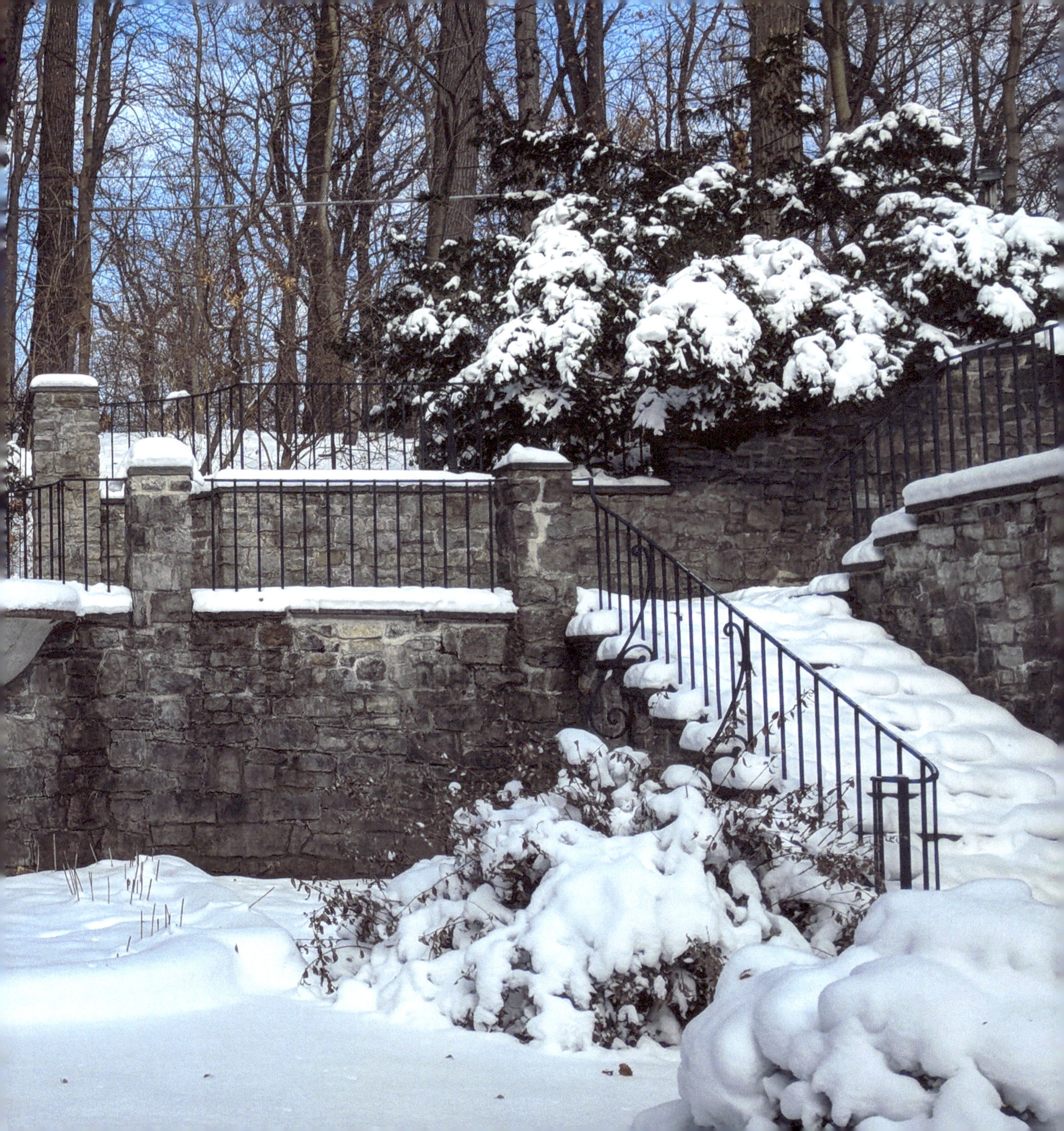

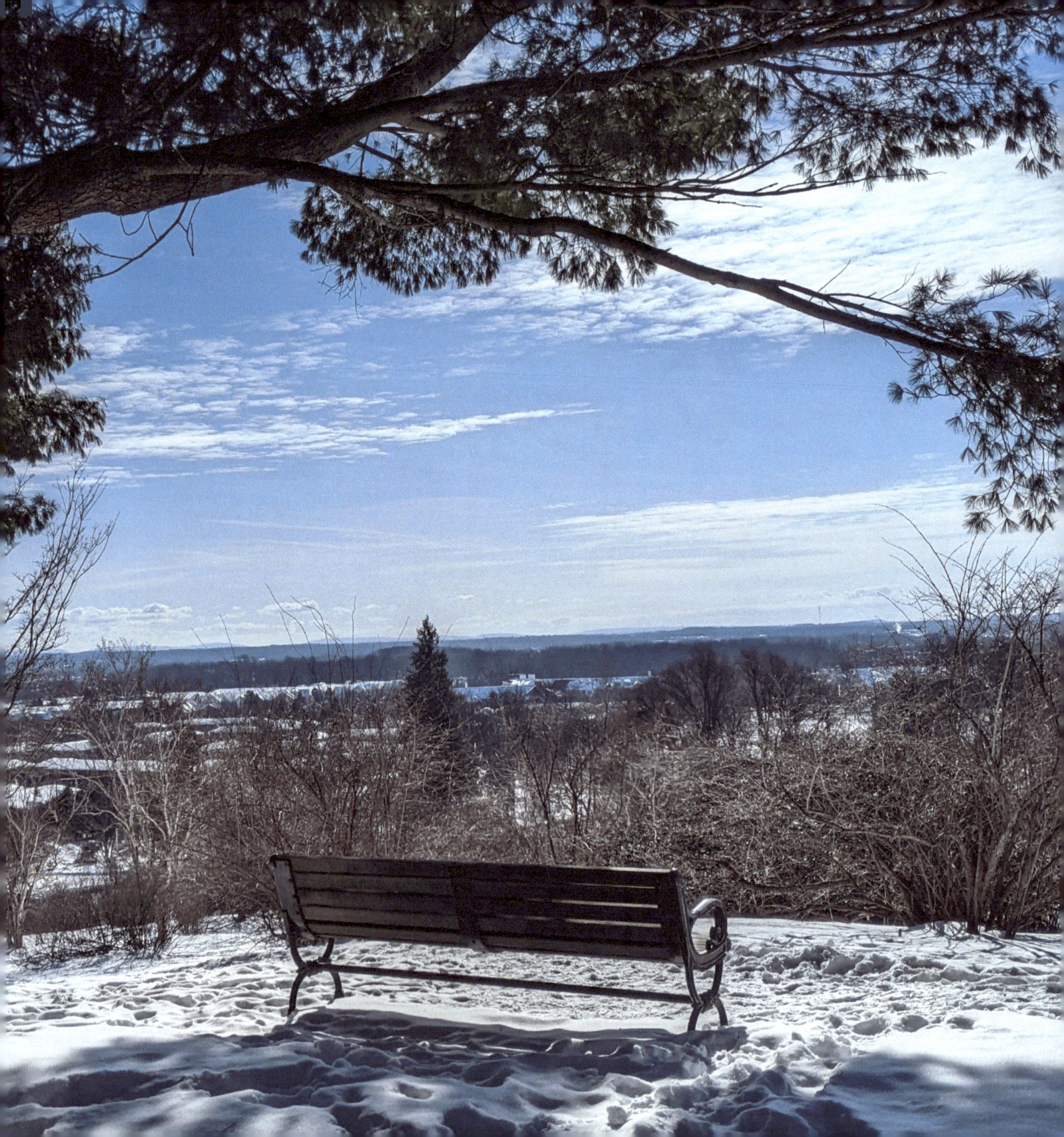

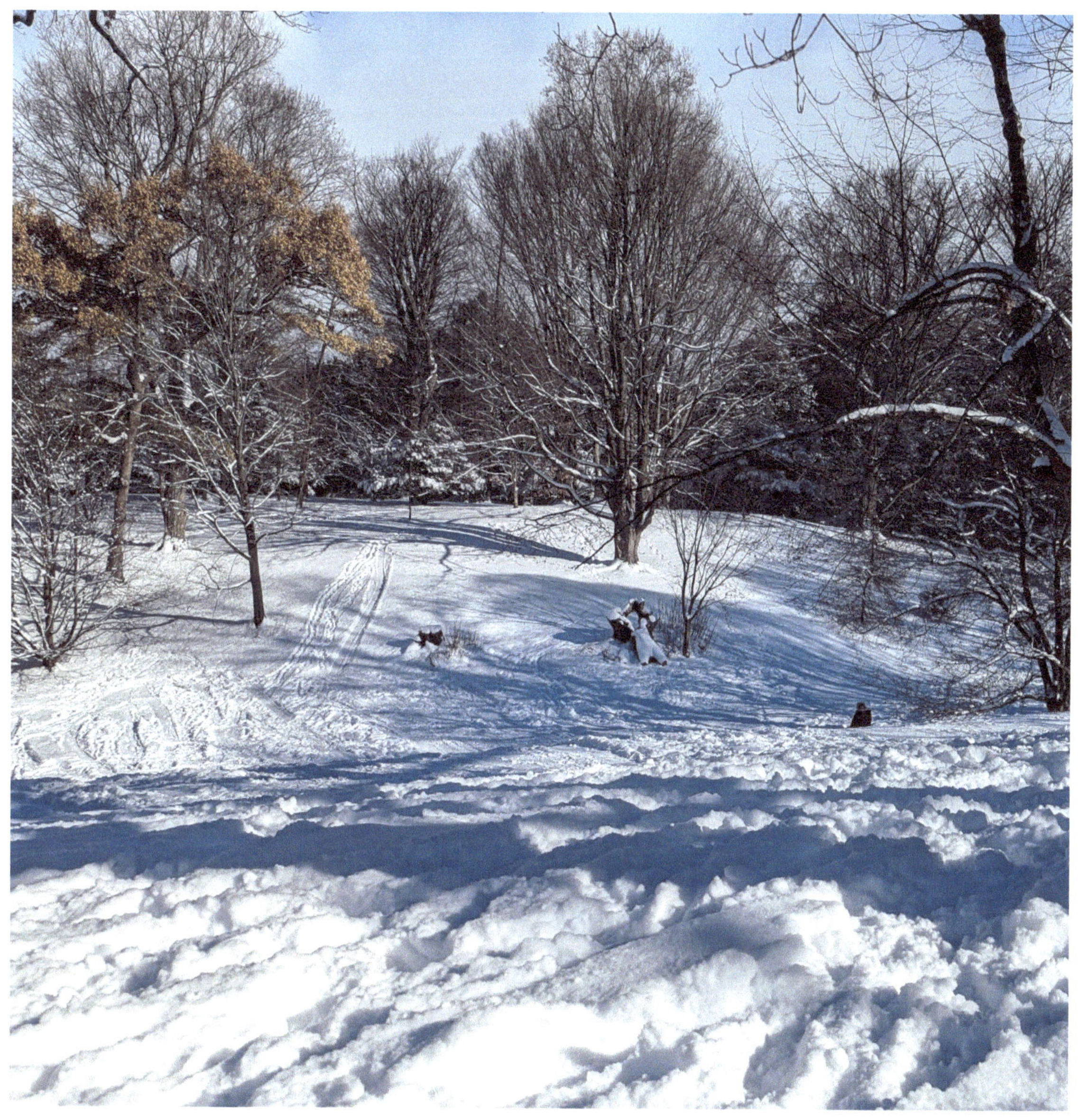

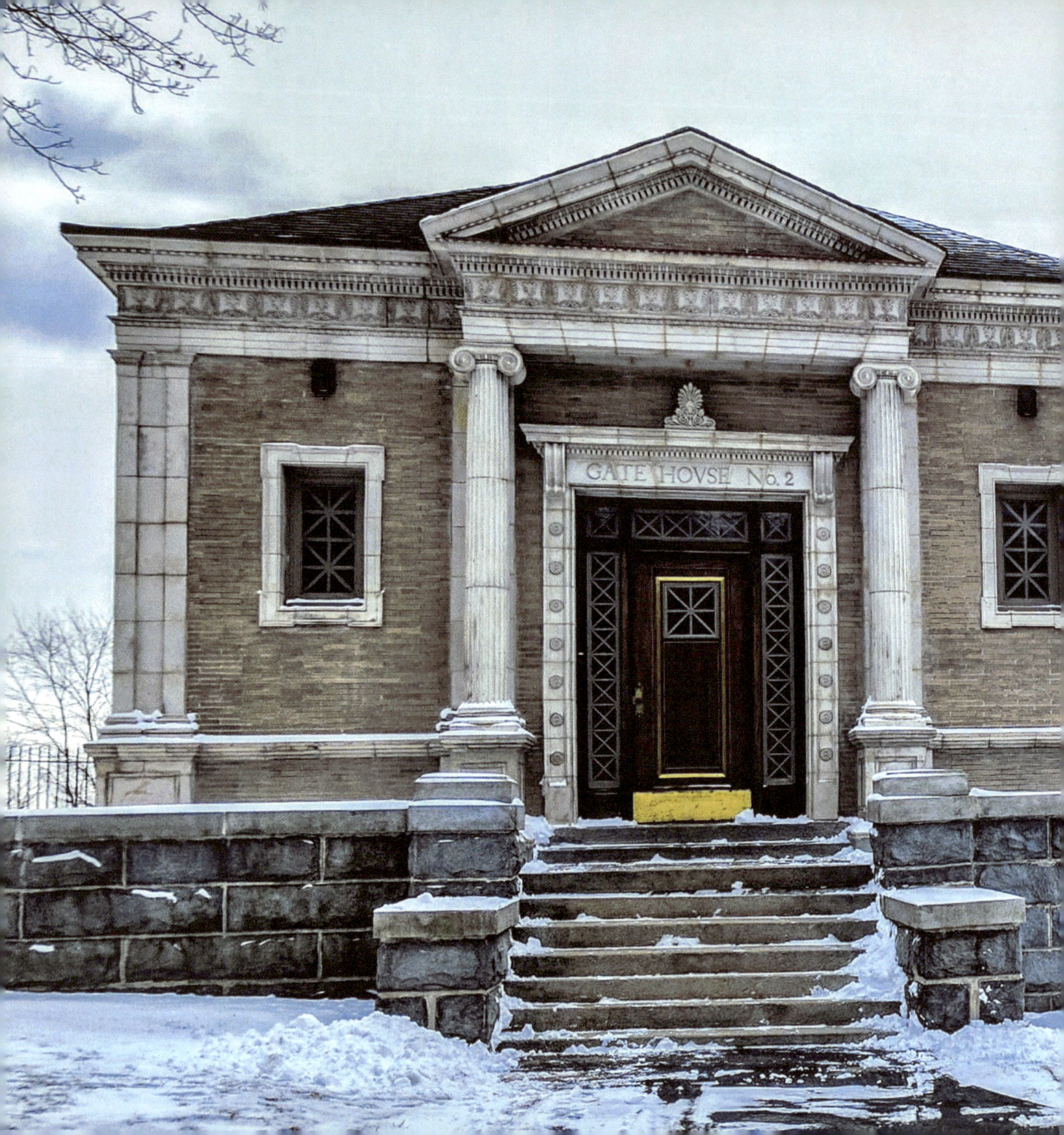

GATE HOVSE No. 2

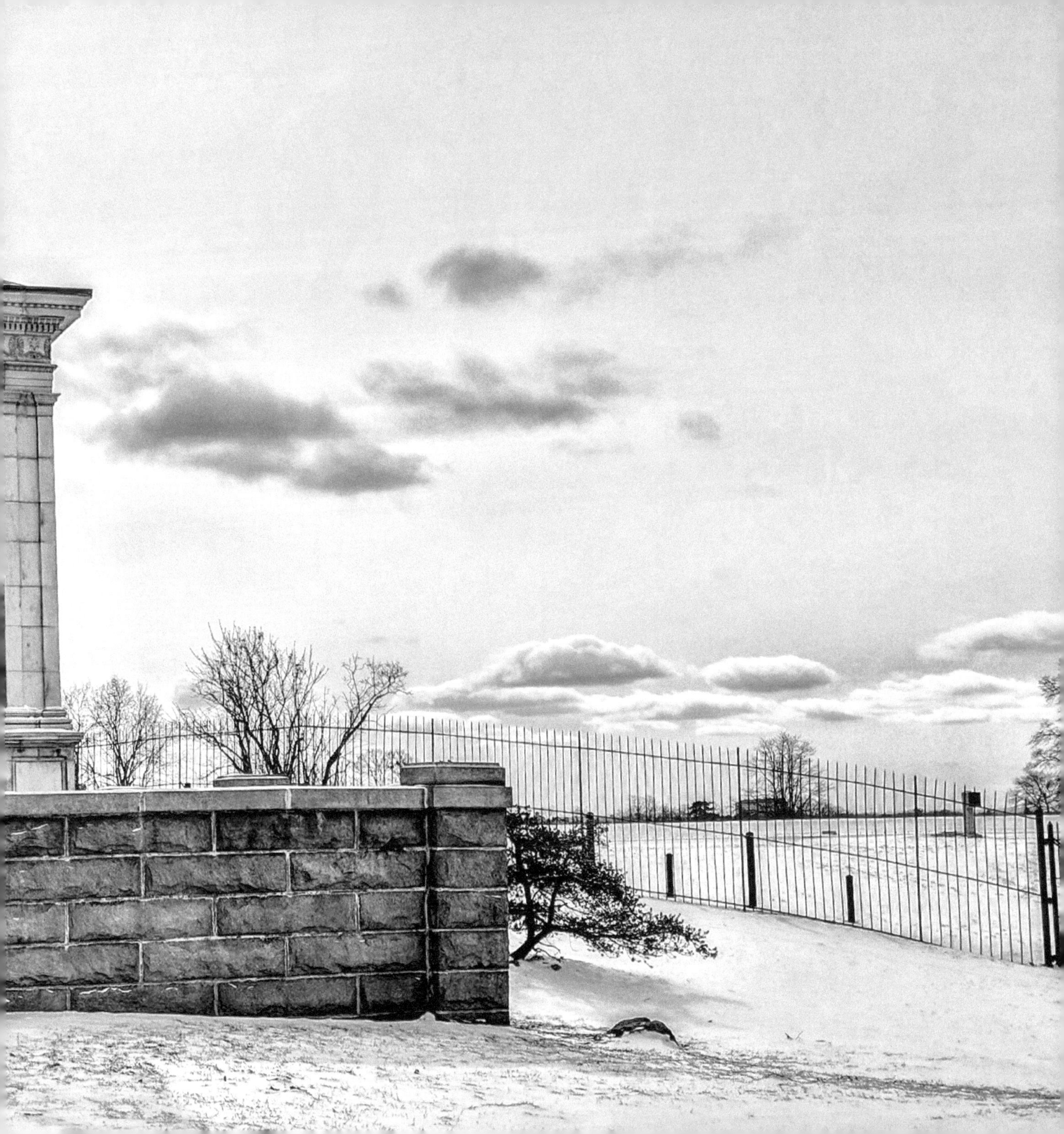

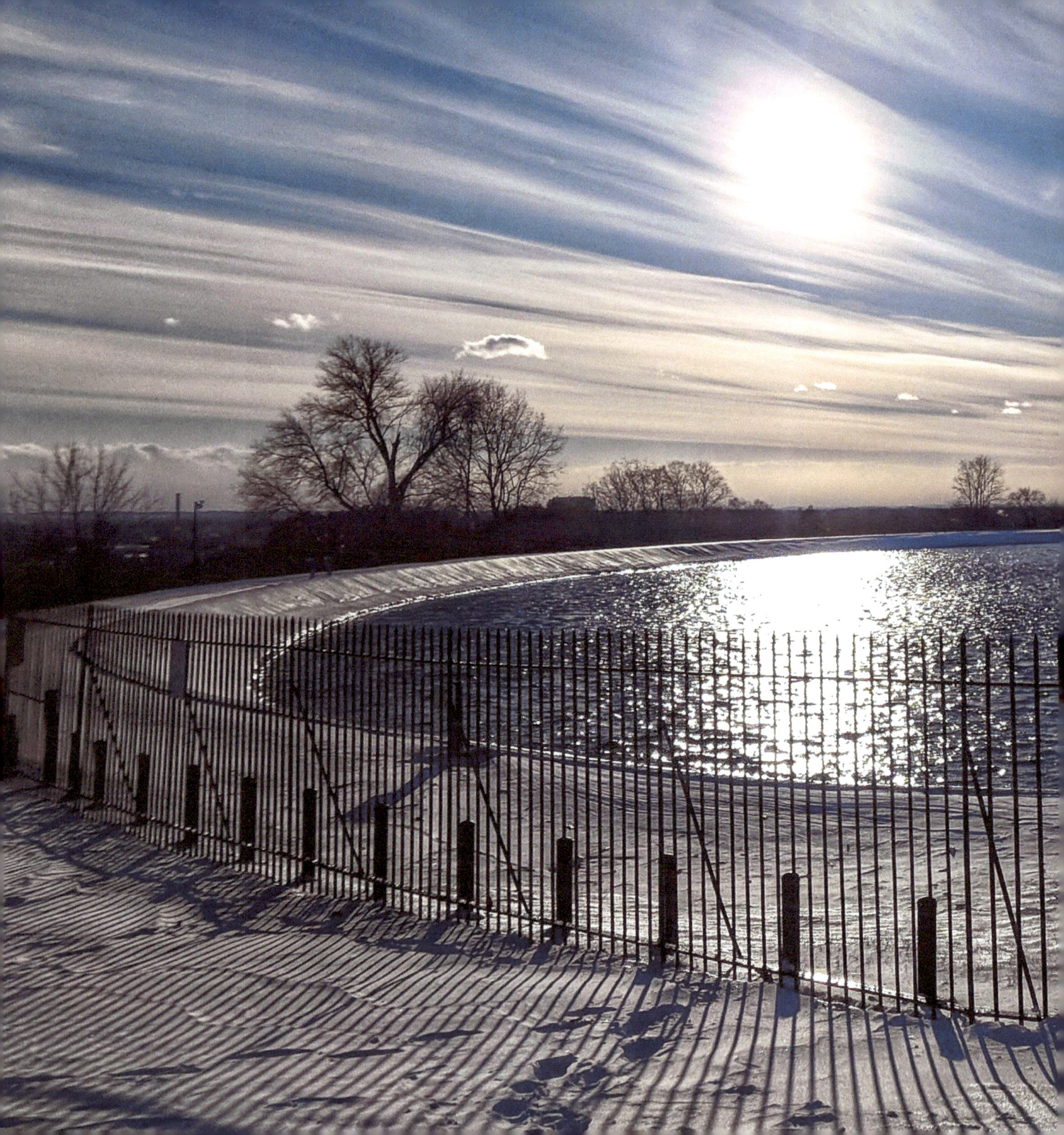

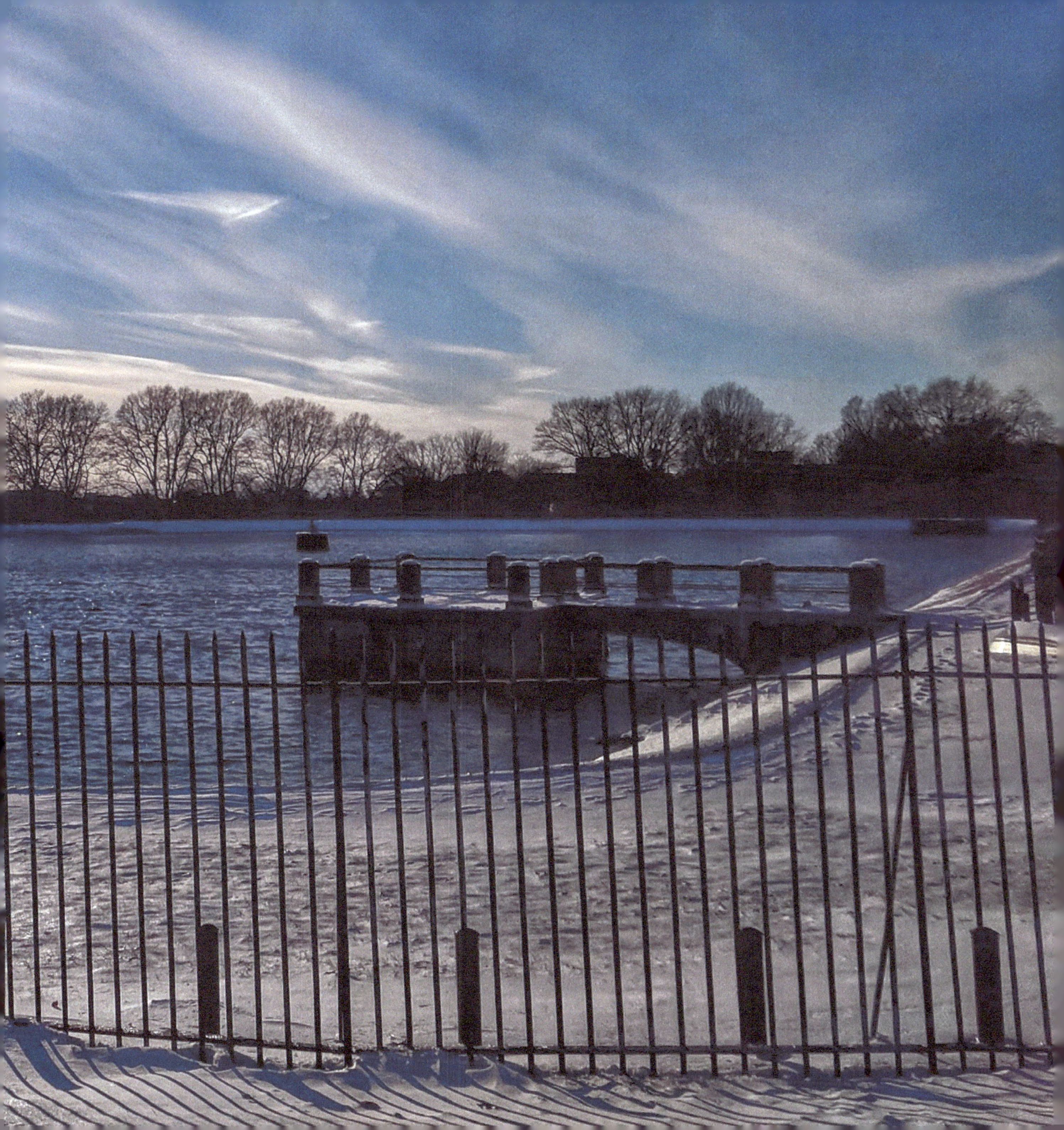

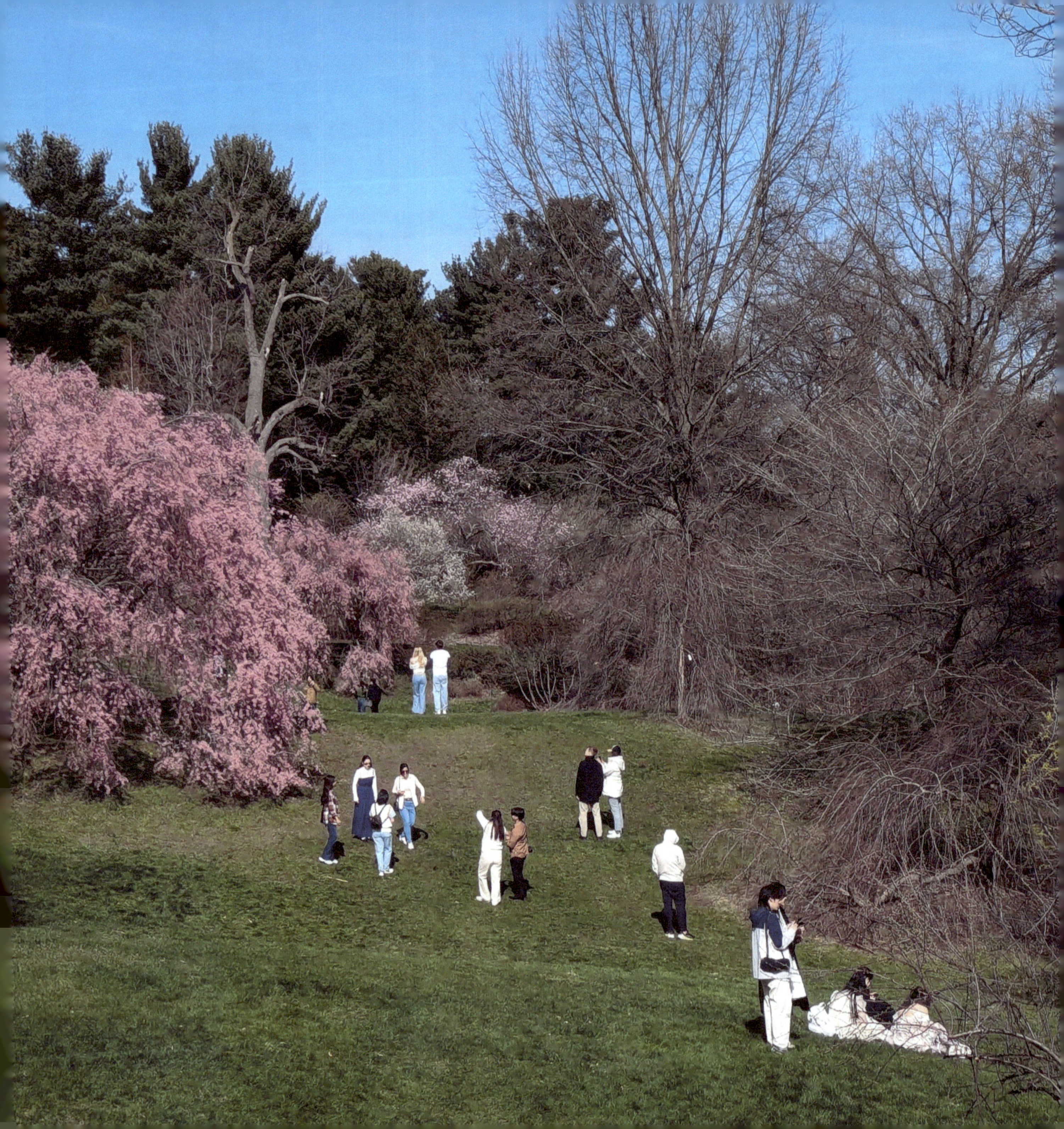

Highland Park Today

Highland Park remains Rochester's living landscape—a place that changes with the seasons yet always feels familiar. More than a century after its creation, it continues to fulfill its quiet purpose: offering beauty, space, and a sense of belonging to anyone who walks its paths.

The seasonal rhythm continues as it has for generations. The park endures not because time has preserved it but because it remains part of daily life. Runners trace familiar loops. Families return to the same slopes for photos. Artists and photographers follow the light as it shifts across the hills. College students from nearby campuses picnic and play between exams.

Intentional public transportation planning makes the park easily accessible to the city it serves, keeping Highland as Olmsted intended—a shared landscape, woven into daily life rather than set apart from it.

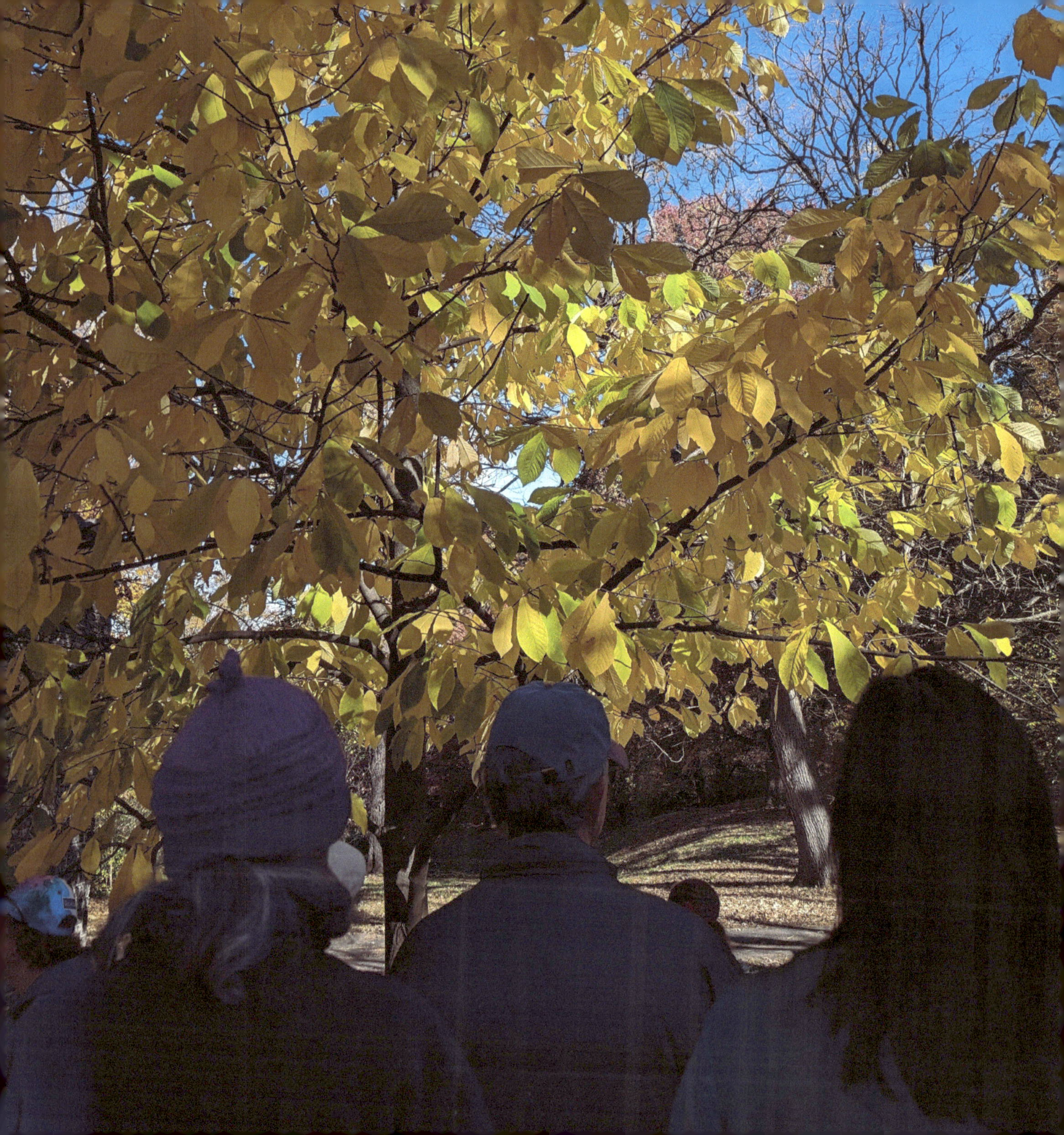

Community and Stewardship

From the beginning, Highland Park has been a collective effort. Every path, tree, and planting bears the quiet mark of attention, imagined by visionaries and sustained by generations of guardians.

From its earliest days, Highland Park has depended on generosity—first through land and public investment, and now through advocacy, fundraising, and volunteer care. The form has changed, but the responsibility remains.

That care continues through the work of the Highland Park Conservancy, the nonprofit partner of Monroe County Parks, the county agency responsible for managing Highland Park and much of Rochester's regional park system.

Guided by historic preservation principles and a close study of Olmsted's plans, the Conservancy preserves the park's design integrity while ensuring it remains relevant, accessible, and welcoming.

Their efforts span restoration projects, volunteer planting and weeding, guided walks, and long-term planning, including ongoing work to reestablish the Children's Pavilion as a fully accessible overlook inspired by the original structure. Each decision balances respect for Olmsted's intent with the needs of today's community.

Visitors play a role as well. When we walk thoughtfully, notice a bloom, or care for the park in small ways, we add our own chapter to its long history of stewardship. Highland Park endures not merely because it was beautifully designed but because it continues to be loved.

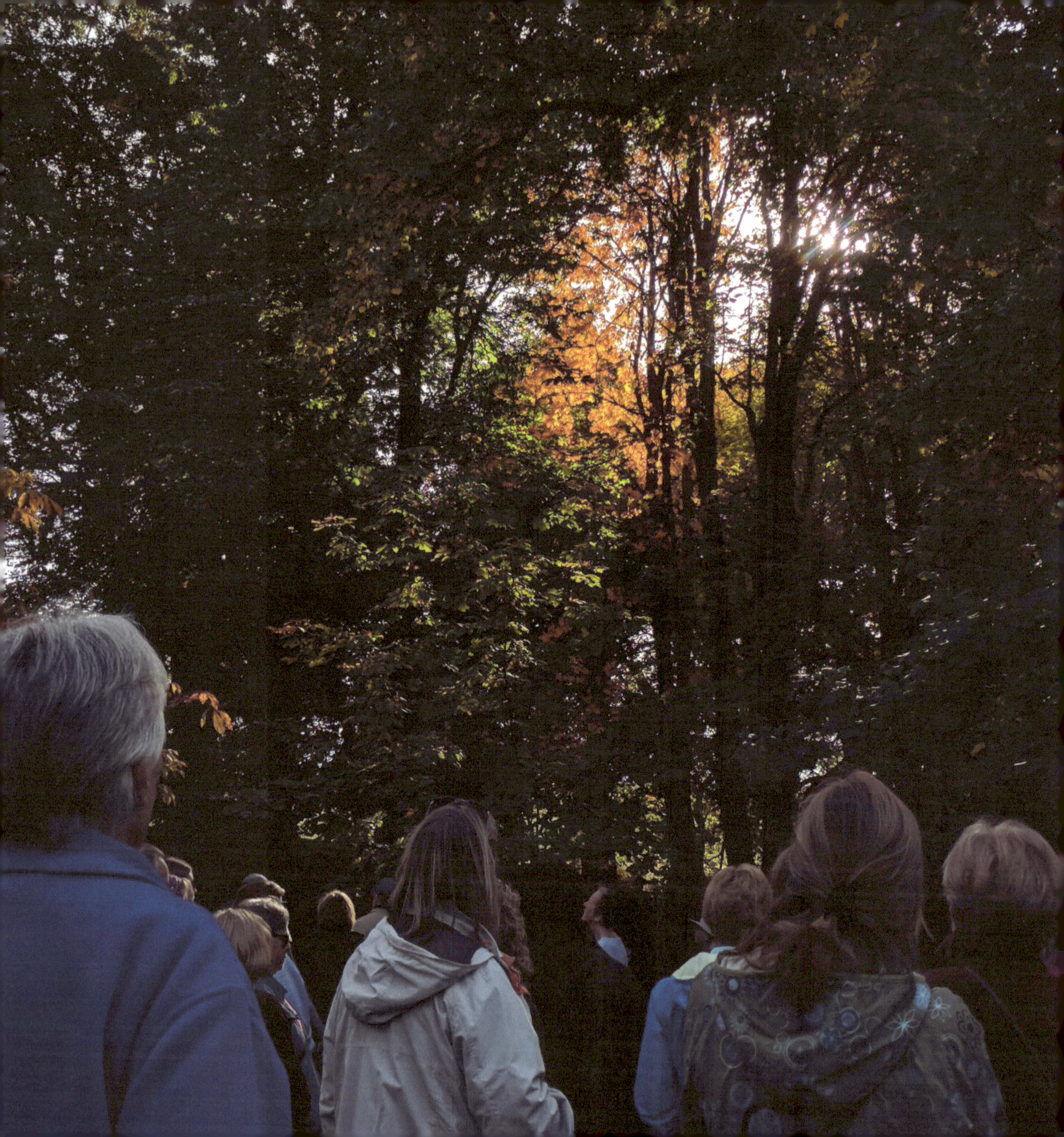

Acknowledgments

This book is written with gratitude to the Highland Park Conservancy—its board, volunteers, and members—for their continued dedication to preserving and nurturing Highland Park and their partnership with the Monroe County Parks Department to sustain Frederick Law Olmsted's vision for generations to come.

Much of the understanding reflected in these pages comes not only from written sources but also from volunteer interpreters, local historians, and horticulturists who lead year-round walks through the park. Through storytelling and shared experience, they educate and inspire the next generation of park stewards, passing knowledge from one season to the next.

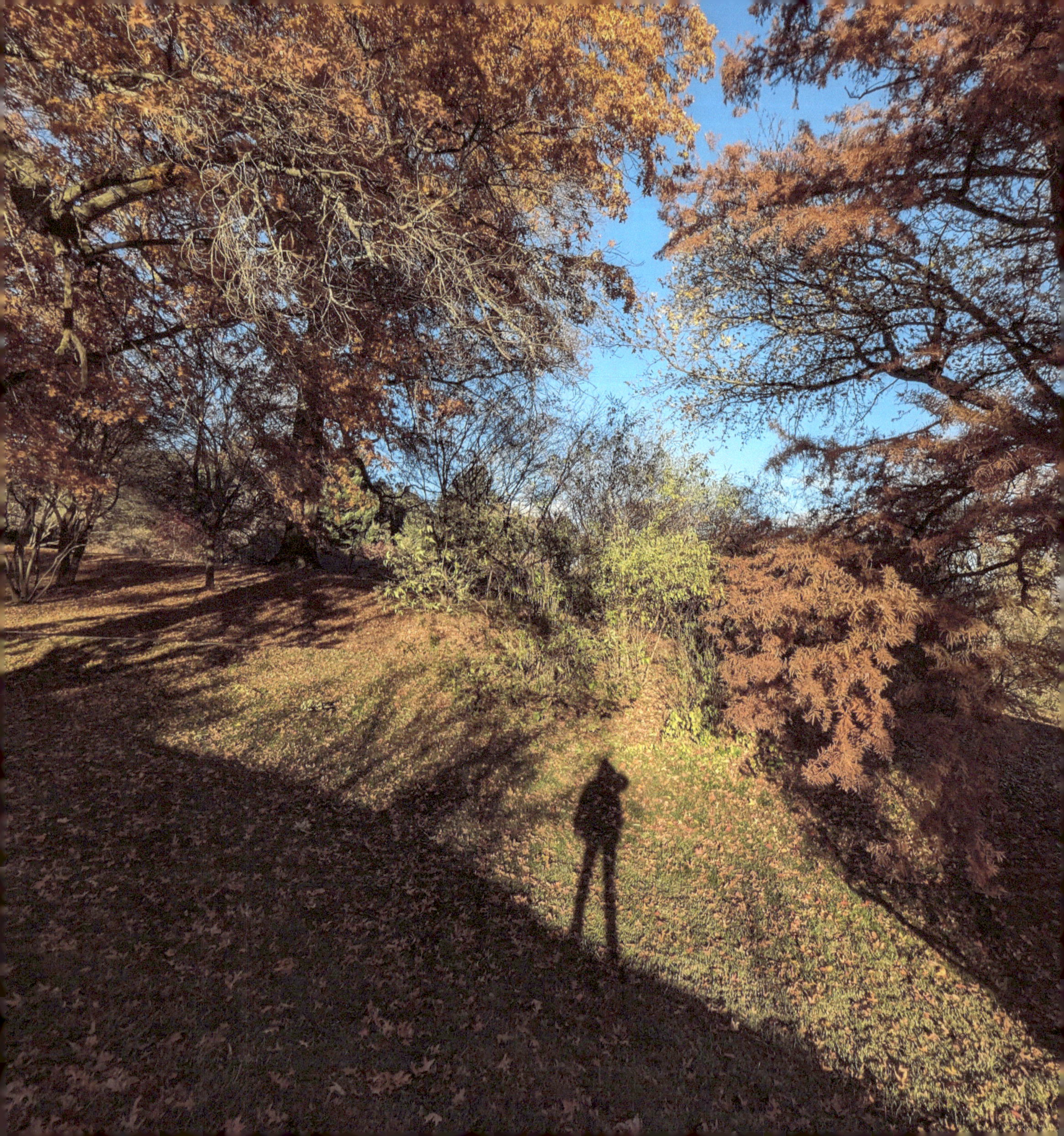

About the Author

Debi Bower is a photographer, travel writer, and web designer based in Rochester, New York. She is the creator of *Day Trips Around Rochester, New York*—a website and collection of books celebrating local exploration throughout the Finger Lakes and Western New York. Through photography and words, she invites readers to slow down, look closely, and rediscover the beauty of familiar places.

A member of the Highland Park Conservancy, Bower finds continual inspiration in the park's light, design, and sense of belonging—a reminder that wonder often waits just beyond the next curve in the path.

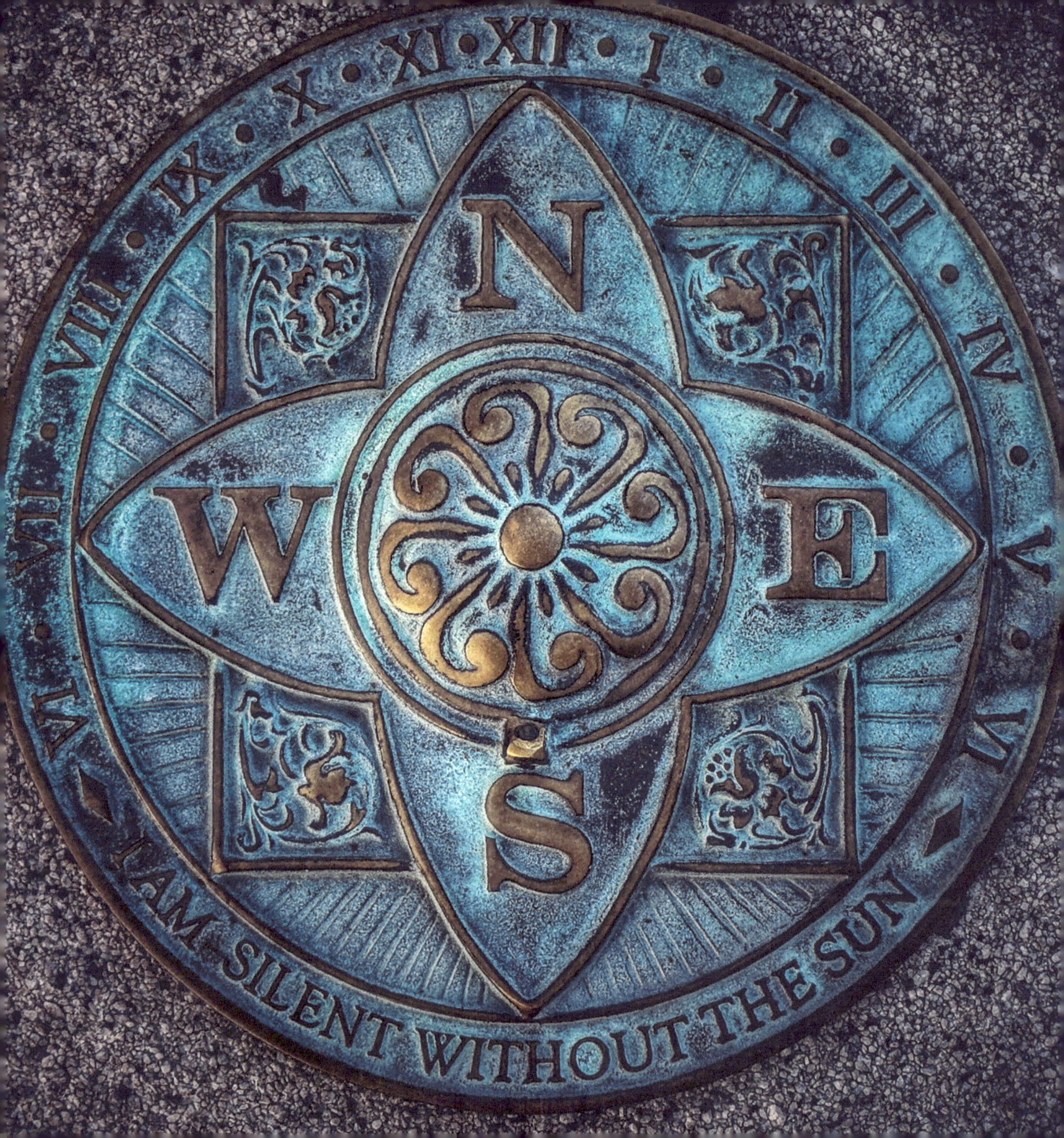

N
S
E
W
IX · X · XI · XII · I · II · III · IV · V · VI · VII · VIII
I AM SILENT WITHOUT THE SUN

Appendix

RECOMMENDED READING

These works shaped the broader historical and cultural context of this book and are recommended for readers seeking to explore Rochester's history in greater depth.

Burd, Camden. *The Roots of Flower City: Horticulture, Empire, and the Remaking of Rochester, New York.* Ithaca: Cornell University Press, 2024.

Grant, Alvan R. *The Plantsmen of Rochester Parks: A History of Rochester's Parks.* Rochester, NY: Arthur Trimble, originally published 1998; 3rd ed., 2014.

McKelvey, Blake. *A Growing Legacy: An Illustrated History of Rochester's Parks.* Rochester, NY: City of Rochester, 1984.

SELECTED PRIMARY SOURCES

Arnold, Bion J., Arnold W. Brunner, and Frederick Law Olmsted Jr. *A City Plan for Rochester.* New York: The Cheltenham Press, 1911.

Horsey, R. E. *Lilacs in the Rochester Parks.* Mimeograph, 1938.

McKelvey, Blake. Selected works on Rochester's civic and park history, including "A Story of Rochester" (1938) and articles published in *Rochester History* (1944, 1949).

Monroe County Parks. *Azaleas and Rhododendrons at Highland Park, Rochester, N.Y.* Pamphlet, 1912.

Rochester Department of Parks. *Parks and Playgrounds: Rochester, N.Y.* Annual Report, January 1, 1919.

Union and Advertiser Press. *The Origin and Development of Rochester's Park System.* Rochester, NY, 1908.

Wickes, Marjorie, and Tim O'Connell. "The Legacy of Frederick Law Olmsted." *Rochester History* Vol. 50, No. 2, 1988.

Left: Sundial in the Poet's Garden

The Children's Pavilion

A View Reimagined

High above the lilac slopes once stood the Ellwanger & Barry Memorial Pavilion, later renamed the Children's Pavilion. Completed in 1890, the three-story structure offered sweeping views of Rochester, the Genesee Valley, and the distant Bristol Hills. Climbing it was to understand the park's design—to see how paths, plantings, and vistas worked together across the landscape.

For more than seventy years, the pavilion served as both a destination and a symbol. Weather and time eventually claimed it, and the structure was lost in 1963. Yet its absence never erased its presence.

Today, the Highland Park Conservancy is working to reconstruct the pavilion as a fully accessible building inspired by the original—an overlook that honors Olmsted's intent and welcomes all visitors.

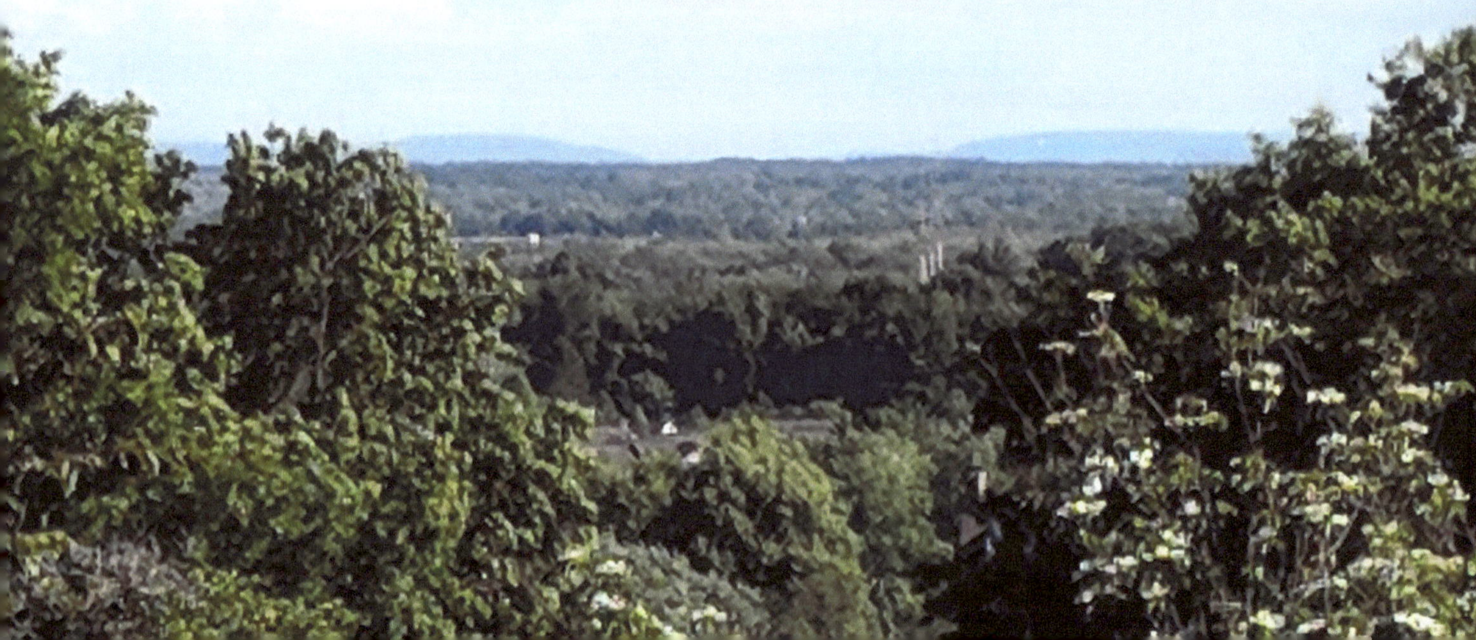